Transnational Crime
& Criminal Justice

SAGE was founded in 1965 by Sara Miller McCune to support the dissemination of usable knowledge by publishing innovative and high-quality research and teaching content. Today, we publish over 900 journals, including those of more than 400 learned societies, more than 800 new books per year, and a growing range of library products including archives, data, case studies, reports, and video. SAGE remains majority-owned by our founder, and after Sara's lifetime will become owned by a charitable trust that secures our continued independence.

Los Angeles | London | New Delhi | Singapore | Washington DC | Melbourne

Transnational Crime & Criminal Justice

Marinella Marmo
& Nerida Chazal

with the contribution
of Andrew Goldsmith

Los Angeles | London | New Delhi
Singapore | Washington DC | Melbourne

Los Angeles | London | New Delhi
Singapore | Washington DC | Melbourne

SAGE Publications Ltd
1 Oliver's Yard
55 City Road
London EC1Y 1SP

SAGE Publications Inc.
2455 Teller Road
Thousand Oaks, California 91320

SAGE Publications India Pvt Ltd
B 1/I 1 Mohan Cooperative Industrial Area
Mathura Road
New Delhi 110 044

SAGE Publications Asia-Pacific Pte Ltd
3 Church Street
#10-04 Samsung Hub
Singapore 049483

Editor: Amy Jarrold
Editorial assistant: George Knowles
Production editor: Sarah Cooke
Copyeditor: Jane Fricker
Proofreader: Audrey Scriven
Indexer: Judith Lavender
Marketing manager: Sally Ransom
Cover design: Wendy Scott
Typeset by: C&M Digitals (P) Ltd, Chennai, India

© Marinella Marmo and Nerida Chazal 2016

First published 2016

Library of Congress Control Number: 2015948822

British Library Cataloguing in Publication data

A catalogue record for this book is available from the British Library

ISBN 978-1-41291-924-1
ISBN 978-1-41291-925-8 (pbk)

At SAGE we take sustainability seriously. Most of our products are printed in the UK using FSC papers and boards. When we print overseas we ensure sustainable papers are used as measured by the PREPS grading system. We undertake an annual audit to monitor our sustainability.

Contents

About the Authors

Dr Marinella Marmo is Associate Professor in Criminal Justice at Flinders University Law School. Marinella researches in the areas of international criminal justice and transnational crime. Currently, she works in the area of migration, border control and human mobility. She has co-authored the books *Crime, Justice and Human Rights* (with Leanne Weber, Elaine Fishwick) and *Race, Gender and the Body in British Migration Control* (with Evan Smith) and co-edited a number of books. Her research has been widely cited in numerous newspapers, including the *Guardian* and the *New York Times*. She is the recipient of an Office for Learning and Teaching Citation for Outstanding Contributions to Student Learning by the Australian Federal Government.

Dr Nerida Chazal is a Lecturer in Criminology at Flinders University, Australia. Her research examines the aims and functioning of international criminal justice in a complex and increasingly global world. In particular, she researches the International Criminal Court and state crime. She is the author of *The International Criminal Court and Global Social Control* (Routledge, 2016) and the co-editor (with W. De Lint and M. Marmo) of *Criminal Justice in International Society* (Routledge, 2014).

Also with contributions from:

Andrew Goldsmith is Strategic Professor of Criminology at Flinders University, Adelaide, Australia. He is also director of the university's Centre for Crime Policy and Research. He is trained in law, criminology, and sociology, and has researched and taught at universities in Canada and the United Kingdom as well as in Australia. He is the founder of the Illicit Networks Workshop, an international collaboration of scholars interested in transnational and organized crime, corruption and terrorism. His research interests include the governance of policing, transnational crime, the impact of new technologies upon crime and policing, and corruption in prisons.

Preface

This book aims to respond to the desire of students of any level and practitioners to know more about the subject of Transnational Crimes and Criminal Justice, and to address the many questions we academics may well often take for granted. Assumed knowledge can be discouraging to those willing to learn more about a topic.

The main concern has been that students and other people new to these topics may feel disenfranchised even in matters where they have shown strong interest. There is a tendency amongst academics to write and deliver complex papers in class; however, after years of teaching this subject at undergraduate and postgraduate level, we have learnt a valuable lesson: the questions received can be basic, for example 'What are transnational crimes? What is the international community?'. Further, we are mindful of Pratt calling for academics to 'relearn how to talk like a real person again' (Pratt 2008: 46) referring to the complicated academic jargon criminologists use when talking about their research to the lay person. We are also aware that the new generation of learners or academics and practitioners approaching this subject for the first time may have a different way of mapping out and building on knowledge.

With this book, we aspire to offer a stepping stone to produce the enthusiasm and inspiration to continue with this topic. Therefore, we see this book as a friendly platform for those students, academics and practitioners who approach enthusiastically these topics for the first time, coming from a range of diverse backgrounds, and would like to expand their knowledge without being intimidated by its complexity and inevitable jargonistic discussion around globalization, transnational matters and human rights.

The chapters are based on several years of lecture notes and discussion with upper level students, postgraduates and academic experts in the field. The material the book offers aims to come across as a conversation both in the structure and content. Examples are given as often as possible to offer a way to engage with abstract material in more concrete terms. In essence, this seeks to be pedagogical material, with the ambition to gain and maintain the interest of the reader.

At times, choices have been made leading to a simplification of complex material. If students feel that they 'want to know more' after reading about one of the many subjects covered, the book has already achieved its purposes.

Our sincere gratitude goes to the Sage commissioning editors and assistant editors for believing in this project from the start to the end; yes, there has been an end product at last! In particular, our gratitude goes to Caroline Porter, Natalie Aguilera, and Amy Jarrold.

We are also indebted to a number of colleagues for their feedback and encouragement: Ryan Conlon, Derek Dalton, Mark Israel, David O. Friedrichs, Mary Heath, Evan Smith, Anne Mignone and the Faculty of Education, Humanities and Law of Flinders University for their financial support during this project.

We are grateful to Andrew Goldsmith for contributing two chapters to the book.

Our research and editorial assistant, Sian Davy, was invaluable in helping us to complete this project. Sian went above and beyond, helping us research case studies, offering comments on drafts, and undertaking the daunting tasks of editing the initial manuscript. Thank you Sian!

Associate Professor Marinella Marmo & Dr Nerida Chazal

Reference list

Pratt T 2008 'Rational choice theory, crime control policy and criminological relevance', *Criminology and Public Policy*, 7:1, 43–52.

1

Introduction

This chapter will look at

- The global nature of social life and crime in the twenty-first century.
- Definitions of international crimes and transnational crimes.
- The role of states and transnational actors in responding to crimes that cross borders.

Keywords

Transnational and
international crime
definitions

Jurisdiction

International
cooperation

1.1 Introduction: Living in a Global Village

In the past three decades we have witnessed a shift in our societies as capitalism, global financial systems, technology and cheap travel have transformed the way we perceive and experience 'locality'. The combination of increased wealth, networks, information sharing and technologies has caused us to spend money, consume commodities, find jobs, organize holidays and use virtual social networks in ways that were unimaginable just decades ago. We expect to find the latest Japanese technological products, South American dance classes and Italian shoes right where we live. We use the internet to book our next holiday to India, check our bank account online and update our Facebook status, allowing us to act at an international level without leaving the comfort of our homes. We have extended our global reach and our ability to export our culture to the world, while we are influenced simultaneously by trends from other cultures and far-reaching global phenomena. These are positive aspects of the globalized economy which we can access through a range of intertwined socio-political arrangements. The positive aspects of globalization have enhanced social inclusion by eroding the borders of time and space and allowing us to reach out to different people and communities across the world, meaning we now live in a global village (McLuhan & Powers 1989).

Although we often view the processes of globalization as positive, there are also many negative aspects to living within this global village. For example, our access to a range of cheap and readily available consumer products is often achieved at the expense of individuals working in appalling conditions in developing countries and to the detriment of the environment. Also, while in the developed world we may be able to easily cross borders, both physically and digitally, there are vast numbers of individuals around the world who do not have access to technology, information or wealth and cannot leave their countries or fully profit from the benefits of globalization. Just think of the numbers of refugees fleeing wars, violence and conflict only to have borders closed down around them. It is, therefore, important to bear in mind that the global village is not experienced equally by everyone and that there are still many boundaries that are both maintained and created by globalization.

Additionally, and most importantly for this book, while we benefit from increased connections, mobility and global reach, which facilitate many legitimate aspects of our everyday lives, so too can criminal actors exploit the processes of globalization for illegitimate means. A major by-product of the global village is a growth in transboundary criminal activities which take advantage of the global

Cocacolonization: Coca-Cola advertising in the High Atlas mountains of Morocco

© Photo by ciukes (Flickr) via Wikimedia Commons

financial system and benefit enormously from economic, media and technological growth. Traditional forms of transnational crimes, such as drug and arms trafficking, and newer forms such as cybercrime and money laundering, have increased consistently. This aspect of negative globalization is a common phenomenon in different countries, notwithstanding whether these countries are more or less developed political economic systems. **Organized crime** and corruption have become widespread phenomena and have infiltrated, at different levels, not only less developed, failed or failing countries, such as Colombia, Mexico, Thailand and Laos, to name a few, but also rich Western countries. Thus, as we benefit from increased global reach, we are also vulnerable to 'being reached' in negative terms by criminal syndicates who exploit the loopholes of the global village.

While there is no need for moral panics and over-reactions, transnational studies in the area of crime and public policy have indicated that local and global criminal activities are often intertwined and have direct and indirect effects on our everyday routine. Are our credit card details swiped if we purchase goods on the internet? Is our identity stolen? Are the drugs we buy at the local pharmacy counterfeit? Can we purchase new synthetic drugs at the local nightclub? Are human beings trafficked to our rich destination countries and exploited by domestic or commercial markets? Should we fear a terrorist attack on our cities? Are we body scanned at the airport against our will for serious security reasons? We all 'suffer' the consequences of widespread global criminal activities, which exploit both illicit and licit venues, such as the local pharmacy, city nightclub, or online store.

And yet, this interwoven network of negative effects of globalization has expanded and reached us in a remarkably unnoticed manner. Local media and politicians mainly address local realities of crime. However, and increasingly so, there are 'triggers' that bring attention to the transnational reality of crime. There are, in particular, three areas which evoke visible and prominent signs that we live in a networked society, the dangers and dark sides of which we cannot escape:

- *Global terrorism:* The most remarkable example of this is the terrorist attacks of 11 September 2001 in the United States, followed by the Madrid and London bombings in 2003 and 2005. The events that followed – the hunt for culprits, the wars in Afghanistan and Iraq, the increased security at checking points and the augmented police powers – had global effects. These responses were justified by the need to defend countries from the spectre of **terrorism** under the rubric of a global war on terror. In the wake of the 2005 London bombings, the mayor of Paris put aside traditional French-Anglo rivalries and illustrated the solidarity of the West in the face of the all-pervasive threat of global terrorism, declaring: 'right now, we are all Londoners' (cited in Samuel & Russell 2005, np). Ten years later, London and the world returned the gesture, following the attacks on the *Charlie Hebdo* offices in Paris, with the collective response 'nous sommes Charlie'. As this statement illustrates, discrete terrorist events in major Western cities have far-reaching, global effects, which continue now as the world reacts to actions by al-Qaeda and Islamic State.

- *Irregular migration:* The movement of irregular migrants, especially when it is visualized as the spectacle of invasion, has caught the attention of the public, the media and politicians. Images of boats full of people reaching European and Australian shores and groups breaching the US–Mexican border have prompted strong reactions from developed countries. This has included: military interventions, regional people-swapping deals and policy initiatives such as excising territory and holding migrants in detention for prolonged periods.

- *Trafficking in drugs:* This has become, from a popular (or populist) perspective, the archetypal form of transnational crime. Here again, we see the narrative of an invasion of destination countries by negative elements, in this case drugs, and a consequent construction of the necessity to defend these countries against evil externalities. Again, this leads to a shutting down of borders, and punitive responses that stem from discourses on the 'war on drugs'.

There are also many other ways that we can see the negative effects of globalization. A recent example is the 2008 Global Financial Crisis, which was the worst financial crisis since the Great Depression. The Global Financial Crisis can be framed in terms of negative globalization as it has had wide-ranging and far-reaching consequences for individuals across the world, including increased levels of poverty, diminished labour opportunities and forced evictions and foreclosures. Another example of the negative effects of globalization is the environmental damage and destruction which is heightened through globalization. For instance, global warming and climate change arise, in part, from the increased travel, mobility and industrialization of modern times. In addition, the effects of these negative environmental situations traverse borders and impact all corners of the earth. No country or population is now immune from adverse environmental changes.

These examples indicate that serious harm is caused to people around the world by the many different aspects of globalization, as well as by **criminogenic** human interventions. Accordingly, there is a pressing need to think about transnational crimes in a broader manner and to go beyond more conventional conceptualizations of transnational crimes as acts which are traditionally deemed illegal, such as drug trafficking, human trafficking and terrorism. A comprehensive consideration of crimes that cross borders should include the wide range of human-made situations that generate harm across the globe and throughout the global village. We will now explore different definitions of crime that crosses borders to form a better conceptual understanding of transnational crime.

1.2 Crimes that Cross Borders: What is Transnational Crime?

There are several different types of crimes that cross borders. While there are many crimes that have transnational characteristics and transboundary implications, the term 'transnational crime' is far more specific than the way it is

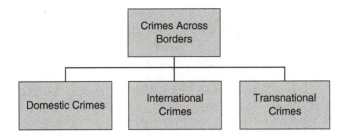

Figure 1.1 Crimes across Borders

commonly used in media and informal debates. As a label, transnational crime refers to particular types of crime, rather than functioning as a generic descriptor for all types of crimes that traverse borders. Figure 1.1 illustrates three different types of crimes that cross borders. As this diagram illustrates, it is important to differentiate between domestic crimes, international crimes and transnational crimes.

Domestic Crimes that Cross Borders

Domestic crimes are acts that are defined as illegal by national (or domestic) laws. Domestic crimes may involve cross-border dimensions. For instance, an offender may engage in criminal activities in a foreign country using the loopholes between domestic criminal justice systems to escape investigation and prosecution. Police and other criminal justice agencies are often under an obligation to collaborate with their counterparts in other countries to bring cross-border offenders to justice. There is increased pressure to resolve criminal matters to the satisfaction of multiple jurisdictions. The crossing of national juridical boundaries is the new element of these illegal behaviours.

Sometimes, cross-border offences are also referred to as conventional or traditional forms of crime because, mainly, they are ordinary crimes, such as homicide, assault, or the selling of illicit goods. The offender, the victim, the investigators and the judges may be in different geographical locations, with different sets of rules, languages and criminal justice aims and systems. In these cases, the concept of domestic criminality is stretched and the weaknesses of nationally bound criminal justice agencies and regulations become apparent. In a globalized world where the national and the international, the global and the local are often intertwined, it is difficult to deal with crimes exclusively through laws and systems that are constrained by the boundaries of the nation-state. The example in Case Study 1.1 illustrates how a crime committed in one country can have implications across multiple jurisdictions, without necessarily being 'transnational'.

Case Study 1.1 – Double Prosecution, Double Jeopardy

In October 2003, Tina and Gabe Watson arrived in Australia from the US to spend part of their honeymoon scuba-diving on the Great Barrier Reef. Five days into the trip, they embarked on a dive expedition in which Tina, a novice diver, got into difficulties when she encountered strong underwater currents. As Gabe attempted to help her, she knocked his mask and respirator and he momentarily let go of her to clear it (Patrick 2010). With his mask replaced he saw Tina was sinking. Assessing she was descending too quickly for him to reach Gabe took the decision to leave his wife and swim to the surface for help. It was a fateful decision.

A number of inconsistencies in Gabe's story prompted a police investigation but it was not until after a Coronial Inquest in 2008 that the Office of the Director of Public Prosecutions in Queensland pressed charges. Given the unclear events surrounding Tina's death and the expensive nature of a murder trial, a plea bargain was negotiated (Flynn & Fitz-Gibbon 2010). Gabe pleaded guilty to manslaughter by criminal negligence and was sentenced to four and a half years' imprisonment, suspended after 12 months (Flynn & Fitzgibbon 2010). This was later increased to 18 months following an appeal.

Meanwhile, dissatisfied with proceedings in Australia, Tina's family had been campaigning in their home state of Alabama for US authorities to prosecute the case. International law allows that in serious cases, in which the accused or the victim is a foreign national, extra-territorial jurisdiction may be sought (O'Brien 2011). As both victim and offender in this case were US citizens, Alabama announced its intention to pursue a murder charge once Gabe was released from custody in Australia. Delicate extradition negotiations ensued in which the Australian government sought assurances that the death penalty would not be applied if Gabe was convicted in the US (Ireland-Piper 2012).

In November 2011, two weeks after his release from jail, Gabe Watson was deported from Australia. He was arrested on arrival in Los Angeles and extradited to Alabama where he was put on trial for Tina's murder in February 2012. Although the charges brought by the state of Alabama were different from those of Queensland, the case raised questions of double jeopardy, whereby a person should not be prosecuted twice for the same criminal conduct (Ireland-Piper 2012). In pre-trial hearings Judge Nail determined that the prosecution would have to address the double jeopardy argument and establish jurisdiction through their evidence (O'Brien 2011). Six days into the trial, the judge dismissed the case citing a lack of evidence. Both prosecution and defence lamented this unsatisfactory conclusion. Despite the efforts of two jurisdictions, the lingering sense remains that neither Tina nor Gabe received justice.

In contrast to domestic crimes, international and transnational crimes are non-conventional and non-traditional crimes, the causes and effects of which go beyond national territory. Both these forms of crime challenge the interests of more than one nation-state, hence they should be considered global issues that go beyond domestic borders. However, they are different in the way their harm is portrayed: **international crimes** are defined as producing harm against the entire humanity, while transnational crimes are often defined as damaging a number of nation-states' interests. In both cases, the consensus of the international community is that solutions should be reached beyond national sovereignty and domestic criminal justice systems.

International Crimes

International crimes are crimes that are in breach of fundamental and universal human rights and therefore constitute serious offences against the international community and threaten world order and security. There are several different ways of defining international crimes, ranging from broad definitions that view international crimes as acts that traverse borders and threaten humankind, to more legal definitions, which conceive of international crimes as acts that contravene **international criminal law**. For conceptual clarity, throughout this book we refer to international crimes as crimes that violate international criminal law.

International criminal law is a body of law that has evolved over the past century and has more rapidly developed since the end of World War II. As with international law in general, international criminal law comes from a broad range of sources including treaties, customary international criminal law, general principles and Security Council resolutions meaning that, until recently, it has not been as clearly defined or codified as domestic laws. It is important to note that international criminal law is different from international law: international law deals with disagreements between states, whereas international criminal law involves individual criminal responsibility for grave acts that threaten the 'conscience of humanity', as defined by the Rome Statute of the International Criminal Court (1998). International law is primarily administered by the International Court of Justice, which was established by the United Nations in 1945 to arbitrate disputes between states. In contrast, there are several different institutions and mechanisms for enforcing international criminal law, including the UN-established ad-hoc tribunals, the International Criminal Tribunal for the Former Yugoslavia (the ICTY), and the International Criminal Tribunal for Rwanda (the ICTR) and, more recently, the permanent International Criminal Court (the ICC or the Court). Chapter 4 provides more details about these institutions, along with more information about different mechanisms for enforcing international criminal law.

Following decades of debate, the agreed position of international law academics and practitioners is that international crimes should be limited to those core crimes listed in statutes of these international ad-hoc or permanent criminal tribunals and courts (Cassese 2003). International criminal law has thus evolved as international society has created different institutions to respond to atrocities (Charlesworth 2002), with each of these institutions using their own statutes and consequent definitions of international criminal law. However, since the 1998 Rome Statute established the permanent International

Criminal Court, this document has been the main source of international criminal law and the primary list of international crimes agreed upon by the international community.

Under Article 5 of the Rome Statute, there are four broad categories of international crimes: the crime of **genocide**, **crimes against humanity**, **war crimes** and the **crime of aggression**. The development of this list of crimes was a process of diplomatic negotiation which occurred during the Rome Conference in July 1998. During the Rome Conference, many countries argued for the inclusion of other crimes in the Rome Statute, for example, India argued for the inclusion of the use of nuclear weapons, and Egypt, Algeria, Turkey, Sri Lanka and the Caribbean states argued for drug trafficking to be defined as an international crime under the Statute. These crimes were not covered in the Rome Statute due to concessions made to other countries (Kirsch & Holmes 1999), and a general consensus that international crimes should be limited to the most serious crimes that 'deeply shock the conscience of humanity' (Rome Statute 1998). As this process illustrates, although we now have a definitive list of international crimes, behind the legal definition lies a series of negotiations, concessions and disagreements about which acts should constitute international crimes, highlighting the contested nature of the legal label of 'crime'.

Spotlight – International Crimes as Defined by the Rome Statute

Genocide includes proscribed acts committed with intent to destroy, in whole or in part, a national, ethnical, racial or religious group.

Crimes against humanity involve a set list of crimes which are committed as part of a widespread or systematic attack directed against any civilian population.

War crimes are comprised of a series of acts that are committed as part of a plan or policy or as part of a large-scale commission of such crimes. 'War crimes' is a relatively broad term which includes acts defined as crimes from several sources, including the Geneva Convention of 12 August 1949 and other laws and customs applicable in international armed conflict.

The crime of aggression is the use of armed force by a state against the **sovereignty**, territorial integrity or political independence of another state.

The Rome Statute's codification of international crimes is important as it establishes the jurisdiction of the ICC, creating a permanent judicial forum to discuss international crime and providing clarity as to which acts constitute international crimes. The Rome Statute provides more specificity in defining international crimes. Although many crimes are included under the categories of genocide, crimes against humanity and war crime, including murder, rape and sexual slavery, torture, enslavement, enforced sterilization and taking hostages, each of these crimes in and of themselves do not constitute an international crime. Rather, the international crimes involve systematic and widespread violence where a range of crimes is committed within a broader context. Thus, 'smaller' crimes must reach a certain threshold to constitute an international crime. These thresholds are illustrated in the definitions in the 'Spotlight' above.

Aggression was a controversial inclusion in the Rome Statute. Although this crime was listed under Article 5 as one of the core international crimes falling under the jurisdiction of the ICC, the international community could not reach a consensus on the exact definition of aggression and the conditions of the court's jurisdiction over this crime. The reason for the lack of agreement is largely political. Aggression describes the use of force by one sovereign state against another sovereign state. As you can imagine, several powerful countries could be accused of committing the crime of aggression for their part in so-called humanitarian wars in other countries. For example, the United States, along with their allies, could be accused of aggression for their invasion of Iraq or their occupation of Afghanistan. Consequently, many different countries held a vested interest in the definition of aggression which made reaching a consensus impossible during the negotiation of the Rome Statute. At the 10-year review of the Rome Statute, which was held in Uganda in 2008, a definition of aggression and the conditions under which the ICC could exercise jurisdiction over the crime was finally reached.

As this sub-section has highlighted, international crimes are the most serious and heinous crimes that violate universal human rights, on a mass scale. Although international crimes may be confined to just one nation-state, they are viewed as international due to their particularly atrocious nature. International crimes thus affect humanity as a whole, with the term humanity being invoked here in a fairly esoteric or conceptual manner and primarily referring to the conscience or morality of the human race. This position accords with the principles of human rights documents that some acts are so immoral and inhuman that they violate inalienable rights and inherent ideas of justice and morality that apply to all of humanity.

Transnational Crimes

While there is now a relatively clear list and an adequate level of consensus as to the legal definition of international crimes, there is no such agreed upon definition of transnational crimes. The major difference between international crimes and transnational crimes is that transnational crimes are not labelled as an offence against the entire world community. Despite this, transnational crime is still considered a global problem that has the ability to cause significant damage to the interests of nation-states and the world order. As Antonio Maria Costa, the former executive director of the United Nations Office on Drugs and Crime (UNODC), announced as he presented the UN's first transnational organized crime threat assessment in 2010, 'transnational crime has become a threat to peace and development, even to the sovereignty of nations' (UNODC 2010a, np). Accordingly, it is conventional to describe transnational crimes as behaviours and activities that have a negative impact on the interests of more than one nation-state, implying that these types of crimes always take place across borders and should, consequently, be dealt with at an international level.

While many accounts of transnational crime describe it as a new form of criminality, or attribute an increase in transnational crime to the advancement of globalization in recent decades, transnational crimes have been a part of the world order for centuries (Roth 2014). Piracy and slavery, for example, were commonplace as early as antiquity and occurred throughout the Middle Ages. Smuggling has also been prevalent throughout history, particularly at times of prohibition. One example is the smuggling of alcohol into the United States via Mexico during the American Prohibition era between 1920 and 1933. Another prominent example is the opium trade between the British East India Company and China during the early nineteenth century.

Although many transnational crimes may not be new, it is clear that the sophistication of criminal activities and the nature and prevalence of transnational crime has increased with globalization. The developments of new technologies and means of transport, the growing interdependence of licit and illicit economies, and the expansion of multinational companies are factors that have facilitated transnational crimes. In the 1970s, criminal activities across borders were loosely linked to the economic expansion of multinational enterprises and considered as by-products of the new world order.

In 1975, the United Nations raised the alarm about changes in forms of national and transnational criminality at the UN Congress on the Prevention of Crime and the Treatment of Offenders (UN 1975). This Congress discussed transnational crime and its implications, identifying certain forms of transnational crime (UN 1975, at paragraph 120 p. 53). However, at this stage there was still confusion about domestic crimes across borders and transnational crimes. These included water pollution, particularly ocean dumping; the sale of harmful products, including drugs; the theft of cultural objects, including archaeological finds; air pollution; kidnapping; currency crimes; crimes related to fishing and the seas (food supplies); and evasion of taxes and exchange regulations.

A lot changed in the following 20 years, and by 1995 the United Nations linked transnational crimes to the globalization process and identified a growing concern over an increasing internationalization of crime which was defined by heighted cross-border mobility and the spread of ethnic conflicts (UN 1995, s.78c 'new areas of concern'). This coincided with the end of the Cold War, after which transnational crime replaced communism and the concerns over the potential for nuclear war as the new threat to international stability and order.

In its 1995 meeting the United Nations defined transnational crimes as 'offences whose inception, prevention and/or direct or indirect effects involved more than one country' (UN 1995, np). The United Nations also devised categories of transnational crimes which included:

- money laundering,
- terrorist activities,
- theft of art and cultural objects,
- theft of intellectual property,
- illicit arms trafficking,
- aircraft hijacking,
- sea piracy,
- insurance fraud,
- computer crime,
- environmental crime,
- trafficking in persons,
- trade in human body parts,
- illicit drug trafficking,
- fraudulent bankruptcy,
- infiltration of legal business,
- corruption,
- and bribery of public or party officials.

When the UN Congress met in 2000, discussions around transnational crimes had evolved into a more sophisticated legal-political analysis. Certain forms of transnational crimes were typified as more conventional, such as trafficking in drugs, stolen goods and human beings as well as money laundering, while emerging forms of crimes were also included. For instance a reference to the interdependence between legal and illegal markets was included in clear terms and examples were provided, such as when legal products, including nuclear material or pharmaceutical goods, are illegally traded. Corruption at governmental level and marketing of banned substances were also mentioned as emerging crimes. At the same meeting a new line of thinking, which connected transnational crimes to organized criminals, emerged (see Albanese 2015). It emphasized border security against the foreigner-other in a revamp of the alien conspiracy theory (Ruggiero 2000).

The consequence of this approach to transnational crime is a legacy that has marked the intervening 15 years with the introduction in 2000 of the UN Convention against Transnational Organized Crime and its adjunct protocols, the Protocol to Prevent, Suppress and Punish Trafficking in Persons, especially Women and Children, and the Protocol against the Smuggling of Migrants by Land, Sea and Air. These documents are now considered a milestone in the area of transnational crime: clear and internationally agreed definitions on specific forms of transnational crimes mean a step forward in the area of multilateral collaboration. It shows that nation-states have shifted from an abstract willingness to cooperate to substantial steps towards teamwork and national responsibility.

Alongside praise for the massive step forward in cooperation represented by the creation of the UN convention and protocols, we can also identify criticism. The most significant one is the slippage between the terms 'transnational crime' and 'transnational organized crime' – the two are often conflated. Ruggiero (2000) has criticized the classification of transnational crimes as being committed by organized criminal groups. Indeed the United Nations has used the term 'transnational organized crime' in its convention rather than 'transnational crime'. This can potentially limit practitioners and researchers in their understanding of transnational crimes: are transnational crimes always related to organized crime? The term 'organized crime' denotes a hierarchical structure and a systematic and controlled nature that conjures images of sophisticated criminal syndicates. However, this picture contradicts the actual experience of many law enforcement officials, who find transnational crime to be more disjointed and organic in nature and committed by groups with horizontal structures and weak ties (Sheptycki 2003, p. 124). As a corollary of this criticism, it is worth pointing out the divergence of policy attention to crimes other than those labelled as organized crime. Ruggiero (2000) laments that discussions over corruption, white collar and corporate crime may be of secondary importance if there is over-emphasis on 'organized crime' and criminal groups. Rothe and Friedrichs (2015) also question a similar attention-diverting policy, which has created a distortion of our understanding of crime and globalization, emphasizing the harm produced by intergovernmental organizations and international financial institutions. These points are important to bear in mind as we explore transnational crime throughout this book.

More recent documents from UNODC reveal a new phase in responses to transnational crime. Even more than before, the negative aspects of globalization and political instability are identified as sources of transnational crimes. While the overarching theme of organized crime is maintained in these discussions, Antonio Maria Costa, the former UNODC executive director, has emphasized that if we overlaid a world map of trafficking in goods and a map of unstable regions, we would easily identify that there is a correspondence between instability and the trafficking of goods (UNODC 2010a). This has marked a new 'official' way to see transnational crimes. Instead of retributive and punitive responses, this approach seeks to understand the needs of origin, transition and destination countries and to plan solutions to address the root causes of transnational crime, addressing issues of both supply and demand. Consequently, peace building and development operations are required to bring a level of stability to source and transit countries, thus advocating a more balanced and holistic understanding of, and response to, transnational crime.

Harm, Human Rights and Crimes of Globalization

The previous three sub-sections have highlighted the differences between domestic crimes with international ramifications, international crimes and transnational crimes. These types of crime all cross borders, but they do so in different ways and with different effects and responses. While we can form lists of the acts that constitute domestic, international and transnational crimes, it is worth noting that the borders of these definitions are not always clear cut and there can be a significant overlap and connection between these categories.

Transnational crimes, such as the arms trade and smuggling in illegal goods, can, for example, contribute to contexts of violence and instability in which international crimes occur. One example is the plundering of precious natural resources including gold and coltan (a metal used in electronic products such as mobile phones) from the Democratic Republic of Congo by neighbouring countries and local and international criminal groups and militias (Samset 2002). Criminal groups may go on to trade these materials illegally and gain significant profit, while locally this trade contributes to numerous deaths and produces anomic conditions in which violence and brutality occur. The ICC is, at the time of writing, investigating and prosecuting the violence in the Democratic Republic of Congo, after preliminary investigations indicated that war crimes and crimes against humanity have been committed in the region. In such situations where do domestic crimes, transnational crimes and international crimes start and end? The answer is not always clear. Even if we attempt to put legal boundaries and classifications around different acts as we label them in a particular manner, complex crimes rarely fit neatly into conceptual categories.

Another issue with legal definitions of different types of crime is that they are often presented as neutral and value-free categories, which can mask the politics that underpins determinations about which crimes are classed as international and transnational and which crimes are not. The conceptual classification of international and transnational crimes sets the agenda of international focus and thus some forms of harm may continue to go under the radar or be considered less important. Legal definitions are not value-free, but rather are constructed through diplomatic processes of negotiation which can be highly political, as the creation of the Rome Statute (1998, p. xx) illustrates.

It is particularly important to note this, as many acts which cause significant harm may fall outside the boundaries of the legal or working definitions of international or transnational crime outlined in the previous two sub-sections. Consider the numerous harms that are caused by globalization and the inequality of the global order. These include: the disproportionate impact of natural disasters on those in poor and underdeveloped areas; the poor living and working conditions of many people in the developing countries who produce consumer goods for the West; the rising obesity rates in Western countries compared with the number of starving and undernourished people in poor countries; disparate access to medical care and pharmaceutical goods; the many individuals forced into prostitution by their circumstances who need to make a living and support their families; and individuals who die at sea trying to flee their home countries, to seek asylum in other parts of the world. Of course, it is difficult to attribute these harms to a particular source, but it is, nevertheless, important to consider the impact of globalization on a more intangible level and the numerous harms that fall outside the rubric of legal definitions of crime.

Indeed, one of the most interesting developments in the area of transnational crime and criminology is that, alongside the most recognizable transnational crimes, we can identify acts that go beyond traditional interpretations of crime, as contained in criminal statutes and codes. This brings with it recognition of multiple forms and causes of human suffering, and marks the emergence of alternative concepts such as harm, violence and power. Since the 1970s, criminologists have increasingly called for criminology to focus on harm, suffering and human rights rather than exclusively examining acts deemed criminal by law (Schwendinger & Schwendinger 1970). Critical criminologists have also called for attention to be paid to the massive amounts of harm and financial damage caused by the immoral activities of corporations, institutions and states (Rothe & Friedrichs 2014).

Examining the different facets of transnational crime goes some way to heeding this call. This is reflected in the material covered in this book. For instance, in Chapter 8 we explore the harmful environmental impacts of globalization, while in Chapter 9 we examine the concept of 'state crime'. State crime is an emerging sub-field of critical criminology which explores the potential of the state to cause harm to the very citizens it is meant to protect, through abuses of its power. In conditions of globalization, state power is, in part, redistributed and now extends to international institutions and organizations. Recently, criminologists have coined the term **crimes of globalization** to highlight how the actions of institutions, such as the World Bank and the International Monetary Fund (IMF), can contribute significantly to harm, particularly in vulnerable regions (Rothe & Friedrichs 2014). We also discuss these crimes in Chapter 9.

In summary: domestic crimes are 'traditional' crimes that are defined as illegal by national laws; international crimes are crimes that threaten the whole of humanity and are listed in various sources of international criminal law, but predominately the Rome Statute of the International Criminal Court; and transnational crimes are crimes whose inception, prevention or effects involve more than one country. This book focuses predominately on transnational crime and responses to it; but, in doing so, it takes a broad approach by considering the impact and harm caused by a range of acts in times of globalization. It also locates responses to transnational crime within wider understandings of globalization and the different criminal justice measures that are emerging in response to crimes that cross borders in our global village.

1.3 Jurisdiction and Cooperation: Who is in Charge?

Throughout this book we will explore the complex relationships between actors at different levels (local, national, regional, international and global) as they respond to transnational crime. In this section we start to unpack some of the different layers of power and authority that constitute global space. Traditionally, criminal justice prosecutions and punishments have been the preserve of nations. Each state has implemented its own systems and process to respond to crime, creating different jurisdictions across the world. Now, however, new difficulties have emerged, as criminal activities challenge the territoriality of national jurisdictions. Increasingly, different jurisdictions must work together to combat and respond to cross-border crime.

Sovereignty, Borders and Geopolitics

The nation-state has been the primary unit of the global order since the seventeenth century when, in 1648, the signing of the treaties of the Peace of Westphalia ended the 30-year war in Europe. The Peace of Westphalia established **sovereignty** as the core principle of the global order, which is also known as the **Westphalian order**. The principle of sovereignty means that a state has full authority and power to govern itself and control affairs within its territorial limit. States also hold a monopoly on violence within their geographical boundaries and gain power through their legitimate use of physical force (the authorized violence of the police and the military) (Weber and Bowling 2004). Under the principle of sovereignty, states are free to govern and enforce their power without any intervention or interference from outside sources. Thus, in the Westphalian model, states are the primary unit of the international order and international cooperation occurs through diplomatic relations between states and heads of states or their representatives.

Considering the above definition of sovereignty, the norm of *non-interference* or *non-intervention* in the affairs of other nations has been a fundamental principle of the Westphalian order. As Oppenheim (cited in Jennings & Watts 1996, p. 428) states, the prohibition of intervention 'is a corollary of every state's right to sovereignty, territorial integrity and political independence'. This is why aggression, or the invasion of other states, is an international crime included in the Rome Statute of the International Criminal Court. However, although in theory non-intervention is a fundamental part of international law, in practice states, alongside other international bodies, have intervened in the affairs of other states since the singing of the Peace of Westphalia. For example, in the nineteenth and twentieth centuries, European colonialist projects in African and Asian countries significantly shaped the global order. During the Cold War (1947–1991) tensions between the Western Bloc (the United States and allies) and the Eastern Bloc (the Soviet Union and allies) were articulated through events in other countries, such as the Vietnam War and the Cuban Missile Crisis. More recently, we have witnessed the invasion of Iraq and Afghanistan by powerful nations including the United States and the United Kingdom. These countries justified the invasions on the grounds of self-defence: in Iraq they claimed that Saddam Hussein was developing weapons of mass destruction, harbouring terrorists and committing wide-scale human rights abuses; in Afghanistan they stated that they needed to dismantle al-Qaeda by removing the Taliban from power in the wake of the 9/11 terrorist attacks.

Other military interventions have been framed as humanitarian interventions and premised on the protection of civilians and their human rights. For example, in 1999, the North Atlantic Treaty Organization (NATO) conducted a series of military strikes in the former Yugoslavia in an attempt to halt atrocities in the Kosovo War. Since the 1990s, humanitarian interventions have increasingly relied on the developing norm of the **Responsibility to Protect** or R2P. The 'responsibility to protect' recasts sovereignty as a partial right, claiming that states forfeit their ability to govern their territory free from external interference when they fail to protect their population from mass atrocities and international crimes (genocide, crimes against humanity and war crimes). The norm of R2P places a duty on the international community to protect humankind and justifies the use of coercive measures, such as economic sanctions and military interventions, to deter or stop states from committing or enabling mass atrocities. In 2011 the responsibility to protect was invoked to substantiate US-led military interventions designed to halt escalating violence in Libya.

It is worth noting that the United Nations Security Council (UNSC) has played a role in sanctioning the use of force against states. Article 42 of the UN Charter gives the Security Council the authority to 'take action by air, sea or land forces as may be necessary to maintain or restore international peace and security'. The UNSC has authorized a number of naval blockades to enforce sanctions in Iraq, the former Yugoslavia, Haiti and Sierra Leone; it has authorized a limited use of force by UN peacekeeping operations in countries such as the former Yugoslavia, Somalia and the Democratic Republic of the Congo (DRC); and it has authorized the use of 'all necessary means' by multinational forces in situations including Rwanda, East Timor, Liberia and Iraq, just to name a few (UN 2015a).

Since the 1990s the UNSC has also mandated judicial intervention in mass atrocities establishing criminal tribunals such as the International Criminal Tribunal for the Former Yugoslavia and the International Criminal Tribunal for Rwanda. In 2001, the International Criminal Court was established as a permanent court to prosecute international crimes as they occurred around the world. The ICC is independent of the United Nations; however, the UNSC still interacts with, and influences, the ICC. For example, in 2011, UNSC Resolution 1970 authorized military intervention and economic sanctions in Libya and simultaneously referred the situation to the ICC for investigation and potential prosecution. If the ICC had not received this referral from the UNSC it would not have been able to investigate, and later prosecute, the situation in Libya as Libya is not a party of the Court.

As these examples illustrate, military interventions and 'just wars' are often legitimated through reference to international law, and international criminal law has become a new form of interference in state affairs. Indeed, international law has often provided moral imperatives to intervene in the affairs of other countries, as is seen in the development of the responsibility to protect norm. This brings us to an important point, the gap between principles and reality in the operation of the international order. The aforementioned examples highlight that although the international order may be based on the principle of non-intervention, reality is often shaped by **realpolitik**. Realpolitik describes politics based on power, practical and material considerations, and strategic interests rather than ethical or moral premises. Viewed through the prism of realpolitik, we can see that more powerful states and blocs (normally Western countries such as the United States and the United Kingdom) are able to operate more effectively within the international order to protect their own interests and achieve their own goals, whereas less powerful (traditionally developing countries) often suffer at the hands of the West. This dynamic means that the idea of an international community is a contested concept and based on power differentials and **geopolitics**.

Some argue that, within this environment, the creation of new international institutions, which adopt powers normally reserved for states, evidences the gradual erosion of sovereignty. While international developments do demonstrate some diminishment of sovereignty, the interference in the affairs of other nations is not a particularly new phenomenon, nor is the state completely withering away. As illustrated in the example of colonialism, borders have always been porous and penetrable, malleable for some, and rigid for others. Sovereignty is ambivalent: it is invoked in particular circumstances and denied in others. Instead of a simple erosion of borders, what we now see is the proliferation of different forms of authority and borders that are constantly renegotiated and shifting. There are times when the state diminishes in power, yet there are also times when state authorities exercise considerable power and enforce their territorial borders. Borders and the concept of sovereignty still play an important role in the international system; the United Nations and the ICC are themselves made up of state parties and rely heavily on state support. Despite this, state power is also often diluted as new layers and levels of power emerge from local, national, regional and international to global.

A Proliferation of Actors

Today, it is difficult to confine crimes to single nations, as people, drugs and weapons flow across borders. Although crime travels across borders, criminal justice systems often remain territorially bound. This necessitates regional and international cooperation, which has created a proliferation of actors working on issues of crime and justice. One development has been an increase in the number of organizations that exist to provide governance and oversight at a global level. The United Nations is the foremost example of an international organization, in which states have handed over some of their powers to ensure global cooperation. The United Nations has a broad range of tasks, with one of these being to combat transnational and international crimes that impact upon global peace and security and threaten human rights. In order to help combat transnational crime, the United Nations has developed the United Nations Office on Drugs and Crime (UNODC), which assists states to fight transnational crime in all its dimensions, and the United Nations Interregional Crime and Justice Research Institute (UNICRI), which carries out research and training and implements technical cooperation programmes in order 'to assist governments and the international community at large in tackling criminal threats to social peace, development and political stability, and in fostering the development of just and efficient criminal justice systems' (UNICRI 2015).

The United Nations has also created a number of other offices and bodies that are involved in different aspects of international and transnational crimes and justice. One example is UN peacekeeping forces, which are comprised of civilians, police officers and military personnel and are deployed to assist countries' transition from conflict to peace. UN peacekeepers have been employed in many different situations around the world, including conflicts in East Timor, Rwanda, Sierra Leone, Haiti and Bosnia and Herzegovina. The role of peacekeepers is to protect civilians and assist in reconstruction efforts. We cannot consider UN peacekeepers as the police or military arm of the international order; peacekeepers work on the consent of the parties, they are impartial, and they are bound by principles of non-force (except in self-defence). The International Criminal Police Organization, or Interpol, is the world's largest international police organization, with 190 member countries. Interpol exists to enhance police cooperation around the world and offers information sharing, communications channels, expert support and training. Interpol is not a supranational law enforcement agency: it is politically neutral and has no powers of arrest. It is, instead, a network that enhances police cooperation, particularly for crimes that cross borders. As Interpol's website states, its role involves 'connecting police for a safer world' (Interpol 2015).

There are also several other prominent examples of international intergovernmental organizations that are broadly involved in crime. The North Atlantic Treaty Organization (NATO) is an intergovernmental political and military alliance that consists of 28 independent member countries. NATO 'promotes democratic values and encourages consultation and cooperation on defence and security issues' (NATO 2015). NATO also has the military capacity to intervene in conflicts and crises, which it has used in interventions in countries such as Bosnia and Herzegovina, Kosovo, Afghanistan, Iraq and Libya. There are also financial institutions, such as the World Bank, which is a UN financial institution that provides loans to developing countries for capital programmes, and the International Monetary Fund (IMF), which consists of 188 countries working to foster global monetary cooperation.

In addition to the United Nations and global intergovernmental organizations, there are several regional collaborations, both formal and informal, that operate to govern different geographical areas of the globe. The European Union (EU) is the most advanced and formalized example of regional cooperation. The EU consists of 28 member states and operates through a system of supranational institutions and intergovernmental negotiated decisions. The EU has created Europol and Eurojust to help coordinate responses to crime across Europe. Europol works closely with law enforcement agencies in EU member states, and around the world, to facilitate information sharing, coordinate expertise and provide strategic intelligence to help tackle criminal organization and terrorist networks that operate across borders. As with Interpol, Europol officers do not have direct powers of arrest, but rather exist to support law enforcement officers in EU member countries and to undertake investigations and analysis to help solve criminal cases in EU countries. Similarly, Eurojust exists to stimulate and coordinate criminal investigations and prosecutions in EU member states. This work involves facilitating the execution of international mutual legal assistance and the implementation of extradition requests and helping to coordinate the complex cross-border prosecutions that arise from transnational crimes. Other examples of regional bodies of cooperation include the African Union, the Arab League, the Commonwealth of Nations, the South Asian Association for Regional Cooperation and the Association of Southeast Asian Nations.

As you will note, the aforementioned organizations are founded on nation-states and exist to increase cooperation and strategic information sharing and policy planning between states. None of these international and regional organizations eclipse state power, and they can sometimes buttress it. While these organizations do have some powers and can undertake important interventions, they often rely on coercive measures to influence state behaviour and have limited powers of enforcement. States are the primary unit of these organizations, as NATO's website proclaims, 'the most important players in the North Atlantic Treaty Organization are the member countries themselves'.

Alongside these intergovernmental organizations are numerous **non-governmental organizations** (NGOs) and actors that exist to protect human rights, respond to transnational and international crimes and help promote justice. The steady increase in the number of non-government actors working in the public sphere has led the rise of the term **global civil society**, which refers to the assemblage of international non-governmental organizations (INGOs), professional organizations, social movements, media and interest groups that engage in dialogue about society and the interests of citizens. Global civil society is a space constituted by a vast array of groups. This includes large INGOs, such as the Red Cross, Amnesty International, Greenpeace and Human Rights Watch, through to smaller and more niche organizations. Often NGOs, working on a shared issue, are drawn together through alliances. The Global Alliance Against Traffic in Women, for example, brings together more than 100 NGOs from all regions of the world, connected by a concern for the victims of human trafficking. Similarly, the Coalition for the International Criminal Court unites over 2,500 civil society organizations in 150 different countries to strengthen international cooperation with the CICC (CICC 2015).

Spotlight – International Conferences and Actors

The vast number of actors operating within global civil space is exemplified during international conventions and conferences surrounding transnational crime. One example is the bi-annual conference convened to discuss, promote and review the implementation of the UN Convention against Transnational Organized Crime. Held in Vienna in 2014 the last conference involved an extensive list of delegates, as demonstrated in Figure 1.2.

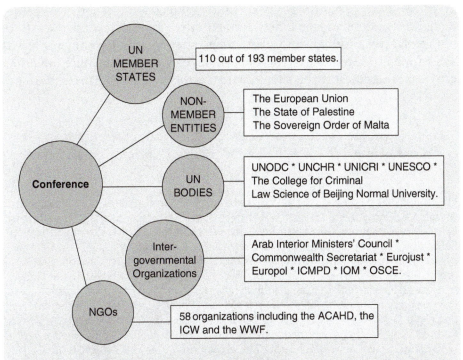

Figure 1.2 Conference of the Parties to the UN Convention against Transnational Organized Crime, Seventh Session, Vienna, 6–10 October 2014

*UNODC = UN Office of Drugs and Crime
UNHCR = UN High Commissioner for Refugees
UNICRI = UN Interregional Crime and Justice Research Institute
UNESCO = UN Educational, Scientific and Cultural Organization
ICMPD = International Centre for Migration Policy Development
IOM = International Organization for Migration
OSCE = Organization for Security and Co-operation in Europe
ACAHD = African Center for Advocacy and Human Development
WWF = World Wide Fund for Nature

Cosmopolitanism and Cultural Clashes

This proliferation of actors and the increased need for cooperation between states to respond to transnational crime bring with them numerous clashes over values, and conflicts over jurisdiction, legitimacy and the correct procedure and punishment for crimes. Some commentators consider that globalization has brought with it an increase in universal or global values, as demonstrated by the idea that international crimes affect the whole of humanity which underpins institutions such as the ICC. These perspectives adhere to **cosmopolitanism**, that is, the *ideology* that all humans belong to a single *community* based on a shared *morality*. However, the idea of an international community is contested as it consists of multiple actors with completely different viewpoints. Additionally, international society is often driven by political interests which can be divisive, creating inequalities and gaps rather than fostering inclusivity and harmony. Despite a need for cooperation, perspectives on crime and justice can diverge significantly between different actors and states. This is illustrated by Case Study 1.2.

Case Study 1.2 – The Bali Nine, Police Cooperation and the Death Penalty

On 17 April 2005, nine Australian citizens were arrested in Bali as they attempted to smuggle 8.3 kg of heroin, worth AU$4 million, into Australia. Michael Czugaj, Renae Lawrence, Scott Rush and Martin Stephens were arrested by the Indonesian National Police (INP) at Denpasar Airport before boarding a flight to Sydney. Police found packages of heroin strapped to their bodies. Andrew Chan, one of the organizers of the group, was arrested separately at Denpasar Airport. Si Yi Chen, Tach Duc Thanh Nguyen, Myuran Sukumaran and Matthew Norman were later arrested in a hotel room where the INP discovered 350 grams of heroin in a suitcase. Police charged each of the nine with trafficking heroin. In February 2006, the Denpasar District Court sentenced Lawrence, Rush, Czugaj, Stephens, Norman, Chen and Nguyen to life imprisonment (Lawrence's sentence was later downgraded to 20 years' imprisonment). The court sentenced the ringleaders, Chan and Sukumaran, to death by firing squad; long processes of legal appeal and demands for presidential clemency against the death penalties ensued; however, the death penalties were upheld and the executions were carried out in the early hours of 29 April 2015.

The case caused considerable controversy in Australia due to the Australian Federal Police's (AFP's) role in facilitating the arrests. On the 8 April 2005, the AFP wrote to the INP with details, including the names and potential travel plans, of the trafficking group. This intelligence led the Indonesian Police to undertake a surveillance operation of the Bali Nine that later enabled the arrest and successful prosecution of the members of the group. The AFP faced criticism for sharing the information with the INP knowing that the traffickers, who were Australian citizens, could face the death penalty if found guilty in Indonesia. Some commentators suggested that the AFP should have ensured that the traffickers were arrested upon arrival in Australia or received assurances that the death penalty would not be imposed before 'tipping off' the INP. The families of Rush and Lawrence even launched court action against the AFP, alleging the police were wrong to pass on information to Indonesia that led to their arrests.

The case illustrated the tensions between Australia's objection to the death penalty, and the need for Australia to strengthen police cooperation to combat transnational crimes such as drug trafficking. In Australia, the death penalty is prohibited under the Death Penalty Abolition Act 1973 (Cth). Australia has also signed and ratified the International Covenant on Civil and Political Rights (ICCPR) and the Second Optional Protocol to the International Covenant on Civil and Political Rights, Aiming at the Abolition of the Death Penalty. Australia's acceptance of these treaties imposes a moral obligation on Australia to ensure that its citizens will not face the death penalty. At the same time, Australia's acceptance of other international treaties, such as the UN Convention against Illicit Traffic in Narcotic Drugs and Psychotropic Substances and the UN Convention against Transnational Organized Crime, obliges it to work with other states to combat transnational crime. To this end, Australia has also signed law enforcement cooperation agreements with other countries, such as the Agreement between Australia and the Republic of Indonesia on the Framework for Security Cooperation and the Memorandum of Understanding between the Government of the Republic of Indonesia and the Government of Australia on Combating Transnational Crime and Developing Police Cooperation.

Within this milieu of international obligations come policy considerations: is the imperative for the AFP to build and maintain strong intelligence-sharing traditions and cooperative relationships with other jurisdictions, particularly with its neighbouring countries, many of which retain the death penalty? In response to criticisms over the handling of the Bali Nine case, the then AFP Commissioner Mick Keelty highlighted that the AFP did not have sufficient evidence to charge the Bali Nine and would not have been able to successfully close down the syndicate if it had waited for arrests in Australia. Keelty also highlighted that the AFP policy of forward engagement had resulted in significant successes in shutting down drug trafficking operations in the past.

While this case illustrates the difficulties and complexities involved in navigating multi-jurisdictional investigations into transnational crime, it also demonstrates the sophisticated nature of state-based criminal justice systems, which have been evolving over centuries. Many countries, and in particular most Western countries operating on democratic principles, distribute the task of administering justice to separate institutions, such as the police, the judiciary and correctional authorities (note that even within these enclosed justice systems we see clashes between different aims and values and difficulties in cooperation between actors). Thus, when we think about and study the criminal justice system, usually the hierarchical pyramid of police–prosecutors–courts is pictured, perhaps at times with some further offices involved, like the Department of Correctional Services. The international criminal justice system stands in stark opposition to this picture. International criminal justice involves numerous actors whose roles are often unclear. There is not a formal separation of powers or a well-defined system through which justice is administered. In fact, international courts operate within any real means of enforcement as there is no international police force. Also problematic is the lack of democratic governance systems to embed these courts within, meaning they risk being politically expedient and entrenching geopolitics.

At this stage, it is difficult to make an argument for an International Criminal Justice System using the tools and knowledge that have been applied so far. If the modern criminal justice system is relatively young and still developing in many areas, an embryonic hierarchical structure of international criminal justice simply does not exist as yet. However, there is increasing interest and space to start talking about international criminal justice, and the beginnings of processes which will establish a more organized structure in the long term. There are areas within this newborn system that are more developed than others, for instance the fight against drug lords has involved several international agencies for some decades now, yet the fight against environmental crimes is seen as a new area of concern, and until very recently this area had minimal organization.

1.4 The Structure of this Book

Throughout this book we examine the phenomenon of transnational crime and responses to it. While the focus of the book is on transnational crimes, we seek to understand these crimes within their broader context. To this end, we explore social theories that assist in conceptualizing the changing nature of the globe and the social space in which transnational crime occurs. We examine the processes of criminalization that are a reflection of many different social structures and influences. We consider how economic and political forces shape transnational crime and responses to it. We do not take the proscribed list of transnational crimes as a given, but rather interrogate the reasons why some acts are defined as crimes while other behaviour, which has the potential to cause considerable damage, is deemed harmful, but not criminal. Thus, we examine transnational crime and justice through a wide lens to understand the myriad complex ways that crime and justice cross borders in the twenty-first century. This brings with it an exploration of how space is being reconstituted, as new levels of authority, new regional and global blocs of power and new virtual spheres emerge, all significantly influencing the way crime is committed and justice administered.

Part 1 of the book explores different theories of crime and justice in the twenty-first century. This part of the book is designed to provide a theoretical backdrop for later explorations of particular forms of transnational crime. Chapter 2 explores different approaches to globalization and examines how borders are both eroding and proliferating as the role of the nation-state and sovereignty is reformulated in a time of heightened mobility. Chapter 3 examines **neoliberal** and risk paradigms, which have a significant bearing on the way crime and justice are framed in times of heightened uncertainty, particularly post-9/11. This chapter also looks at the increasing role of networks and cyberspace. Chapter 4 explores how trends in crime and justice, such as a focus on **penal populism** and **punitiveness**, can travel around the globe through **policy transfer**, convergence, information sharing and the development of new international criminal justice mechanisms and institutions. As this chapter highlights, some of these mechanisms are more developed than others, yet overall the international 'system' of justice remains quite piecemeal, often negotiated through states and intergovernmental organizations and facilitated by cooperation and communication rather than force.

Part 2 looks at different forms of transnational crime. Chapter 5 explores issues around mobility, sex and the human body, examining human trafficking, sexual exploitation and tourism, trafficking in organs and the trade in surrogacy as examples of the increasing movement and **commodification** of the body. Chapter 6 looks at organized crime as a transnational phenomenon, exploring domestic, regional and international responses to various forms of organized crime and considering how and why organized crime is seen as an international problem. Chapter 7 examines terrorism and focuses on ways of explaining the nature and significance of terrorism, as well as how both nation-states and the broader international community have responded to terrorism and constructed it as a threat. Chapter 8 explores crimes against the environment, which range in severity and impact. Some crimes against the environment represent mass disasters and significantly impact on particular regions and populations of the globe. Some environmental issues, such as climate change, may have devastating global impacts yet are not currently considered criminal. Other acts against the environment include harm to wildlife, such as poaching, and smuggling flora and fauna. Chapter 9 examines the field of **state crime** to consider how we can reframe transnational crime to include a broader range of acts and actors. This chapter discusses the role of the state and the degree to which the state can be held criminally responsible for its actions, some of which may cause significant harm to people and territory. In Chapter 10, the conclusion to this book, we look at the future of transnational crime and consider the possibility of a global criminology that can more adequately understand and respond to the wide variety of ways that crimes traverse borders and constitute global space.

Questions: Revise and Reflect

1. What are some of the differences between domestic, transnational and international crimes?

2. Are countries legally obligated to uphold the treaties and conventions to which they are signatories? Who holds them to account if they don't?

3. Consider your thoughts on the Bali Nine case. Do you think it was right for Australia to tip off the Indonesian forces?

Further Reading

Aas, K 2012, *Globalization and crime*, Sage, London.

Findlay, M 2013, *International and comparative criminal justice: A critical introduction*, Routledge, London.

Natarajan, M (ed.) 2011, *International crime and justice*, Cambridge University Press, New York.

Reichel, P & Albanese, J (eds) 2014, *Handbook of transnational crime and justice*, Sage, Thousand Oaks, CA.

Websites to Visit

Australian Institute of Criminology Organised and Transnational Crime: www.aic.gov.au/crime_types/transnational.html

Eurojust: www.eurojust.europa.eu/Pages/home.aspx

International Criminal Court: www.icc-cpi.int/en_menus/icc/Pages/default.aspx

United Nations Office of Drugs and Crime: www.unodc.org/

UN Repertoire of the Practice of the Security Council: www.un.org/en/sc/repertoire/

PART 1
APPROACHES TO TRANSNATIONAL CRIME AND JUSTICE

2
Globalization and Mobility

This chapter will look at

- Theories of globalization.
- Global–local interactions and relationships.
- Mobility and social exclusion.

Keywords

Globalization	Glocalization	Mobility
Late modernity	Social stratification	

2.1 Introduction

Globalization is a buzzword that has significantly shaped the start of the twenty-first century. The term has been used by academics, journalists, politicians, economists, corporations and advertising professionals alike to describe a growing sense of global interconnectedness that shapes political, economic, social and cultural life. Sociologist Anthony Giddens (2002, p. 7) stated, 'globalisation may not be a particularly elegant word. But absolutely no one who wants to understand our prospects at century's end can ignore it.' In this chapter we will explore the variety of approaches towards globalization and unpack the concept to better understand the nature and structure of the world in which crime is enmeshed. We examine the key social theories that explain the connected, fast-paced and global character of the world at the beginning of the twenty-first century, including theories on mobility. We consider how the changing nature of social, economic and political relations constitutes new spaces, different levels of control and regulation (local, national, regional, international, global), and shifting and dynamic relationships where power and influence are constantly renegotiated and reconfigured in processes of **glocalization**. As we move through these theories and explanations we can see that the increasingly transnational nature of crime and its control is entwined within broader changes in social, political and economic relations that structure the world.

Globalization involves a complex series of processes and conditions. There are many different ideas about the causes, conceptualization, periodization, impacts and trajectories of globalization (Held et al. 1999) and these ideas raise numerous questions. Is globalization a new phenomenon? Does globalization signal the start of a new epoch? Is globalization defined by economic, political, or social forces? Does globalization create positive opportunities or does it negatively impact on the environment and local populations? Who and what is driving globalization? Is globalization a top–down process by which cultural differences are diminished or does it enrich culture and deepen social life? Based on their views on these questions globalization theorists can be grouped into three categories: **radical globalists**, **globalization sceptics** and **global transformationalists**. We explore each of these approaches in this chapter to highlight the many different facets of globalization. To do this we refer to Case Study 2.1 to demonstrate how approaches to globalization construct events differently and to illustrate the complexity of globalization. At first glance, the case study may appear to be confined to one country, Bangladesh, but throughout this chapter we will see how it highlights the far-reaching impacts of globalization. Globalization creates a world in motion (Aas 2007a). In the final part of this chapter we explore how mobility and movement significantly shape contemporary social life.

An important part of the discussions throughout this chapter is the exploration of how the changing nature and shape of the world produce new forms of social stratification, the system by which society ranks categories of people in a hierarchy, on a global level. We question how different groups and individuals are marginalized or excluded from dominant discourses through prevailing paradigms and ways of seeing the world. Social stratification is often examined at state level when we consider how some groups have greater status, power and wealth than other groups. In a world of increasing global connection, interaction and interdependence, it is important to consider how social stratification operates at a global level. Why is this important? The structure of society significantly influences how crime is constructed, committed and controlled. Critical criminology frequently examines the genesis of crime and the nature of 'justice' through the lens of class structure and inequality. As space, place and society are transformed through processes of globalization it is necessary to locate crime within global social structures. Globalization and mobility theories change the way we view place and space and thereby influence the construction of crime and responses to it at both global and local levels.

2.2 Globalization: Towards a Borderless World

When you woke up this morning and decided what to wear did you pull on a pair of jeans? This simple and seemingly benign act of wearing jeans may appear to be a straightforward and uncomplicated personal choice based on your fashion preferences, but it is, in fact, the product of a series of global forces in which you are inextricably enmeshed. Wearing jeans is an act influenced by global mobility, multinational corporations and cultural imperialism. Your jeans travelled a long way to get to you this morning: they may have been designed in the United States, the cotton harvested in India and the yarn spun in Turkey. The yarn might then have been dyed in Taiwan, with indigo from Italy and the textile woven in Poland. The thread could have been manufactured in Hungary, the zip made from brass from Japan and the buttons from Australian zinc. Finally, the jeans could have been sewn together in Tunisia, pumice stonewashed in Turkey, and the final product sent to your local department store. Or perhaps you bought your jeans online and they were parcelled up and sent to your door, wherever you happen to live in the world.

Your choice of jeans may have been an easy one, driven by current fashion, comfort and price, but behind that choice lie decades of cultural evolution; jeans were transformed from a utilitarian garment to the embodiment of the American ethos and then exported to the world, becoming one of the most popular fashion items today. As this brief tour of a pair of jeans highlights, forces of globalization reach and influence almost every aspect of our daily lives.

In its simplest form globalization is 'the widening, deepening and speeding up of worldwide interconnectedness in all aspects of contemporary life' (Held et al. 1999, p. 2); however, globalization is a nebulous and contested concept. There are many different perspectives on the causes and consequences of globalization and debates over its extent and novelty. Some view it as a phenomenon that accelerated towards the end of the twentieth century, as transport and telecommunication technologies rapidly developed and brought the world closer together in time and space (Giddens 2002). Certainly in the twenty-first century we see a level of mobility and connection that far exceeds that of just 50 years ago. However, others disagree, arguing that globalization is not a new phenomenon and that the human race has always been globally inclined, as evidenced by the first migrations of people out of Africa 100,000 years ago. Since these early movements, humans have sought global connection through trade, religion, conquest and travel.

The term 'globalization' first appeared in the 1960s, yet it only gained popularity and momentum from the 1990s before which the term 'internationalization' was more common. Globalization differs from internationalization as it describes the emergence of a global space, whereas internationalization alludes to the ongoing primacy and importance of states and the relationships between them. Consider the etymology of the words: inter-national as opposed to global. In this departure from thinking 'internationally' to thinking 'globally' we see the crux of what we mean when we refer to globalization, the creation and conditions of a space which transcends the national border. These conditions mean that nations are not insulated frontiers of power and economics and arbiters of identity and culture. Instead, the local can rarely escape the influence of global forces while, simultaneously, local events are magnified to have global import.

Case Study 2.1 – Dying for Fashion

Wall of missing photos

© Photo by Sharat Chowdhury via Wikimedia Commons

When deep cracks appeared in the walls of the Rana Plaza building in Savar, Bangladesh, no one could have foreseen the scale of the tragedy that was soon to unfold. The building, which contained a shopping centre and five garment factories, could house approximately 5,000 workers (Motlagh 2014) who were sub-contracted to supply Western clothing chains such as Primark, Joe Fresh, Kik and Benetton, and Walmart (*Economist* 2013a; Kuttner 2013). Workers were crammed into the large floors and worked long hours in dangerous conditions, yet the owner of the building, Sohel Rana, was unmoved by the appearance of the cracks, declaring his building to be safe for another hundred years (Motlagh 2014).

The police did not agree. On 23 April 2013, they evacuated the building following advice from local technicians, who deemed Rana Plaza to be vulnerable and unsafe. It and surrounding businesses shut their doors. The next morning, however, Rana ordered workers to return to work. A well-known supporter of the ruling Awami League Party, Rana had ulterior motives for this insistence: he did not want the workers taking part in strike action, called by opponents to the party, and instead had plans to mobilize them for possible street protests later that day (Motlagh 2014). The factory owners, conscious that orders were overdue, also pressured workers and threatened to withhold their monthly pay if they did not return (Motlagh 2014; Yardley 2013a). Accordingly, many workers, who would have been unable to survive without their wage, entered the building to work.

At 8.45 a.m. the power in the building went off, a common occurrence in the greater Dakar area. The building's four heavy diesel generators, located on the upper floors, kicked in and their vibrations were felt throughout the building (Yardley 2013a). The vibrations caused the structurally unsound upper floors to fall in quick succession and the lower floors pancaked under their weight (Burke 2013). Rana, who was trapped in his basement office, was dug out by his bodyguards (Motlagh 2014). Within minutes the site was besieged by panic-stricken relatives, who attempted their own rescues, hindering access by emergency services who failed to control the site (*Economist* 2013a). More concerned with national pride than saving lives, the government declined offers of international help to send rescue teams with machinery and sniffer dogs (Motlagh 2014).

The official death toll from the tragedy came to 1,138 people (*Washington Post* 2014). More than 2,500 people were injured; many suffering serious injuries, amputations and disabilities that dramatically affected their ability to support themselves and their families (Siegle 2014). The Rana Plaza collapse became the worst industrial accident in South Asia since the Bhopal disaster in 1984 (*Economist* 2013a).

Radical globalists hold a strong and optimistic view of globalization, believing that it marks the start of a new epoch when borders are eroded through global economic flows and technological advancement. The perspective of radical globalists is not interchangeable with radical ideas on politics and society and it is not aligned with **radical criminology**, which views crime as caused by economic forces in society. Instead the term 'radical globalists', also referred to as 'hyper-globalists' (Held et al. 1999), refers to those who agree that globalization is a new phenomenon that is significantly shaping the world and social, political and economic life as we know it. From the radical globalist perspective, states can no longer control or regulate financial markets and corporations that extend beyond national borders, meaning that state power is significantly diminished. From this position **neoliberalism**, and its emphasis on free market principles, drives globalization and creates the conditions through which a truly global space is created. The impact of economic globalization is a reconfiguration of global social stratification in which the traditional structure of core and periphery states (or the **global north** and the **global south**) is replaced by a stratification based on the division of labour and a complex architecture of economic power. Reflecting this perspective, management consultant and organizational theorist Kenichi Ohmae describes globalization as the 'end of the nation state' (Ohmae 1995) and the start of a 'borderless world' (Ohmae 1994).

While Ohame's analysis is primarily economic, the borderless world theory of radical globalists extends beyond the global financial sector to shape other aspects of society. For example, **international criminal law** and human rights advocates suggest that international courts are needed to provide justice beyond the nation-state as serious crimes and mass atrocities affect the whole of the human race. This sentiment is reflected in the Preamble of the Rome Statute of the International Criminal Court which declares that the ICC exists to address atrocities that 'deeply shock the conscience of humanity', 'threaten the peace, security and well-being of the world' and concern the 'international community as a whole' (Rome Statute 1998, p. 1). Within these phrases, we see the idea of interconnection and shared experience, which transcend state borders and create a global cosmopolitan community. We also see kernels of this idea of a universal or shared fate in responses to transnational crimes, which highlight the limitations of the national authorities in combating highly mobile and global criminal networks that operate beyond the confines of states and benefit from global economic flows.

The Rana Plaza example clearly demonstrates the impact of global economic flows and multinational corporations on local lives. The erosion of economic boundaries means that the fashion industry has become a global enterprise with corporations able to outsource the manufacture of clothing to countries where production costs are lower. Nations and state authorities play a minor role in these arrangements with negotiations occurring between global corporations and local factory owners. Of course, within these relationships multinational corporations hold significantly more power than local factories as they can shop around to find the factory that will complete the job for the lowest price. As radical globalists highlight, this demonstrates the development of global social stratification based on differences between those who produce (individuals working in Bangladeshi sweatshops) and those who consume (individuals in countries such as the United Kingdom and the United States who can buy cheap clothing from major retailers).

There are some benefits of this global restratification. The globalization of the fashion supply chain, for example, creates employment opportunities in developing countries with large populations and high rates of poverty. It is estimated that the textile industry employs 3.5 million people in Bangladesh alone. Most of these individuals come from poverty and many are women who are supporting their families (Bearnot 2013). Although workers earn little more than a dollar a day and the working conditions are arduous (Kuttner 2013), the pay is generally better than other industries – clothing factories pay three to seven times more than other unskilled labour in developing countries (Gregory 2013) – and the work is less taxing than alternative employment. Since the EU relaxed its rules, allowing the poorest countries to import fabric to be stitched into garments (rather than produce it themselves), Bangladesh has become the second largest exporter of textiles in the world behind China, and its GDP has grown by an average of 6% every year for the past decade (Bearnot 2013). The number of Bangladeshis living in poverty has dropped 25% since 2000, largely due to the meteoric rise of the garment industry (Gregory 2013).

In addition, the erosion of borders and the global competition over lucrative manufacturing contracts means that the international community can exert pressure on local governments and business owners in countries such as Bangladesh to ensure working conditions are improved and better outcomes are achieved for victims in the wake of accidents. For example, following the Rana Plaza collapse a combination of bad publicity and the risk of losing favourable tariffs has forced the government to make legislative changes. At the time of the collapse the minimum wage for garment workers was the lowest in the world at just US$37 per month (Greenhouse 2013). In November 2013, ahead of elections, the government pressured the Bangladesh Garment Manufactures and Exporters Association to raise it to US$68 per month (Motlagh 2014). It has also allowed more workers to unionize, with more than 140 new unions registering since the start of 2013 compared to just two for the previous three years (*New York Times* 2014). These examples illustrate some of the benefits of globalization as seen through the hyper-globalist, or radical globalist, framework that views the current era as the end of the nation-state.

2.3 Against Globalization

Despite the aforementioned benefits of globalization and its diminishment of borders, there are also many negative effects of globalization. Globalization, particularly when it is linked to advanced industrialization and capitalism, can have a detrimental impact on the environment, on marginalized social groups and on developing countries. Terms such as **Americanization**, McDonaldization (Ritzner 1993), or Disneyization allude to these negative impacts. These terms view globalization as a process by which Western values of turbo-capitalism, consumerism, democracy and individualization are exported from America out into the world. Certainly, there is a trend towards heightened capitalism and consumerism that is pushed forward by global financial markets and a culture of consumption spread by global marketing and shared cultural products. Coca-Cola, for example, is one of the biggest global brands today, selling over 1.8 billion drinks every day (BBC 2012). Founded in 1886 in Atlanta, United States, the iconic red and white packaging and branding can now be seen all around the world and the drink is a popular, everyday choice, from Argentina to Afghanistan. Through this lens globalization can be seen as a top–down process driven by corporate capitalism and economic imperatives.

There are wide-reaching side effects of global economic development and global financial markets driven by capitalism: financial crises can echo across the world, global inequality and poverty increase as the rich get richer and the poor get poorer, environmental destruction ensues as profits are pursued at all costs, and we all feel the need to 'keep up' as life gets faster and more mobile and global. Rampant capitalism and consumerism can entrench global inequalities, the likes of which are illustrated by the Rana Plaza example. The contrast between the lives of those who purchased cheap clothing made in Rana Plaza, and those who made it, is extreme. Consumers in the **global north** increasingly demand cheap, fashionable clothing and there is no limit on where they can find it. Primark in the United Kingdom, for example, sells t-shirts made in Bangladesh for as little as £2 (approximately US$1.6).

This consumer demand places pressure on retailers and manufacturers throughout the supply chain, meaning manufacturers hunt for ways to keep production costs down in a globally competitive market. The solution is often to produce clothing in countries where standards around working conditions, pay and building safety are low. Bangladesh has more than 5,000 garment factories but only 40 building inspectors (Harris 2013) and the Prime Minister has declared that 90% of all buildings meet no building code (*Economist* 2013a).

Alongside these low standards is a culture of corruption and cronyism that further compromises safety as local businesses scramble to make profits from international textile contracts. Huge economic power is tied up in the garment industry, which constitutes 80% of Bangladesh's exports (Yardley 2013b), and factory owners finance political campaigns which gives them broad influence. Rana Plaza exemplifies this. Although Rana Plaza was eight storeys high, planning permission had only been granted for five stories with the top three floors constructed illegally to house garment factories (Yardley 2013a). A ninth floor was also under construction. Construction quality was poor, disregarding building codes and using sub-standard materials. It has been alleged that Mr Rana bribed local officials for construction approvals (Yardley 2013a). Furthermore, Bangladesh's Fire Service and Civil Defence had signed off on Rana Plaza's building and safety compliance multiple times, giving it an A rating most recently on 4 April (Motlagh 2014).

The burden to carry the impacts of price-reducing measures falls on the most vulnerable groups and individuals, those who are desperate for work to support their families in poor and developing countries such as Bangladesh. Individuals work long hours in appalling conditions with low job security. Machinist Paki Begum, for example, worked 12–14 hours a day, six days a week, to earn US$110 a month before the Rana Plaza collapse (Motlagh 2014). Such vulnerable individuals have no choice but to put their safety at risk by working in these conditions. This cost 1,138 people in Rana Plaza their lives and injured more than 2,500 others, many of whom will be unable to work and support their families in future, due to the serious nature of their injuries.

Large fashion brands continue to make profits in the wake of Rana Plaza. In the aftermath of the disaster, it was proposed that Western garment purchasers should accept more corporate responsibility for what happens in the factories they buy from (Kuttner 2013). The Accord on Fire and Building Safety in Bangladesh was created to this end. Currently, 190 brands, retailers and importers have signed the Accord (Accord 2015); however, 15 major US retailers refuse to sign, citing issues of unacceptable liability (Bearnot 2013). Some corporations have paid compensation to Rana Plaza victims, yet this remains sporadic and inadequate (Motlagh 2014). In neoliberal globalization, multinational corporations create the conditions where low standards are accepted in the name of profits. However, it is difficult to regulate or punish multinational corporations that exist beyond the apparatus of the state and thus represent a law unto themselves. In this context, profits rely on the exploitation of workers in developing countries leading to inequality and deep, yet often hidden, social stratification. Eminent sociologist Zygmunt Bauman (1998) analyses the human consequences of globalization, highlighting how globalized consumerism and consumption have entrenched differences between the haves and have nots, creating a stratified global order.

In the global marketplace, the gap between workers and consumers has increased such that the plight of the workers is all but invisible to those who commission and purchase the goods they produce. At the other end of the supply chain, multinational corporations are also hidden behind a cloak of invisibility, afforded by being located half way across the world. As geographical distance and the complexity of the supply chain increase, the visibility of harms and the connection to those responsible for them become harder to distinguish.

Anti-globalization Protests

This dark side of globalization has prompted an **anti-globalization movement**, which brings together heterogeneous groups, including NGOs, social activists, environmental action groups, socialist and anti-capitalist campaigners and anarchist groups. These groups oppose various aspects of globalization such as uncontrolled neoliberalism, global injustice, war and the proliferation and power of international financial institutions and transnational corporations. Anti-globalization groups often identify key organizations, such as the World Trade Organization (WTO), the International Monetary Fund (IMF) and the World Bank, as responsible for negative aspects of globalization (Fotopoulos 2001).

The anti-globalization movement can be traced back to 1984 when the New Economics Foundation of London organized 'The Other Economic Summit' to coincide with the tenth G7 Summit (a meeting of the finance ministers and central bank governors of seven major advanced economies) (Pianta 2001). The following year mass protests occurred around the G7 Summit in Bonn, West Germany, with 30,000 protesters rallying for 'a world without exploitation, submission and intervention' (Holzapfel & Konig 2002, np). In 1988, those numbers had swelled to 80,000 when the World Bank and the IMF held their annual meetings in Berlin (Gerhards & Rucht 1992). Sporadic protests continued throughout the 1990s. By the mid-1990s a fully-fledged global civil movement had emerged (Pianta 2001). This included protests in Seattle in 1999, where between 40,000 and 100,000 protesters (reports vary) coalesced around the Third Ministerial Conference of the WTO, and protests on the 1 May 2000 (referred to as MayDay2K), where anti-globalization demonstrations were coordinated in 75 cities on six continents to coincide with International Workers' Day (Buttel 2003).

In recent years, attendance, passions and media interest in anti-globalization protests have waned. The turning point may have been 9/11, which dramatically diminished any appetite for anti-Americanism (Dwyer 2013). The movement has never recovered. Since then, the Middle East and the threat of terrorism have become more pressing issues. The American domestic and global economies have also declined. May Day protests now reflect a greater preoccupation with local, domestic issues. The impact of organizations such as the World Bank and the IMF has also declined, while private finance has become more important – but private funding does not provide a convenient single target to protest against (Dwyer 2013).

Globalization Sceptics

In contrast to the anti-globalization movement, **globalization sceptics** debate the extent (or sometimes the very existence) of globalization. They disagree that a major shift is occurring in the nature and shape of social life. The views of globalization sceptics can be placed on a continuum. There are scholars who concede that economic flows are intensifying but debate the extensiveness and newness of these flows and other phenomena, such as global movement and social and political interdependence. On the other end of the continuum are scholars who deny that we are entering a new globalized epoch, as global movement and increasing connectedness have been features of human evolution since the first tribes migrated from Africa. Technological developments, such as the internet and jet planes, are often heralded as the drivers of globalization; however, from a sceptical viewpoint we can see such technology as part of the longer, continuous march of human progress throughout history.

Earlier technological inventions, such as newspapers, telegram, radio and telephone, also facilitated a global sharing of ideas, knowledge and news, while developments such as steamships and railways enhanced modes of production and transportation. Groups, from Vikings to slave traders, whalers to pirates, have long traversed seas and borders, and the ramifications of many significant events, such as World War I and II, have reverberated across the globe. Thus, our current era of connection and globalism can be seen as an extension of forces that have been gaining momentum for centuries.

While globalization sceptics concede that economic flows do traverse borders, they often view states, transnational cooperation and regional blocs as the dominant forces that construct global structures. This view maintains the primacy of the state and state-driven, international, regulatory structures in ordering the globe. This position can be drawn out from the Rana Plaza example, which demonstrates the ongoing role of state regulation and international cooperation in structuring trade, social services, economic distribution and legal and judicial institutions. For example, following the Rana Plaza tragedy, the Bangladesh legal system is prosecuting a Bangladeshi factory owner in the garment industry (Motlagh 2014). The owner of Tazreen Fashions has been charged with the culpable homicide of 112 workers who died in a fire at his factory in November 2012 (Harris 2013). Since then, Sohel Rana and 17 other individuals involved in the construction of Rana Plaza have been charged by the Anti Corruption Commission with building irregularities which led to the collapse (bdnews24.com 2014; Paul 2014). As we can see, if the Rana Plaza collapse is viewed as a crime, it is viewed primarily as a domestic crime rather than a transnational or international crime, and it is the national judicial system and government who must respond.

Thus, globalization sceptics view clashes between dominant blocs as a more accurate depiction of current global ordering, as opposed to stratification based on producers and consumers, or the 'winners and losers' of global neoliberal politics (anti-globalization proponents), or a global community with supranational bodies of governance and justice (radical globalists). Samuel Huntington (1996), for example, divides the globe into civilization blocs based on cultural and religious identities (Western blocs, Eastern Blocs, the Muslim world, etc.) and predicts that these divisions will cause a 'clash of civilizations' that will demonstrate the myth of global culture, solidarity and governance. This thesis highlights that the management of global affairs is the ongoing preserve of Western states rather than a cosmopolitan project based on global community.

Another scholar who denies the newness of globalization is sociologist Immanuel Wallerstein. Although his work theorizes the operation of society beyond the level of the state, Wallerstein has been dismissive of the concept of globalization, preferring instead to look at social changes over a much longer duration, beginning with the emergence of capitalism in 1500 (Robinson 2011). Wallerstein is famous for developing **world-system theory**, which divides the globe into regions based on capitalist divisions of labour. World-system theory suggests that the world is shaped by three great regions, or hierarchically organized tiers: the core, or the powerful, dominant centres of the system that exploit peripheral countries for labour and raw materials; the periphery, or regions that have been subordinated to the core (via colonialism, for example) and are dependent on the core for capital; and the semi-periphery, or those regions that share characteristics of both the core and periphery countries. While this approach looks at regional clashes, it is necessarily international as countries remain the primary entities that comprise the regional groupings (Robinson 2011). This differentiates world-system theory from radical globalization perspectives that posit the end of the nation-state through processes of global flows and thus views social stratification as based on individuals who are producers and consumers (rather than states as capitalist/labourer states).

2.4 Global Transformations

The perspectives of radical globalists and global sceptics can be reductive in that they view globalization as an all or nothing proposition; either the state is withering away and diminishing in significance through the proliferation of global flows, or the state remains the primary unit in a continually connected world in which the impact of global flows remains minimal. Of course, as with any academic labelling exercise, the division of perspectives on globalization into distinct categories is somewhat artificial, and within the radical/sceptical groupings is a range of different perspectives on globalization. It is difficult, for example, to clearly classify the work of Immanuel Wallerstein, who rejects the term 'globalization', yet examines the complex processes of social stratification that are occurring at a global level; he criticizes a sociology based solely on the nation-state, yet employs the state as a unit of analysis. The labels of radical/ sceptical do provide a schematic and conceptual tool that helps us better understand divergent positions on the complex phenomenon of globalization. What we can see is that neither the radical view nor the sceptical view of globalization is adequate. Radical convictions about the declining power of the state fail to sufficiently acknowledge the continuing role of nations in global affairs and the structuring of global order. Sceptical positions that deny or minimize globalization do not sufficiently capture the unique, profound and extensive changes in the social world that have intensified in previous decades.

While we may disagree about the conditions and consequences of globalization, it is impossible for us to step outside the paradigm of global flows as they constitute the world and social life as we know it. Even the most isolated of groups that live outside the boundaries of modern social life are affected by events that take place on a global stage. For example, native Amazonian Indian tribes, living near the border of Brazil and Peru, recently made contact with Peruvian locals as they were being forced from their land and threatened by environmental destruction caused by illegal loggers and cocaine traffickers (Alexander 2014). These previously unconnected tribes were unable to escape the negative side effects of global economic and criminal flows. Similarly, even those anti-globalization activists who protest against the negative effects of globalization deploy tools of globalization, such as telecommunication networks, to facilitate their protests.

As these cursory examples highlight, globalization entails a set of complex processes that we cannot evade. Radical/sceptical positions on globalization do not reflect this complexity. Accordingly, a third perspective on globalization has emerged, that of global transformationalists. Advanced by sociologist David Held, the global transformationalist perspective theorizes that globalization heralds major changes for the nation-state, but does not necessarily mean that the nation-state and its borders are waning. On the contrary, globalization is less about erosion and more about a reshaping of the nation-state. Held (2004, p. 10) explains:

> Globalization is not simply a monolithic process that brings in its wake wholly positive or negative outcomes. It is formed and constituted by complex processes with multiple impacts that need to be carefully dissected and examined. But one thing is already clear: globalization does not simply lead to the 'end of politics' or the demise of regulatory capacity. Rather, globalization is more accurately linked with the expansion of the terms of political activity and of the range of actors involved in political life. Globalization marks the continuation of politics by new means operating at many levels.

Held et al. (1999) elucidate four key factors that define globalization: the extent of global networks, the intensity of global interconnectedness, the velocity of global flows, and the impact propensity of global interconnectedness. These changes can be located within the conceptual framework of **late modernity**, which defines contemporary society as an extension and universalization of the project of **modernity** and a reconfiguration of modernity's institutions and social, cultural and political traditions (Giddens 1990). The period of modernity is linked to Enlightenment principles of human progress through science, bureaucracy and technology underpinned by rationality, individual freedoms, capitalism, industrialization and a rejection of tradition. Modernity conceives history as having a single, progressive direction, marked by rational progress and grounded in reason and the desire for order and control (Elliot 2007). Giddens (1990) highlights three core aspects of society that define modernity:

- a set of attitudes towards the world as open to transformation by human intervention;
- a complex array of economic institutions, industrial productions and a market economy;
- and a range of political institutions, especially the nation-state and mass democracy (Giddens & Pierson 1998).

Modernity involves three interconnected movements: the uncoupling of time and space, the disembedding of social institutions through the 'lifting out' of social interaction from particular locales through the media, expert systems and symbolic tokens (such as money), and far-reaching **reflexivity** (Giddens 1990). Reflexivity describes the use of knowledge to reflect on practices and improve the human condition. These processes are intensified and extended in late modernity.

From the late modern perspective, the uncoupling of time and space, which Giddens (1981) also refers to as **time–space distanciation**, is a core aspect of globalization. Time–space distanciation is the process whereby remote interaction (as opposed to face-to-face interaction) becomes increasingly significant. As a consequence, systems that were previously discrete have become connected and interdependent and cause and effect are distanced, meaning local events are magnified to have global import and what happens globally simultaneously shapes the local. David Harvey (1990) labels this phenomenon as time–space compression, describing how technologies of communication (telephone, internet, travel – cars, rail, jets) and economics (global financial markets and systems) condense spatial and temporal distances. Similarly, Virilio (2005) talks about the annihilation of space in an age of extreme speed. Virilio's work highlights that speed is an important factor in the compression of time and space, mirroring Held et al.'s (1999) point that the velocity of global flows is a key condition of globalization. Giddens (2002) uses the metaphors of a runaway world and a 'juggernaut' (Giddens 1990, p. 139) to capture the increasing speed and connection of the current era which is propelled forward by 24/7 news cycles, constant networking (social and professional) and global financial markets that appear to have a life of their own.

These processes lead to a world defined by ambivalence (Garland 2001) and complexity (Urry 2003). Global transformationalists explore this complexity, viewing globalization as an ongoing process involving both fragmentation and unification. Globalization entails increasing use of connection and cooperation through the creation of collaborative organizations, treaties and practices. At the same time, it splinters power and authority as multiple actors and voices emerge. Over the past decades we have seen an intense proliferation of actors that operate outside, and often above, the state. At the beginning of the twentieth century there were only 37 **inter-governmental organizations (IGOs)** and 176 international non-governmental organizations (INGOs). Today, there are an estimated 7000 IGOs and over 50,000 INGOs as well as millions of private firms that operate across borders (Elliot 2009). Refer back to Figure 1.2 for an example of the plethora of actors involved in negotiating treaties on transnational crime. The increasing plurality of actors changes the shape and role of the state, which is 'increasingly embedded in webs of regional and global interconnectedness permeated by supranational, intergovernmental and transnational forces and unable to determine its own fate' (Held & McGrew 2007, p. 27). Yet the state still plays an important role and in some ways globalization has bolstered state power, as is evidenced through punitive national responses to migration, which we will explore later in this chapter.

Let's return to the Rana Plaza example to see some of these transformationalist principles in action. It is difficult to trace a direct line of cause and effect that led to the Rana Plaza collapse. Where does responsibility for the tragedy begin and end? Are consumers in the global north complicit in these events? Think of how far we can stretch the chain of cause and effect in this example. An individual in America buys a $2 t-shirt from a chain store such as Walmart – perhaps this individual has been affected by the global financial crisis and cannot afford to pay any more for such an item. Consumer demand for disposable, low-cost fast-fashion creates an environment where global corporations hunt for the cheapest way to produce items. After a competitive process they settle on a factory in the Rana Plaza complex in Bangladesh, overlooking the poor working conditions and safety standards in favour of higher profits. The social structure and poverty in Bangladesh create the environment where desperate workers accept poor conditions and wages out of the need to support their families. Local factory owners exploit this in the pursuit of profits and neglect workers by maintaining unsafe buildings. Local government and other officials turn a blind eye to building and safety violations in order to foster desperately needed private enterprise or because they have been bribed. Local factory owners escape prosecution and continue to build more factories and exploit more workers. Sub-contracting of labour blurs the picture still further and encourages the devolution of responsibility. In this example it is impossible to untangle the local from the global, in terms of how and why the tragedy occurred or to place boundaries around the event in time and space. We clearly see that the stretching of social relations, development of technologies (production, transport and communication), collapsing of time and space and the reflexivity of actors who improve institutions to achieve their desired outcomes (profits in a capitalist system) result in this tragedy.

Processes of both integration and fragmentation are also evident and a wide range of actors was implicated in creating the conditions in which the Rana Plaza tragedy occurred. Additionally, many actors were involved in responses to the building collapse including the Government of Bangladesh, international corporations (Primark, Benetton among others), intergovernmental

Aerial view of the Rana Plaza building following the disaster

© Photo by rijans (Flickr) via Wikimedia Commons

organizations (the WTO, International Labour Organization) and non-government organizations representing a variety of perspectives (Human Rights Watch, Clean Clothes campaign). The large number of actors involved in Rana Plaza does not indicate a diminishment of the state; the Bangladeshi state still held authority for criminal justice prosecutions and the enforcement of workplace and building standards, but the government of Bangladesh also interacted with, and was influenced by, a number of external actors who held considerable power. In essence, the transformationalist perspective captures aspects of the previous positions discussed as it illustrates the fragmented nature of global order. Both the state and a range of actors operate in a vast, multilayered structure of **global civil society**.

The concept of **glocalization** provides another way to conceptualize global–local interactions and relationships in a more nuanced manner. The term 'glocalization' stems from Japanese business methods of the 1980s which sought to adapt a global outlook to local conditions through tailoring and advertising global goods and services to local and particular markets. Sociologist Roland Robertson (2012) adopted the principle of glocalization to counteract some of the totalizing myths and grand narratives of globalization as a homogenizing force in contemporary society. As Robertson (2012) highlights, globalization is often seen as a large-scale phenomenon that obliterates the local and in which universalism overrides particularism. The local is superseded by the global and 'the very idea of locality is sometimes cast as a form of resistance

Transnational Crime & Criminal Justice

to the hegemonically global' (Robertson 2012, p. 195). This leads to a standardization of locality, as culture and identity are defined from above. Counteracting this dominant globalization discourse, Robertson (2012) suggests that glocalization involves the simultaneity of both universalizing and particularizing tendencies, meaning globalization produces cultural pluralism as well as homogeneity. Thus, instead of viewing globalizing trends as in tension with local assertions of identity and culture, glocalization highlights the dialectical processes whereby both the local and the global are transformed in the contemporary era. This parallels global transformationalist perspectives; as Giddens states, 'local transformation is as much a part of globalization as the lateral extension of social connections across time and space' (Giddens 1990, p. 64).

2.5 Mobilities

The previous section demonstrates that globalization creates a 'world in motion' (Aas 2007a), as technologies intensify and extend global connections and the flow of ideas, culture, material objects and people across borders. Modernity was a time of solid, heavy, static systems, institutions and process. In contrast, late modernity is a time of constant change as systems and institutions emerge, evolve and dissolve, and as identity and power are fragmented and pluralized. The movement associated with globalization materializes in several ways. We can theorize social life (relationships, institutions, processes, structures) as being fluid, changeable and mobile. Another term for the period of late modernity is **liquid modernity**, a concept developed by Bauman (2000) to capture the fluidity, movement and fast pace of contemporary society. As Bauman (2000) points out, liquids do not keep their shape for very long, they are constantly prone to alterations and continuous change. Accordingly, the liquid modernity metaphor highlights that movement, or mobility, and change is a core part of globalization and the current era. Bauman has written a series of books using this metaphor including, *Liquid Modernity*, *Liquid Life*, *Liquid Fear* and *Liquid Love*. These books explore how change and movement characterize all aspects of social life, from relationships, work and leisure to political institutions, as the bonds and structures that formerly held social life, institutions and identities together are broken apart and liquefied.

Examples of this liquidity surround us and impact upon our daily lives. Work and careers were once relatively structured and linear: it was common for people to hold a job in the same company, and certainly in the same field, for their entire working lives, and work hours and years were often well-defined (9–5 Monday to Friday with set holidays each year). Commitment, loyalty and gradual progression were valued in the workplace. Now, short-term and casual contracts are the norm, and there is pressure to do more, progress quickly and be available 24/7 (Sennett 1998, 2006). It is common for people to completely change careers and employers, often multiple times throughout their working lives. Flexibility, resilience, dynamism and mobility (the ability to travel or work unencumbered) are valued in the marketplace of work. These changes demonstrate a shift from thinking long-term to short-term (Sennett 2006).

Similarly, personal relationships have significantly changed shape (Bauman 2003). Romantic relationships are more transient, divorce has become commonplace, and family units take many different forms. Once ingrained gender roles have also been transformed, and our understandings of sexuality have shifted. As people no longer live and work in the same place for the course of their lives, closely knit communities have been dismantled. In essence, the traditions, structures and stable roles and bonds that once underscored society have loosened (or come undone) and are now more malleable and transient, meaning we have more freedom to construct our own identities. This freedom can result in profound insecurity and anxiety (Salecl 2004, 2010) as it impacts on our sense of stability in the world. Of course, it can also be extremely positive as we are not constrained by rigid, inequitable and often oppressive norms and roles.

This environment affects the way that crime is constructed, committed, controlled and punished. A sense of uncertainty and instability causes the 'projection of feelings of insecurity onto particular groups (criminals, asylum seekers, terrorists)' (Daems & Robert 2007, p. 94), and often, the poor. Bauman (in Daems & Robert 2007, p. 94) explains that 'the poor now serve as the (partially effective) "safety valve" for social anxiety which otherwise would be bound to accumulate to self-combustion point in the world of flexible labour, crumbling human bonds, and the spectre of social redundancy'. Paralleling this position, criminologists such as Aas (2007a), Garland (2001) and Simon (2007) have examined the rise of **punitiveness** and the use of crime as a governing tool in environments of uncertainty and insecurity. We discuss this in more depth in Chapter 4.

Associated with this liquefaction of society is an increase in the physical movement of people, information, ideas and things (Urry 2007). This has led to a new 'mobility' paradigm in social sciences (Sheller & Urry 2006) which focuses on movement and flows, and the routes connecting places and people (Clifford 1997). From this perspective, mobility becomes the linchpin for understanding the operation of global structures and relationships. Within this environment of heighted mobility, movement is a prized quality. Individuals are expected to be mobile and so many of us freely traverse borders as we holiday in exotic locations and attend conferences and business meetings in foreign cities and countries. The nomad is the archetypal figure of this mobile world. Someone with a short-term work contract, a fragmented family structure and few durable commitments (mirroring the qualities of liquid modernity) can be highly mobile (Bauman 2000).

However, not everyone is free to roam the globe as they please and mobility has become a major stratifying force in the global social hierarchy (Aas 2007a).

Bauman (1998) distinguishes between tourists and vagabonds to highlight the gaps that constitute the global mobility regime. Tourists (often from the global north) travel freely for business and pleasure; whereas vagabonds (often from the global south) are constricted in their movement, and if they do move it is because they are forced to flee poverty, war, or discrimination. Just think of the many thousands of asylum seekers who are unsuccessful in their attempts to seek refuge as they are stopped short by the precarious nature of their journeys or the punitive border control policies of **destination countries**. As this indicates, individuals and groups have vastly different access to opportunities for movement, and bodies are differentiated by their mobility, as we explore in Chapter 5.

Spotlight – Death at the Border

For many, the border is the site of death and harm. The coffins shown in the photograph are a monument for those who have died attempting to cross the US–Mexican border. Each coffin represents a year and the number of dead. It is a protest against the effects of Operation Guardian.

Memorial coffins on the US–Mexico barrier for those killed crossing the border fence (taken at the Tijuana–San Diego border)

© Photo by Tomas Castelazo via Wikimedia Commons

As Elliot and Urry (2010) highlight, there is no increase in fluidity without extensive systems of immobility. The idea that borders are diminishing is, therefore, misleading. For the global nomad or tourist borders are eroding, yet for the vagabond borders are proliferating and solidifying. The destination countries of the global north are becoming fortresses, secured by both physical and virtual borders. The border is physically manifested in guarded walls (such as the US–Mexico border) or maritime patrols (such as those surrounding Europe and Australia), yet it is also diffuse and virtual as individuals may be controlled by passport checks and biosocial profiling, even beyond territorial frontiers (Salter 2004; Weber & Bowling 2004). There is ambivalence between the immovable and solid apparatus of control and the desire for fluidity and mobility in the contemporary era, as states attempt to 'harden the border for some, while making it more elastic and porous for others' (Wonders 2007, p. 34). The border is therefore a symbol of global social exclusion as 'others' (Schmitt 1996) are rendered immobile, while tourists and nomads are encouraged to become global citizens. From this perspective, global social stratification is based on mobility/immobility. As with other forms of social exclusion, the control of undesirable individuals and groups (asylum seekers, terrorists) stems from a sense of insecurity caused by the uncertainty and unpredictability of contemporary social life in a globalized, mobile, liquid world. Figure 2.1 schematizes the different ways we can conceptualize the border.

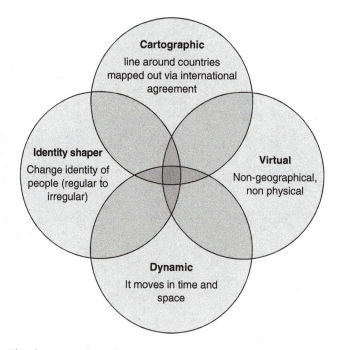

Figure 2.1 The Conceptual Border

Adapted from Weber (2006) and Tazreiter (2013)

In cartographic representations of the world, we rely on state borders and a traditional understanding of territorial divisions to visually represent the globe. Maps are usually based on a Euro-centric vision of space; this is a visual representation that reflects the domination of European countries and their colonial conquests of the nineteenth and twentieth centuries (see Figure 2.2). But is this still a realistic way of visualising the world? Could we alter maps based on the changing power differentials that constitute the current era? The second map is a US-centred map which reflects the strength of the US as a superpower that carries much weight in international affairs. Perhaps we could reconceptualize the world in a radical new way. The third map depicts an 'upside down' version of the traditional world map. This gives us a vastly different picture of the world that challenges our traditional understanding of states and regions and the relationships between them. Note how many less powerful regions and countries are placed on top of the world in this map (Africa, South America etc.). From space, this type of picture of the world could be possible and accurate. Our understanding of the world through traditional, Euro-centric maps is a human-made social construct that has been determined by history, politics and power. These maps highlight that our understanding of the globe and the operation of international relations is not fixed, but is significantly linked to geopolitics and power.

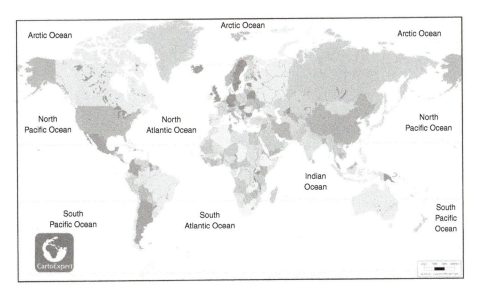

Figure 2.2 Traditional Eurocentric Map

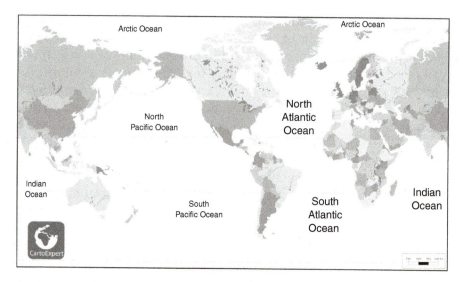

Figure 2.3   US-Centred Map

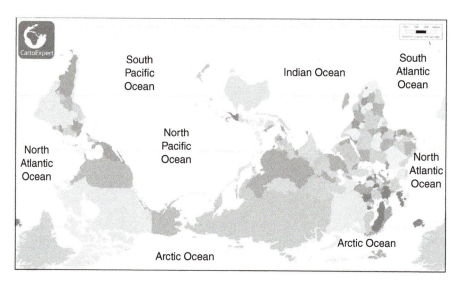

Figure 2.4   An 'upside down' world map

Adapted from Weber (2006) and Tazreiter (2013)

2.6 Conclusion

Globalization is a complex series of occurrences that shape and change social relations and structures in a myriad of ways. It manifests differently in different locales and regions. Globalization can be divisive, not just unifying, producing inequalities and stratification as well as a cosmopolitan sense of a shared fate. Globalization can have both positive and negative effects, as anti-globalization protesters highlight. Throughout this book we adopt a global transformationalist perspective, viewing globalization as a multifaceted phenomenon that materializes in many different ways. The role of states is changing as many different forms of power and regulation emerge at regional, international and global levels. Regions, states and locales do not, and often cannot, exist in isolation but rather influence and are influenced by outside events. This means that events that occur in one corner of the globe now have the potential to affect the entire world. However, the reality remains that it is difficult for us to think outside the framework of the nation-state. States continue to hold considerable influence, power and autonomy and they are important units in the global order. Globalization and mobility theories capture the increasing movement of the contemporary era, which results in change, uncertainty and insecurity. In the following chapter we explore the ramifications of this insecurity through the framework of risk and regulation.

Questions: Revise and Reflect

1. Which approach(es) to globalization do you agree with and why? What trends and phenomena do you think shape twenty-first century society and life?

2. Consider the role of the ethical shopper. What responsibility do we, as the ultimate consumer of a product, have in contributing to harm to workers worldwide?

3. How could the harm caused by the Rana Plaza collapse be considered criminal? What do radical and critical criminological theories say about this?

4. What role do borders play in a global world? Are borders different for different people and groups?

5. Visit the Human Costs of Border Control project website: www.borderdeaths.org/?page_id=5. This website provides a database that measures instances of deaths at the border. As the website states 'the Deaths at the Borders Database is an "evidence-base" derived from official sources generated by the death management systems of Spain, Gibraltar, Italy, Malta and Greece. It aims to fill some of the gaps, and serve as a new, complementary resource to enable further analysis and research, and ultimately to move the discussions about border deaths forward towards concrete recommendations and policy changes.'
   What do you think about the information on this site? Are there any data that surprise you? What does this information tell us about the nature of the border and inequality on a global level?

Further Reading

Bauman, Z 1998, *Globalization: The human consequences*, Columbia University Press, New York.

Bauman, Z 2000, *Liquid modernity*, Polity Press, Cambridge.

Elliot, A 2009, *Contemporary social theory: An introduction*, Routledge, Abingdon.

Giddens, A 2002, *Runaway world: How globalisation is reshaping our lives*, Profile Books, London.

Held, D & McGrew, A 2007, *Globalization/anti-globalization: Beyond the great divide*, Polity Press, Cambridge.

Urry, J 2007, *Mobilities*, Polity Press, Cambridge.

Websites to Visit

The Border Crossing Observatory: Borders, Crime, Justice: artsonline.monash.edu.au/thebordercrossingobservatory/

The Human Costs of Border Control: www.borderdeaths.org/

Global Policy Forum: www.globalpolicy.org/index.php

International Labour Organization (ILO): www.ilo.org/global/lang—en/index.htm

Open Democracy: www.opendemocracy.net/editorial-tags/globalisation

Social Theory Rewired: theory.routledgesoc.com/book-themes

3

Risk, Networks and Cyberspace

This chapter will look at

- The risk society.
- The role and functioning of networks.
- The emergence of virtual space and cybercrime.

Keywords

Risk	Governing through crime	Networks
Control		Cybercrime

3.1 Introduction

What do nuclear war, climate change, terrorist attacks, environmental catastrophes, Ebola outbreaks and **cybercrime** have in common? They are all examples of the extreme and pervasive risks that we face in the contemporary era. Such risks surround us and shape our understanding of and interaction with the world. These risks arise from, and reflect, the uncertainty and insecurity of contemporary social life. They are human-made risks that are produced as side effects of the globalized, **neoliberal** economy, yet they are largely unpredictable and uncontrollable: we do not know where or when they may occur or how they will affect us. The centrality of risk in modern life has led sociologists to talk of a **risk society** (Beck 1992; Giddens 1990) and a **world risk society** (Beck 1999) in which the concept of risk is central to the structure and operation of social life.

In this chapter, we explore risk and its role in shaping global social relations. We examine how risk leads to a desire for control, which consequently influences the way that governments respond to crime. **Crime control**, based on the classification of dangerous populations and actuarial calculations, is symptomatic of a society preoccupied with risk. This means that crime control is often used to govern society through discourses of insecurity, a phenomenon that we see increasingly at a global level through responses to **transnational** and **international crimes** (Findlay 2008).

Another concept that reflects the unpredictable and fluid nature of social relations and crime is **network theory**. Advanced by sociologist Manuel Castells (2000, 2004), network theory proposes that society is increasingly constituted by global networks that capture and direct flows of information, people and money. Networks are decentralized, flexible and changeable. The metaphor of networks is reflected in crime as we see **organized crime** syndicates operating in dispersed, network-like structures. Individuals and groups are also able to use existing licit networks, such as the internet, for illicit ends such as dealing in drugs, weapons and even body parts. As this illustrates, the networked society creates new spaces, such as **cyberspace**, that are difficult to govern, or are even ungovernable. Our growing reliance on the internet to facilitate all aspects of our lives, from social connection to the operation of business and finance, and the sense that these networks are uncontrollable, leads to new manifestations of risk.

3.2 The World Risk Society

In Chapter 2, we discussed how the changeability of modern life, the loosening of social ties and the fast-paced, mobile nature of the globalized world create a pervasive sense of anxiety, uncertainty and insecurity which shapes contemporary society. Uncertainty is heightened in conditions of globalization under which **reflexivity**, that is, the use of knowledge to reflect on practices and improve the human condition, is intensified. The intensification of reflexivity causes recognition of the changeability of knowledge – what we know today may be undermined tomorrow as we acquire new information (Heaphy 2007) – and a greater reflection on the principles, institutions and processes of **modernity** itself, creating an amplified awareness of the unintended consequences of social life (Beck et al. 1994). Within this environment of increased anxiety and insecurity, the concept of risk emerges as a defining factor of contemporary society.

Beck (1999) examines the centrality of risk to contemporary society through his 'world risk society' thesis. Beck highlights how we are increasingly aware of the contingent nature of social life and the existence of uncontrollable, global risks that could impact on us at any moment. In pre-modern times dangers such as famines and floods were attributed to gods, nature or demons. Conversely, in contemporary society risks are attributed to human activity, such as the use of nuclear energy, human genetics and gene technology, nanotechnology and advanced industrialization. Beck (1999) identifies three main types of global risk: ecological disasters, global financial crises and global terror networks. These risks are global in their causes and consequences and can be linked to globalization, the advancement of neoliberal ideals of free markets and the pursuit of profits above all else. Trends such as population growth alongside economic and technological developments are putting enormous pressures on the environment and natural resources. The disposal of hazardous products, overuse of land, environmental exploitation of less legally developed economies, the dumping of rubbish in oceans, air pollution and new diseases are just some of the examples of environmental problems that a globalized economy is creating or accelerating (we explore these issues further in Chapter 8). Alongside these ecological risks, the meltdown of global financial systems poses a real threat to individuals, groups and societies around the world. For example, the 2008 Global Financial Crisis, which had origins in the US sub-prime mortgage crisis, created a global recession that led to poverty and austerity measures around the world, as explored in Case Study 3.1.

Case Study 3.1 – The Melting of Iceland's Economy

There is no greater illustration of the extent of globalization than the widespread fallout which emanated from the collapse of two US financial institutions. Banking giant Lehman Brothers filed for bankruptcy on the morning of Monday 15 September 2008 and two days later policy makers intervened to save the multinational insurance corporation AIG. The fall of these financial heavyweights precipitated the global financial crisis, the effects of which continue to be borne by millions of people. As global economies are intricately linked, the shockwave reverberated around the world, causing mass job losses and negative trade effects (Kucera et al. 2011).

The true scale of the harm is incalculable but organizations such as the ILO and the World Bank have attempted to assess it. According to the World Bank (2009), export-oriented industries were particularly badly hit: India reported half a million job losses in these industries in the last quarter of 2008; and in China, 25 million migrant workers had reportedly lost their jobs by April 2009. Global unemployment increased by nearly 30 million persons during 2009 (Kucera et al. 2011, p. 196). These figures are likely to be conservative as many industries took temporary measures to minimize job losses, for example, in Russia 10 times as many people were on administrative leave or employed part-time in early 2009 compared to the previous year (World Bank 2009). It was the poorest who were the hardest hit: worldwide, an estimated 40 million extra people were pushed into the category of the working poor by 2011 (earning less than $1.25 per day) and an additional 95 million people became malnourished, resulting in 30,000–50,000 additional infant deaths in Africa (Kucera et al. 2011, p. 196).

(Continued)

(Continued)

Iceland, a small European island with a thriving economy, was one of the first and biggest casualties. In 2005, the IMF judged Iceland to be the third richest country in the world in per capita terms (Hart-Landsberg 2013). However, like the US economy, the economic gains that Iceland had made in the previous 20 years were fuelled by privatization of state assets (including banks) and deregulation of the financial sector. This allowed the banks and financial markets to speculate heavily, particularly in the four years prior to the economic collapse. The end of year assets of the three largest banks rose from less than twice GDP in 2003, to almost 10 times GDP within a five-year period (Hart-Landsberg 2013). Frenzied investments created stock market and housing bubbles. When the crash came it was spectacular and sudden.

Within a month of Lehman Brothers' bankruptcy, all three of Iceland's major banks failed and were taken over by the government (Hart-Landsberg 2013). Over the next two years Iceland suffered one of the worst economic declines ever seen in the developed world. It affected every household. Unemployment rose from 1% to 8%. Those that managed to retain their jobs had their hours reduced. Many people, unable to repay loans, lost their homes or cars. Early in 2009 the government resigned, the only one to do so as a result of the Global Financial Crisis (Hart-Landsberg 2013). The new government brought in a series of unconventional recovery measures, quite different from the types of austerity measures most governments were choosing. These measures have succeeded in steering Iceland towards a strong economic recovery.

Iceland is also the only country to have taken bold steps to prosecute those who were responsible, convicting chief executives of all the major banks with charges ranging from breach of trust to market manipulation and fraud (Scrutton & Sigurdardottir 2015). Even the former Prime Minister, Geir Haarde, was put on trial for failing in his duty to prevent the demise of the banks – although only one charge was upheld (Neate 2012; Stothard 2012). Other European countries have taken sporadic action and there is growing attention being paid to white collar crime and a greater willingness to prosecute (Mount 2014).

By contrast, the United States has shown little appetite for bringing to justice those responsible for the banking crisis that almost brought down the world's financial system and precipitated the worst recession in 80 years (*Economist* 2013c). Not one Wall Street banker has been brought to trial to date, partly because financial incompetence is not illegal as such (*Economist* 2013b). However, there is precedent in the concept of 'wilful blindness' in US criminal law and some indication that reckless management might be brought under the scrutiny of the law in future in the United Kingdom and Germany (*Economist* 2013b; Rakoff 2014).

Under current US federal law, unarmed bank robbery of any amount over $1000 is subject to a fine and a maximum 10-year sentence (Legal Information Institute n.d.). For running a bank into the ground, however, there is no proscribed sanction, as the law does not criminalize those who make business mistakes, even reckless ones (Irwin 2013). Most executives not only avoided prosecution but also kept their jobs or moved to new positions, retaining the proceeds and vast bonuses they had been given (Ferguson et al. 2010). It was ordinary taxpayers who had to foot the bill for the multi-trillion dollar bailouts, necessary to save the institutions bankrupted by these bankers' actions (Irwin 2013).

Although these risks, such as the Global Financial Crisis discussed in Case Study 3.1, are human-made, they are largely non-quantifiable and uncontrollable. Risks are often non-calculable – they are unknown situations that can produce effects that are difficult to quantify – and they generate fear and anxiety. These incalculable risks can be considered products of negative globalization (see Chapter 2). Fear and anxiety are our reactions to the notion that calamities can occur unannounced. A central point in Beck's (1999) discourse is that risks are now invisible, at least until they produce a negative impact on society. For instance, Beck (1999) refers to pollution by nuclear radiation, generated by the 1986 Chernobyl disaster, which has had impacts across borders and through time. The nuclear power station in Chernobyl served a positive purpose, to generate electric power, which, in turn, had negative consequences that could not be escaped by neighbouring ecosystems. Giddens (1991) describes these situations, in which negative consequences are difficult to identify or foresee, as 'high-consequence risks'. He (Giddens 1991, p. 122) claims that: 'the more calamitous the hazards they involve, the less we have any real experience of what we risk: for if things "go wrong", it is already too late'.

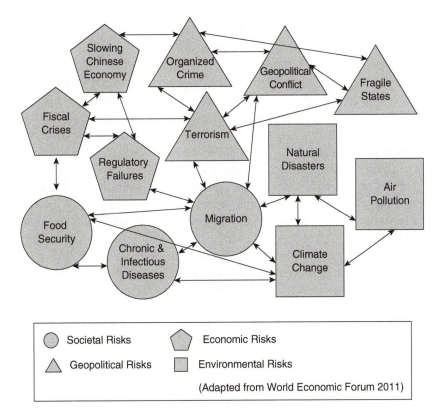

Figure 3.1 The Interconnection of Risk

Giddens (1991, p. 124) adds to this evaluation of the invisibility of risk by stating that 'the risk climate of modernity is thus unsettling for everyone: no one escapes'. New forms of risk affect everyone, human beings, animals and the eco-system, and can occur anywhere. This succinctly synthesizes the vision of the modern risk – differently from wars – directly created and produced by human beings, with impacts that cannot be escaped or contained. Risks have the potential to arbitrarily affect all of humanity (Beck 1999). Beck (1992, p. 47) focuses on 'communities of danger' to demonstrate how risks erode class-consciousness as everyone is threatened by global risks. Climate change, for example, affects all corners of the world, meaning no one, no matter their status or wealth, can escape the damaging impacts brought about by global warming. Figure 3.1 demonstrates the interconnection of many different types of risk.

While risks are now global in nature, this does not mean that they are necessarily distributed or experienced equally. Beck's work has been criticized for its overly simplistic and reductive rendering of risk which asserts that risk affects all strata of social life (Elliot 2002; Stenson 2003). Beck claims that risks have an 'equalising effect' on global society uniformly (Beck 1992, p. 35). This assessment denies the continuing role that race, class, gender divisions and power differentials have on structuring people's experiences and the global order. For example, while climate change has universal implications, it is widely argued that the impact of climate change will be felt more acutely by vulnerable populations and marginalized groups that already experience social exclusion. As the Governance and Social Development Resource Centre (GSDRC 2008, p. 1) highlights, 'poor people in developing countries are most vulnerable to the negative effects of climate change, due to their precarious socio-economic position which exacerbates their vulnerability to shocks and limits their adaptive capacities'.

Other marginalized groups, such as children, the elderly and the disabled, may suffer the negative impacts of climate change more profoundly than wealthy individuals, and research indicates that men and women will experience the impact of climate change differently (Denton 2002). This is because climate change will impact upon many aspects of social life, including public health, agriculture, natural resources and migration patterns, changes to which affect excluded groups more keenly. As this illustrates, if a key theme of globalization is interconnection, it is important to see how social exclusion and stratification infuse all aspects of life and how risk operates differentially within existing social groups and hierarchies, rather than operating outside them. Risk may minimize the significance of social division as global communities of common fate appear, but it does not completely override or transcend existing social divisions. Even the way we identify and experience risk changes, according to our place and socio-economic status: not all individuals, groups and societies perceive risk in the same way. Risk and an expectation of security and safety are largely Western constructs, as Case Study 3.2 illustrates.

Case Study 3.2 – Risk and Cultural Relativism

Many citizens of Western countries expect their governments to minimize the risks that they face both at home and abroad. Domestically we expect governments to monitor and minimize the risk of negative events such as terrorist attacks, the outbreak of infectious diseases, street crime and contamination within food supply chains. Our expectation of domestic safety and governments' risk-based approach to safety is evidenced by initiatives such as terrorist alert systems. For example France has a national security alert system called *Le Plan Vigipirate*, which defines four levels of threat, represented by corresponding colours. The threat level dictates measures that the government may take to protect citizens at particular times, including increased police patrols and military presence.

Western expectations of safety also extend to our overseas travels. French citizens, for example, can consult the *Conseils aux Voyageurs* (Advice for Travellers) website, which provides an overview of threat levels in different countries and precautionary information for travellers. If they are caught up in risky events overseas, French travellers can also expect assistance from their government as well as travel and insurance companies. For example, when the Arab Spring revolution broke out in Tunisia, a former French colony and popular travel destination for the French, major travel companies such as Ceto and Thomas Cook airlifted French tourists out of Tunisia as the situation became more dangerous, and therefore more risky for travellers (*Australian* 2011). The French government also provided consular assistance to tourists stuck in the region.

But did Tunisian citizens view the events of the Arab Spring through the framework and language of risk? Did they expect their government to offer them safety and reduce the risks they faced in daily life? Quite the contrary, the Tunisian uprisings were the result of protests against the dictatorial regime of former President Zine El Abidine Ben Al. Under Ben Al's dictatorship Tunisians experienced high costs of living, unemployment, police brutality and food shortages, all of which were fuelled by the corruption of the president, who lived an opulent life. The contrast in this example is stark. While a Western country such as France is strongly underpinned by risk-based principles and driven by expectations that governments and corporations protect the safety of citizens, citizens of a country such as Tunisia cannot expect the government to assure even their basic needs, such as affordable and accessible food, let alone protect their safety or monitor the levels of risk the country and its citizens face from external threats. The risk–insurance–security discourse is not prevalent in Tunisia and, in fact, many Tunisians viewed the uprisings as an opportunity to overthrow the corrupt president and secure a more democratic government and better way of life.

3.3 Governing through Crime and Risk

The risk society thesis characterizes the current era as driven by the increasingly pervasive logic of manufactured uncertainty (Adam et al. 2000). This uncertainty causes a politics of insecurity (Ericson 2007) whereby risks are defined and managed by national governments, in partnership with corporate bodies. Here politics can be conceived of as dealing with the 'contingent event' and a state of 'living with ambiguity' (Hannien, quoted in de Lint & Virta 2004, p. 473).

Beck (1992) highlights that this approach allows key players, such as industries and governments, to regulate different sectors of social life at a regional level, even if the effects (both direct and indirect) are felt at a global level. For example, genetically modified food is produced locally or regionally, but is distributed and consumed globally. The issues associated with the stretching of the food supply chain were demonstrated in 2015 when imported frozen berries were linked to Hepatitis A infections in both Europe and Australia, affecting populations far from their original source. The Australian government was urged to bring in stricter regulations for the importation of food products to minimize the risk of such an outbreak in the future. A further risk to blood supplies was identified by the Australian Red Cross, who quarantined blood from potentially infected donors.

This situation highlights a paradox in risk discourses: although risks are territorially debounded and disembedded from the nation-state, in a risk society the state gains new levels of authority as it is tasked with securing or responding to risks. In the aftermath of 9/11 the state has been reinforced due to the constructed need for it to provide security for its citizens. The result is that Western societies are now governed through the problem of uncertainty, which is often achieved through new forms of criminalization (Ericson 2007), therefore producing the phenomenon of 'governing through crime' (Simon 2007). In late modern conditions of uncertainty, reflexivity, contingency and risk, crime proves to be the strongest expression of authority in the face of a lack of trust in public institutions and an increasing sense of ungovernability (Ericson 2007). The notion of governing through crime as a response to the ungovernability of contemporary society is closely associated with the risk society framework as 'risk inherently contains the concept of control' (Beck 2002, p. 40), meaning that crime can be used as a means of feigning control over the uncontrollable, thereby creating a 'culture of control' through crime and justice discourses (Garland 2001).

Accordingly, crime plays a key role in establishing order and governing societies by implementing a veneer of control. Crime control functions to counter feelings of insecurity and uncertainty, by providing a seemingly solid and reassuring response to the unknown and unpredictable future, through a familiar classificatory and exclusionary framework that delineates the 'dangerous others'. As Garland and Sparks (2000, pp. 17–18) highlight, 'the mobile and insecure world of late modernity has given rise to new practices of control and exclusion that seek to make society less open and less mobile: to fix identities, immobilize individuals, quarantine whole sections of the population, erect boundaries, close off access'. However, while crime and the criminalization of dangerous populations (such as terrorists, migrants and organized criminals) may offer some sense of security, crime also provides another site of anxiety and insecurity as 'the threat of crime has become a routine part of modern consciousness' (Garland 1996, p. 446).

As this discussion demonstrates, the pervasive sense of risk and uncertainty that characterizes contemporary social life leads to attempts to calculate and mediate risks (and risky populations) and control the future. The combination of risk and uncertainty in late modernity means that 'catastrophic imaginations are fuelled, precautionary logics become pervasive, and extreme security measures are invoked in frantic efforts to pre-empt imagined sources of harm' (Ericson 2007, p. 1). These conditions produce actuarial models of justice (Ericson 2007; Feeley & Simon 1994) that focus on evaluating and responding to risk through initiatives such as risk profiling of offenders (rather than responding to individuals and their unique needs), managing risks through targeted treatment programmes based on risk profiles, and looking to the future rather than punishing purely for past behaviour. This uncertain, future-orientated environment parallels the logic of the risk society, as Beck (1992, p. 34) highlights, 'the centre of risk consciousness lies not in the present, but in the future. . . . We become active today in order to prevent, alleviate, or take precautions against the problems and crises of tomorrow and the day after tomorrow'. This leads to a society based on 'pre-crime' which Zedner (2007, p. 261) explains: 'conventionally, crime is regarded principally as harm or wrong and the dominant ordering practices arise post hoc. In the emerging pre-crime society, crime is conceived essentially as risk or potential loss, ordering practices are pre-emptive and security is a commodity sold for profit'.

As Zedner (2007) highlights, precautionary approaches to crime and justice have become more prevalent at national and international levels over the past decade. At the national level the pre-emptive politics of crime control can be seen through initiatives such as antisocial behaviour laws, criminal possession, transience and private policing. Precautionary approaches are also reflected in the increasing use of preventative sentencing, which seeks to exclude and segregate dangerous sections of the community (Findlay 2008). On a global scale, this future-orientated focus is exemplified in reactions to terrorism, which is one of the most politicized risks in contemporary society (Findlay 2008). The 'new' terrorist threat, as exemplified by 9/11 and the London bombings, typifies the precarious, risk-based nature of the current era, and this invokes strong precautionary and pre-emptive reactions which attempt to control the uncontrollable (de Goede 2008). In Australia, reactions to terrorism have involved preventative detention and control orders (McCulloch & Pickering 2009). Here the risk-based nature of terrorism, and the uncertainty and unpredictability involved, justify the prioritization of 'human security' over human rights (McCulloch 2003), leading to precautionary interventions which violate political freedom, civil liberties and constitutional rights (Head 2002).

Mirroring domestic developments, the amplified sense of risk and security evidenced at national levels also pervades the international scene. There is an increasing construction and use of crime and punishment to govern the globe

(Findlay 2008), a situation which arises as a response to an environment of risk and insecurity. The erosion of state borders and the escalating inability of governments to control risks which are increasingly global in nature '[invite] the discussion of governance in terms such as law, justice and bureaucracy without or above the state' (Findlay 2008, p. 326).

3.4 Networks

As the discussion in the previous section highlights, risks are now global and interconnected. One way to look at this interconnection is through network theory. Spanish sociologist Manuel Castells' work views contemporary society as a network society constituted by information networks that are digitally mediated (Castells 2000, 2004). Network theory is related to the mobility theories discussed in the previous chapter. Networks are an important part of mobility as they facilitate and organize the flow of information, people and material objects (Castells 2000, 2004). If networks direct flows, then nodes become important points of connection. In a mobile society, nodes include airports, stations, hotels and cosmopolitan cities. Sassen (2001) explores the operation of global cities, places where flows of information and capital converge. Global cities, such as London, Tokyo and New York, act as nodes in interconnected systems of information and money. These cities are no longer deeply embedded within the countries and regions in which they sit; instead they function as junctions for global flows and mobilities (Sassen 2001). A consequence of this is the growth in the marginalized population of global cities as individuals find it difficult to earn a living in a global marketplace.

It is clear that networks, and particularly online and virtual networks, are becoming increasingly entrenched in our everyday lives. We organize our social lives and connect with others through online social networks such as Facebook and Twitter. We rely on online financial systems to conduct everyday transactions, from online banking to using a credit card in a local shop. We search for information using websites such as Google and from here we can book holidays, choose restaurants, shop for food, clothes and electronic products and find vast amounts of information about any subject. On top of this, we can easily share our opinion on information and goods and services with individuals across the other side of the world. This means our networks are getting wider and wider and are disembedded from our physical location.

Digital networks are a core part of our lives and, as Castells (2000, 2004) argues, they make up the very structure of contemporary society. Social and financial networks can give more power to individuals to act globally and become more informed world citizens. Recently, online engagement has allowed individuals to become part of global social movements calling for justice at both local and international levels. For example, the Kony 2012 campaign involved the worldwide dissemination of a human rights video by US-based NGO group Invisible Children (Chazal & Pocrnic, 2016). The video (www.youtube.com/watch?v=Y4MnpzG5Sqc) highlighted the atrocities occurring in Uganda and, in particular, looked at the alleged crimes of warlord Joseph Kony. The video asked for individuals to share and like the video, a strategy that tapped into the social media trend of 'liking' and 'sharing' information with our wide online social networks. This strategy worked for Invisible Children and their video quickly became a worldwide phenomenon; within only six days of its release, Kony 2012 received over 100 million views, making it the most watched human rights video to date (Visible Measures 2012).

While online networks offer us the ability to act in a global forum, often our engagement in online social movements can be superficial and inconsequential. For example, while the Kony 2012 campaign sought to bring Kony to justice, in 2015 he remains at large and many online activists will have forgotten about the ongoing violence in Uganda. As such, terms such as 'slacktivism' (Morozov 2009) and 'clicktivism' (White 2010) have been used to describe our digitally mediated engagement with social movements. Often, online support is fleeting and requires little effort, but makes us feel good as we are acting as globally savvy citizens to promote justice (Chazal & Pocrnic 2016).

Additionally, although access to new forms of information and communication technologies (internet, mobile phones, personal computers, etc.) helps us connect with the world and in doing so breaks apart traditional social hierarchies, it also creates new forms of inequality. The term 'the digital divide' refers to the gap between those who have access to technology and those who do not (Norris 2001). This includes vast gaps between countries (often those from the global north and the global south), regions (cities versus rural settings) and individuals (significant differences between the rich and poor, young and old). As we become increasingly reliant on online networks to conduct many aspects of our lives, it is important to bear in mind those who are left behind or stuck in the slow lanes of the global information superhighway.

Another drawback of the growth of online networks is that potential offenders (in particular, organized criminals and terrorists) are also able to access and use technology and build physical, virtual and online networks to facilitate the commission of crime across borders. Network analysis is an approach to studying, measuring and understanding crime that involves mapping criminal networks. These maps illustrate the different nodes (often individuals) and the connection or ties between them. Network analysis is often used in organized crime studies to look at the structure and operation of crime rings (see Chapter 6). These studies highlight that contemporary criminal groups often lack hierarchy and are instead loosely connected, dispersed and fluid. Organized crime networks often build on legitimate networks. This is demonstrated in Case Study 3.3, which discusses how criminals can use the internet and online marketplaces to their advantage.

Similarly, Nordstrom (2000) explores the operation of shadow networks, that is international mechanisms and powers that shape world economics and policies and facilitate criminal activities and war, yet often remain invisible in formal analysis. Nordstrom's (2000) analysis demonstrates that states and shadow networks operate simultaneously and that different licit and illicit practices are intertwined, creating a complex environment of multiple, overlapping networks that flow around the world. By way of example, Nordstrom (2000, p. 40) states that goods such as precious gems (legal or illegal) 'don't flow in a vacuum – they flow along informal food and supply lines, along illegal drug and weapons routes, along undocumented immigration passageways, along legal and diplomatic channels'. While we often disaggregate practices such as the trade in illegal weapons, sex slavery, war crimes and the trade in precious metals and goods, these acts are often closely connected and are reliant on existing legitimate networks. Viewing society and crime through network theory is useful as nodes and the connections between them offer a way of conceptualizing space beyond the territorially bound prism of traditional maps based on nation-states. For example, instead of conceiving of crime as something that occurs across defined state borders between actors in set locations, we can see crime as a series of fluid interactions between debounded actors operating in multiple global networks.

Case Study 3.3 – The Dark Net Rises

In the deepest recesses of the internet, below the browsers with which we are familiar, is a subterranean online world, which has been dubbed the **Dark Net**. It is accessed via The Onion Router or Tor for short, an alternative navigation tool, developed originally by the US Navy (DEBKAfile 2015; Martin 2014). Tor was created specifically to allow secret, untraceable communications on the internet. Constructed like an onion, encrypted messages are transferred from source to destination via layers of computers (DEBKAfile 2015). It has provided the perfect tool for those who wish to transact their business in secret and retain their anonymity because it is extremely difficult to discover someone's real identity or their location once communication has been relayed via multiple ports (Martin 2014).

A second business tool was provided with the arrival of **cryptocurrencies**. The first of these, Bitcoin, began operating in 2008. Cryptocurrencies enable transactions to take place outside the view of financial institutions and are the currency of choice for online black market operations (Goodman 2013; Martin 2014). These two technologies combined have produced the conditions necessary to spawn a new and diverse black market economy, transacted online in the back alleys of the internet. There, cryptomarkets have mushroomed, where it is possible to buy an array of illegal goods and services, including firearms, dangerous drugs, counterfeit currency, body parts and the skills of hackers or hitmen (DEBKAfile 2015; Goodman 2013).

Silk Road was one of the best known of these sites, established primarily to facilitate the sale and purchase of illegal substances (DEBKAfile 2015). It was a mecca for underground drug dealing, a drugs Ebay as it were (Martin 2014). Its architect and administrator, the mysterious 'Dread Pirate Roberts' (also known as DPR), set up Silk Road in approximately January 2011 (FBI 2015). In September 2013, when the FBI shut down the site, there were 13,000 individual listings for controlled substances, ranging from a few grams of marijuana to a kilogram of cocaine (FBI 2015; *Manager Magazin* 2013). Like Amazon, it relied on feedback and customer ratings and, aside from the merchandise on offer, appeared to be a civilized marketplace with rules forbidding the sale of weapons, child pornography and stolen credit cards (Cadwalladr 2013; Goodman 2013).

Some argue that cryptomarkets allow illegal transactions to be made in relative safety, without the purchaser having to physically step foot on a drug dealer's turf, and that the incidence of associated violence is therefore reduced (Martin 2014). They also, however, allow illicit drugs – some 4,400 kinds are available – to be purchased with relative ease and sent to any address worldwide, thus increasing the trade's reach and spreading addiction (*Manager Magazin* 2013; Martin 2014). There is no doubting the Dark Net's success as a conduit for criminal enterprise and, unsurprisingly, since Silk Road was closed down, other sites such as Sheep and Black Market Reloaded have readily sprung up in its place (Cadwalladr 2013).

The Dark Net may not, however, be as hidden as its users would like to believe. Tor was developed by the US military, and National Security Agency researchers operate deep within it (DEBKAfile 2015). They had been monitoring DPR for some time. Despite the apparent anonymity offered by Tor and Bitcoin, it was in seeking help on the internet for a technical problem with his servers that DPR inadvertently revealed his true identity. The problem with swimming in the deep is at some point you have to come up for air. Finally unmasked, its creator was revealed to be 29-year-old Ross William Ulbricht, a University of Texas physics graduate. Despite Silk Road making him an estimated US$13 million, money did not appear to be Ulbricht's primary motivation: he was a libertarian and was keen to demonstrate 'what it would be like to live in a world without the systemic use of force'. He was found guilty on seven counts related to his operation and ownership of Silk Road (FBI 2015).

3.5 The Emergence of Ungovernable, Virtual Space

It is increasingly important to reconceptualize our understanding of space as the online environment becomes a more prominent aspect of our lives. Virtual space, or cyberspace, sits outside state-defined territory and the physical environment. The evolution of the virtual world has created new types of crimes and has made it easier for individuals to commit traditional crimes at both domestic and transnational levels. As was demonstrated in the previous section, actors can use the online space to facilitate illegal behaviour. A further example of this is provided in Chapter 7 which explores how terrorists use cyberspace to recruit potential participants, communicate with other group members and finance their crimes. The Australian Crime Commission (ACC) (2013a, p. 2) explains that, 'the internet is particularly attractive to criminals and organized crime groups. It is globally connected, borderless, anonymous, fast, low-risk, easily accessible and has high volumes of rich data including financing data, personal information, military information and business information'.

Cybercrime is known by a variety of names, including computer crime, virtual crime and high-tech crime. The key aspect of cybercrime is the use of international and communication technologies to commit an offence. There is a broad range of crimes that come under this banner including fraud, hacking, money laundering and theft, cyberstalking, cyberbullying, identity theft, child sexual exploitation and child grooming (AIC 2015). These crimes can be divided into two categories: crimes directed at computers where offences exist only in the digital world (hacking is one example); and crimes where computers or information and communication technologies are an integral part of the offence (for example online fraud or identity theft) (ACC 2013a). The second category defined above describes the way that traditional crimes are committed in new ways through the use of new technological platforms.

Cybercrime is difficult to measure as it is often hidden and underreported. It is also challenging to respond to and control cybercrime. Online actors are often anonymous and these individuals can act in physical locations far from that in which they are based.

This causes significant problems in terms of how we respond to crimes that often have such dispersed cause and effect. For example, an offender could be based in Nigeria and lure a computer-user located in Canada to provide financial details via email. Investigations and prosecutions of such crimes require cross-jurisdictional cooperation and collaboration. In addition to this barrier, it is often very difficult to identify offenders, who can remain anonymous in the vast recesses of the internet. This is why we can consider the online environment as a largely ungovernable space. Accordingly, prevention is often a key strategy of officials in the fight against cybercrime. Prevention involves informing and educating potential victims about safe online practices and target hardening computers and internet sites and databases to make it more difficult for offenders to access these.

While some crimes may be committed wholly within virtual space, this does not mean that there are no tangible impacts of cybercrime. Crimes committed online can cause significant ramifications and harm in the physical world. One case of a purely virtual crime is explored in Case Study 3.4. Is there real life harm caused by this virtual crime?

Case Study 3.4 – When is Rape Not a Rape?

LambdaMOO is a Multi-User Dungeon or Dimension (MUD), an interactive space created for gameplay. The purpose of a MUD is to allow participants to explore and experience a variety of virtual worlds in any guise they choose – in short, to create and live in an alternative reality and to experience things they could not in real life. What happens in a MUD occurs in real-time, using online characters or avatars, which are created and controlled by users.

In the early 1990s, one LambdaMOO user, whose avatar was a clown-like character called Mr Bungle, armed himself with a voodoo doll programme that allowed him to take control of other users' avatars. With this he forced one character (legba) to perform sexual acts on Mr Bungle. Then, he turned his attentions to a second character (Starsinger), forcing her to perform sex acts with three other characters. Finally, both legba and Starsinger were made to carry out violent and degrading acts upon themselves. During the attacks Mr Bungle was heard laughing evilly in the background. His victims were powerless against his rampages and he could not be stopped until a character was finally summoned who possessed a gun that, when fired, could contain and immobilize Mr Bungle in a virtual cage (Dibbell 1994).

Those involved directly or as witnesses to these events found them highly disturbing and a prolonged online discussion began about how best to deal with Mr Bungle. Mr Bungle himself made several appearances in LambdaMOO in the days following the attacks, coolly wandering about but engaging little with the community. He was finally despatched by a 'wizard', a MUD technician, who could access a toading tool, which summarily destroys unwanted characters. A few days later Mr Bungle was reincarnated in the form of a new character, Dr Jest, who continued to rile the populace of LambdaMOO, albeit in a more subdued form (Dibbell 1994).

So what can we make of these virtual 'crimes' and how should we respond? As Dibbell (1994) states, these actions fall in a gap between real life and the virtual world. A virtual rape is not a rape in the technical sense, but certainly some harm has been caused. Despite the passing of the Communications Decency Act 1996 (US), which attempted to address the proliferation of pornography and indecent material on the internet, there are few controls to regulate actions in deep cyberspace (Michals 1997). Violent sexual fantasies, gang-rape, incest and unprovoked attacks are commonplace and many women in particular have reported being subjected to unwanted attacks (Arnold 1998; Michals 1997). Anonymity is the driving force, allowing users to behave in socially unacceptable ways without censure. Since the LambdaMOO incident online communities realized that solutions to unacceptable online behaviour could not be provided by real-life legal avenues, and began to organize their own norms, rules and sanctions. These vary depending on what is allowable in each individual community but broadly they mirror real-life punitive responses, such as reintegrative shaming, retribution and expulsion (Byassee 1995; Williams 2000).

3.6 Conclusion

This chapter has demonstrated some of the new vulnerabilities that are emerging in a globalized world defined by risk and structured through fluid, dispersed networks. The risk paradigm reframes the way we view the world and shapes our attitudes towards and responses to crime. Avoiding risk entails calculating the likelihood of future events and enforcing harsh, preventative measures on groups and individuals identified as dangerous. The result of this risk-based approach can be a diminishment of rights for 'risky' (often vulnerable) people such as irregular migrants, potential terrorists and organized criminals. The new frontier – the virtual world – extends our sense of risk and defencelessness as we can be reached by anonymous criminals from around the globe. Although the internet can be a risky place, we are still searching for ways of governing and controlling virtual landscapes.

Questions: Revise and Reflect

1. Does risk operate as an equalizing force in a global world? In what ways might risk actually create more divides and who might be disadvantaged in a risk-based world?

2. How has 9/11 affected policy decisions related to law and order? In the United States? In your country?

3. How do the media and politicians contribute to a climate of risk? What effect do they have on public perceptions of risk? How do those perceptions feed back to policy decisions?

4. Can virtual crime be considered a crime in the traditional sense? Should virtual crimes be addressed by the criminal justice system?

Further Reading

Beck, U 1999, *World risk society*, Polity Press, Cambridge.
Castells, M 2004, *The network society: A cross-cultural perspective*, Edward Elgar, Cheltenham.
Ericson, R 2007, *Crime in an insecure world*, Polity Press, Cambridge.
Findlay, M 2008, *Governing through globalised crime: Futures for international criminal justice*, Willan, Portland, OR.
Garland, D 2001, *The culture of control*, Oxford University Press, Oxford.

Websites to Visit

AIC Cyber Crime: www.aic.gov.au/crime_types/cybercrime.html
University of Cambridge Centre for Risk Studies: www.risk.jbs.cam.ac.uk/

4

The Creation and Circulation of Justice Norms

This chapter will look at

- Policy transfer and convergence.
- Penal populism and punitiveness.
- International criminal justice mechanisms and structures.

Keywords

Penal populism	Capacity building	Alternative justice mechanisms
Policy transfer	International criminal courts	

4.1 Introduction

This chapter looks at the many different ways that ideas about crime and justice circulate, transfer and converge around the world. It examines the emerging structures and mechanisms that exist to respond to transnational and international crimes and considers how concepts, norms, principles, policies and processes of justice are incrementally built through these mechanisms leading to the development of an evolving body of criminal justice that operates at several different levels: local, national, regional, transnational, international and supranational. Concepts of crime and justice are diffused through a variety of outlets, including formal justice institutions, such as courts and tribunals, as well as through more informal mechanisms, which include policy transfer, capacity building and the encouragement of national jurisdictions to harmonize their policies with international standards. This chapter explores how dominant approaches to crime emerge and evolve and considers how themes such as **punitiveness** and **penal populism** operate at a global level.

4.2 Policy Transfer and Convergence: Penal Populism and Punitiveness

In the globally connected world of the twenty-first century, music, ideas, theories, news and 'memes' can circulate the world in an instant. In this climate, it is not surprising that crime and justice policies may also be transported from one jurisdiction to another. When one country implements a seemingly successful crime policy, other countries can access this information and employ a similar policy in their own local area. The adoption of policies that originate in another jurisdiction is known as **policy transfer**. Dolowitz and Marsh (2000, p. 5) describe policy transfer as the process by which 'knowledge about how policies, administrative arrangements, institutions and ideas in one political setting (past or present) is used in the development of policies, administrative arrangements, institutions and ideas in another political setting'. In Britain, the Centre for Management and Policy Studies (CMPS) has highlighted the benefits of policy transfer in a globalized age stating:

> Looking abroad to see what other governments have done can point us towards a new understanding of shared problems; towards new solutions to those problems; or to new mechanisms for implementing policy and improving the delivery of public services. International examples can provide invaluable evidence of what works in practice, and help us avoid either reinventing the wheel or repeating others' mistakes. (CMPS 2002)

Policy transfer occurs through many different processes and at many different levels.

Bennett (1991) lists four ways in which policy transfer may be achieved:

- Emulation – where one jurisdiction directly emulates a policy that originated in another jurisdiction;

- Elite networking – where transnational groups of actors share expertise and information about a common problem, creating an international policy culture;

- Harmonization – where policy transfer is driven by formal intergovernmental organizations and structures established to coordinate policies on a certain subject;

- Penetration/coercion – where nation-states are forced to conform to particular policy developments driven by other nations or external organizations and structures, for example third world countries must develop certain economic policies as a condition of aid or loans from the World Bank or the IMF.

As this list highlights, there are many different forms and degrees of policy transfer. Policy transfer encompasses simple lesson drawing and informal sharing of ideas about 'what works' to direct coercion by which nation-states are cajoled to align their policies with other jurisdictions. We can think of a policy transfer as a continuum; on one end of the continuum is informal lesson drawing from other jurisdictions, and on the other end is direct, coercive transfer, where external policies are imposed on jurisdictions via international organizations or other countries (Dolowitz & Marsh 2000). Sitting towards the coercive end of the continuum is a process known as regionalization. The best example of a formal process of regionalization is the European Union. The EU relies on the harmonization and convergence of the policies of its member states – in many ways this is the raison d'être of the EU. Under this model, candidate countries must emulate EU standards and policies prior to accession. This means that countries that wish to join the EU are coerced into adopting certain policies. While this may be a voluntary coercion as states can choose not to implement EU mandated policies, and in doing so remain separate from the EU, the benefits for countries in joining the EU lend strong coercive weight to policy decisions. The EU therefore demonstrates how policy transfer can occur in a vertical manner with states complying with directives and regulations driven by an overarching body. However, the EU also offers a forum for more informal, horizontal policy sharing and discussions, as it establishes communication networks (what Adler & Haas 1992 call 'epistemological communities') among officials where policy actors can learn from other countries.

In the realm of criminal justice, there are several examples where crime control policies have been transferred from one country to another. One prominent example is the policy of 'zero tolerance' policing, which was introduced in New York following the election of Mayor Rudolph Giuliani in 1993. Zero tolerance policing is premised on Wilson and Kelling's (1982) Broken Windows Theory, which asserts that minor incivilities and disorder (such as vandalism and graffiti) lead to more serious crimes. Broken Windows Theory describes high-crime areas as caught in a vicious cycle: petty crimes and disorder create a generalized fear of crime in a local neighbourhood which leads to a growing reluctance by citizens to use public space, a diminishment of natural surveillance in the area, a loosening of social ties and the loss of a sense of community, all of which can contribute to more serious crimes and a heightened crime rate (Newburn & Jones 2007a). Accordingly, the model of zero tolerance policing focuses on taking authoritative action on minor crimes and incivilities, including aggressive enforcement against street crimes and harsh law enforcement responses and a non-discretionary approach to minor crime and disorder (Newburn & Jones 2007a).

Following the New York Police Department's adoption of zero tolerance policing methods, crime rates in New York fell and this decline in crime was attributed to the new, strict and non-discretionary approach to policing (Bratton 1997). Although the role that zero tolerance policing played in reducing crime rates was contested (crime rates had also dropped in other US cities during the same period) (Brereton 1999), zero tolerance policing was widely viewed as a success and became a mainstay in the US crime control landscape. This apparent success prompted governments in other jurisdictions, particularly in the United Kingdom and Australia, to adopt similar zero tolerance policies. In their comprehensive study of criminal justice policy transfer, Newburn and Jones (2007b) found clear evidence of policy transfer between the United States and the United Kingdom in the use of zero tolerance policing. Policy actors in the United Kingdom (civil servants, politicians and police officers) visited the New York Police Department, with the explicit aim of observing and drawing lessons from their practices (Newburn & Jones 2007b). Following such visits, similar policies appeared in the United Kingdom. In addition to this explicit transfer of policies, Newburn and Jones (2007b) also found that the spread of zero tolerance was apparent in the use of rhetoric and symbols. The mantra of zero tolerance is now deployed in a range of circumstances in jurisdictions around the world, where actors wish to convey a tough, punitive stance on crime. We can see manifestations of zero tolerance in mandatory sentencing regimes, the wars on crime and drugs and harsh policing of street crimes.

Another example of criminal justice policy transfer is the spread of private prisons in developed countries around the world. As with zero tolerance policing, the concept of private prisons began in the United States; the first mainstream, commercially operated prison, run by the Corrections Corporation of America, opened in Houston, Texas in 1984. The mid-1990s saw a wave of private prisons open across the United States, particularly in western and southern states, such as Texas, Oklahoma, Florida and Tennessee. Today, there are over 100 private prisons in the United States. The popularity of the private prison stems from the expensive nature of building and maintaining prisons and from governments' desire to reduce costs, which is increasingly a measure of success and effectiveness in prisons. In 1992, Wolds Prison became the first privately managed prison in the United Kingdom. There are now 14 privately run prisons in the UK (Justice UK 2014). Again, Jones and Newburn (2007b) found examples of direct policy transfer of the private prison concept between the United States and the United Kingdom. This trend has also spread to Australia, with private prisons opening around the country.

Although the examples of zero tolerance policing and privately run prisons appear to indicate the existence of clear and direct policy transfer practices between states, there are some issues with policy transfer both as a concept and in practice. Transferring policies between countries requires attentiveness to local conditions and cultures. What is appropriate and successful in one context may be unsuccessful in another, and indeed may be insensitive to the cultural, social, economic and political specificities of a particular location. Take private prisons, for example. Melossi (2004, p. 84) has shown that 'punishment is deeply embedded in the national/cultural specificity of the environment which produces it'. The concept of the private prison originated in the United States, which has a culture of strong individualism and a suspicion of state and government regulation. Other countries, such as the United Kingdom, have not always subscribed to such doctrines with the same fervour as the United States (although this is changing, as future examples will illustrate). This means that the way that society views the individual subject, the relationship between citizens and the state and the role of governments differ greatly between the United States and the United Kingdom. The United Kingdom also has its own, unique punishment conventions which have evolved throughout the country's history and has a stronger welfare state tradition than the United States. Accordingly, the transfer of a corrections policy such as the introduction of private prisons may not be as successful or appropriate.

In addition to this practical pitfall, the concept of policy transfer is itself flawed. Policy transfer is based on the assumption of rationality in the policy process, but is the making of policy really so linear, or is it more complex and serendipitous? There are numerous actors involved in the policy process, including activists and advocates, NGOs, politicians, citizens and civil servants. As any of these experienced policy actors would tell you, the process of implementing policy is bumpy and often circular, susceptible to the vagaries of politics. Many different voices can emerge and influence the process and a policy may change shape many times before it comes into being. This messy, complicated process of policy implementation can be difficult to trace, quantify and measure. It is clear that this process is not captured in the idea of policy being directly transferred from one jurisdiction to another.

Policy convergence is perhaps a more salient way to understand how policy norms and practices circulate in a **globalized** (and **glocalized**) environment. Policy convergence describes the process by which policies are influenced by the social forces that shape social life. For example, in Chapter 2 we explored how the principles of **late modernity** and a focus on **reflexivity** and control characterize the current era. In Chapter 3, we considered how the concept of risk profoundly influences society. These discourses often traverse borders, particularly in Western, Anglo-Saxon countries such as the United States, the United Kingdom and Australia. Consequently, different countries may be shaped in a similar manner by the social forces that operate as a homogenizing influence at a global level. Indeed, much literature on globalization demonstrates the tendency of societies to grow more alike under conditions of industrialization, **modernity** and globalization. This homogenization process can mean that similar policies appear in different jurisdictions without the direct influence suggested by policy transfer.

The influence of global social forces on criminal justice policy is discernible in our examples of zero tolerance policing and private prisons. The authoritative tough on crime stance of zero tolerance policies can be linked to the crime control predicament of late modernity. In his seminal work on late modern crime control, Garland (2001) describes how capitalist societies seek to denounce crime and reassure the public by taking visible, punitive measures in response to high crime rates (refer back to Chapter 3 for more discussion). A punitive approach clearly underpins zero tolerance policies that operate in several different countries, such as the United States and the United Kingdom, and function to assuage public anxiety over petty crime and disorder. Similarly, penal populism (that is an environment in which politicians compete to be 'tough on crime'; Pratt 2007) has been increasing around the world. The rise in penal populism is complex, but can be partly linked to discourses of risk and the spread of **neoliberalism**. These forces create a desire for preventative detention (as discussed in Chapter 3) and punitive punishments for individuals who threaten the social order or the freedom of others (individual freedom being a cornerstone of neoliberalism). Punitive punishments for the 'other' also channel some of the anxiety associated with neoliberal risk environments, meaning incarceration offers a politically popular option.

Additionally, criminologist Nils Christie (2000) has examined how a culture of neoliberalism creates a 'prison-industrial complex' driven by an international alliance of commercial penal and industrial interests that profit from expansionist penal policies. Within this environment, a punitive approach to crime creates the need for more prisons, which benefits those corporations responsible for privately run prisons and simultaneously justifies their existence. In these examples, we can see that crime and justice policies may converge or they may be similar across different jurisdictions because of a shared punitive culture of mass incarceration and penal populism that is a product of global social forces and structural factors, such as the spread of neoliberalism and risk.

As the above discussion suggests, direct policy transfer and even the more complex concept of policy convergence predominately operate between Western nation-states with similar cultures and traditions. These countries share roughly comparable approaches to crime and justice, law and criminology. The idea of policy transfer rests on the notion of determining 'what works' in crime policy, a position that emerged from the rationality of the Enlightenment project and its belief in empirical research and scientific evidence (a largely Western approach).

It is important to note that research and 'evidence' are themselves contestable as they rely on certain taken-for-granted assumptions. For example, quantitative research into crime and justice (involving measuring crime and justice policies using statistics) makes clear assumptions about which acts constitute a crime. From this perspective, the idea of whether certain acts should be defined as criminal remains unquestioned and punitiveness is justified and normalized. A reliance on numbers and unquestioned 'facts' to determine the success of justice policy, such as measuring the success of prisons purely through their cost-effectiveness, obscures the complex processes of criminalization, the role of crime and punishment in society, and the humans at the end of the punitive policy line.

4.3 Responses to Transnational Crimes

In Chapter 1, we outlined how responses to **transnational crime** have emerged and evolved throughout history. As this discussion demonstrated, responses to transnational crime largely rely on two approaches: urging national jurisdictions to respond to transnational crimes in a particular way, and encouraging cooperation between states, with the involvement of many different intergovernmental agencies, NGOs and regional bodies. There are no international courts to prosecute transnational crime as such. Interestingly, in 1989, Trinidad and Tobago revived long-standing discussions on the development of an international criminal court, calling for a court to deal with the illegal drug trade. While Trinidad and Tobago's requests for an international criminal court eventually resulted in the Rome Conference and the establishment of the ICC, the ICC was not tasked with responding to drug crimes at all, instead it was confined to the international crimes of **genocide**, **war crimes**, **crimes against humanity** and **aggression** (see Chapter 1 on the distinction between transnational and **international crimes**).

Due to the lack of formal justice institutions, national jurisdictions are tasked with responding to transnational crime, alongside other states. To this end, there are a number of conventions that seek to coordinate state responses to transnational crime. For example, the UN Convention against Transnational Organized Crime is a multilateral treaty that was adopted in 2000 in Palermo, Italy (it is also referred to as the Palermo Convention). There are three protocols associated with the convention (the Palermo Protocols):

- Protocol to Prevent, Suppress and Punish Trafficking in Persons, especially Women and Children;
- Protocol against the Smuggling of Migrants by Land, Sea and Air; and
- Protocol against the Illicit Manufacturing and Trafficking in Firearms.

The convention and its associated protocols encourage appropriate responses to transnational crime. This includes advising states to criminalize particular acts (trafficking in human beings, for example), to introduce legislation that aligns with international standards and to undertake appropriate criminal investigations and prosecutions. Under this approach it is clear that a form of policy transfer is encouraged, as national jurisdictions are persuaded to harmonize their national legislation with overarching international standards which are presumed to be neutral and desirable examples of best practice.

Sometimes, more coercive measures can be introduced to encourage nations to adhere to these international standards. For example, the US Department of State has created an Office to Monitor and Combat Trafficking in Persons which produces an annual *Trafficking in persons report* (US Department of State 2014). The report is based on a three-tiered ranking of countries, according to the government's actions, to confront and eliminate trafficking in persons. Countries ranked as Tier 1 are countries whose governments fully comply with the Trafficking Victims Protection Act's (TVPA) minimum standards (this is a US piece of legislation). Tier 2 countries do not fully comply, but are 'making significant efforts to bring themselves into compliance with those standards' (US Department of State 2015, np). Tier 3 countries 'do not fully comply with the minimum standards and are not making significant efforts to do so' (US Department of State 2015, np).

The ranking system is a way to name and shame governments for their inability or unwillingness to enact legislation and implement policies that align with US (and international) standards on trafficking in persons. As with other measures that attempt to place pressure on countries in order to initiate reform, the consequences for countries that are not ranked favourably primarily involve a loss of international reputation and esteem. The report is also described as the US government's 'principal diplomatic tool to engage foreign governments on human trafficking' (US Department of State 2015, np), meaning that a country's tiered placement may influence the way the United States engages with its government in terms of aid and assistance programmes. However, the United States is often driven by its own **realpolitik** considerations, which can be capricious. Even though the United States is a self-proclaimed leader in the fight against trafficking in persons, its role as arbitrator can be seen as self-interested as the United States is a major **destination country** for trafficked people and therefore carries the burden of dealing with the end-point of the trafficking process. Additionally, some governments may not care about the image they project to the West and their ranking on the Department of State's report will have no bearing on their actions in regard to trafficking in persons.

Another way that national jurisdictions are encouraged to harmonize their policies with international standards in relation to transnational crime is through capacity building efforts. Capacity building describes the process of strengthening the skills, competencies and abilities of local governments and communities. Organizational capacity building is encouraged by NGOs and international organizations who work on development projects in third world countries. It is also a component of post-conflict measures to rebuild society after war and mass atrocity.

Spotlight – Police Capacity Building in East Timor

Conflict in East Timor in 1999 left the country's criminal justice infrastructure devastated and the local police force significantly weakened. The United Nations consequently sent peacekeepers to the area to help rebuild the country's justice system. The Australian Federal Police also sent a contingent to East Timor to work with the country's officials to redevelop the local police force (Goldsmith & Dinnen 2007).

This form of transnational police building demonstrates how international experts can act to diffuse norms and embed them in other jurisdictions, by working with local officials to build functional democratic systems. Strong justice systems and police forces can help combat transnational crime at its source.

The example in the Spotlight above highlights that cooperation between nation-states is another key factor in successful responses to transnational crime. The Palermo Convention and its Protocols highlight the importance of cooperation and information sharing between law enforcement agencies. For example, the Protocol to Prevent, Suppress and Punish Trafficking in Persons, especially Women and Children (UN 2000, p. 6), states that 'law enforcement, immigration or other relevant authorities of States Parties shall, as appropriate, cooperate with one another by exchanging information, in accordance with their domestic law'. As already highlighted in Chapter 1, there are a multitude of international and regional agencies that exist to coordinate responses to transnational crimes, including Interpol and Europol.

The causes of transnational crime are broad and varied, meaning that a multifaceted approach is needed to help address both the conditions that cause crimes and the symptoms of those crimes. This section has provided a very brief overview of some approaches to transnational crime control. The reason for the brevity of this discussion is that a lot of material on responses to transnational crime features in other sections of this book. Chapter 1 introduces several core concepts on transnational crime. The second half of this book is dedicated to comprehensive discussions of different types of transnational crime, including trafficking in persons and **organized crime**. These chapters go into more depth on responses that are specific to particular types of transnational crime. The point of the discussion here has been to outline how responses to transnational crime facilitate the circulation of ideas and norms about crime and justice beyond the border of the nation-state. As there is no formal international justice structure to deal with transnational crime, responses can be piecemeal, relying on cooperation between different countries and the development of strong policing capability to address transnational crime.

4.4 International Criminal Justice Mechanisms and Structures

In many ways, responses to international crimes (genocide, war crimes, crimes against humanity and aggression) are the opposite of responses to transnational crimes. As the previous section illustrated, transnational crimes are often dealt with through policing measures and cooperation between states and existing domestic criminal justice structures, with no formal international courts to prosecute transnational crimes beyond the state. Conversely, responses to international crimes are primarily focused on the end-stage – the prosecution of crimes in a trial setting. Thus we see many international criminal courts and tribunals concerned with punishing international crimes, but no international police force to facilitate the work of these courts, and no system of democratic governance to constrain the powers of the courts and develop legislation. These courts are, therefore, disembodied from a broader system or hierarchy of justice. In contrast to transnational crime, international criminal justice norms have been diffused by the establishment of more formal structures of justice and by a flurry of institution building, as we shall see in this section.

Institutional Development

The decades since the end of World War II have seen the rapid development of international courts, tribunals and war crimes trials to prosecute international crimes. Following World War II, two international criminal tribunals were established by the Allied Forces to prosecute Axis Powers. The Nuremberg Trials, or the International Military Tribunal (IMT), were held in 1945 to prosecute prominent members of the political, military and economic leadership of Nazi Germany. The trials were held in Nuremberg, Germany, and were presided over by judges from the Soviet Union, the United Kingdom, the United States and France. The first round of trials saw 24 accused of war crimes, with 12 defendants sentenced to death. Subsequent trials prosecuted 183 high-ranking German officials for their role in implementing the Nazi plan of Jewish extermination. Other countries affected by the war concurrently prosecuted individuals through domestic courts. In 1947, Poland sentenced Rudolf Höss, commandant of the Auschwitz camp, to death. After its liberation from German occupation in 1944,

France undertook a wave of trials known as 'the legal purge' in which over 300,000 cases of Nazi collaboration were investigated by the French justice system, resulting in 791 executions.

Alongside these domestic prosecutions and the famous Nuremberg Tribunal, the Allied Forces also established the International Military Tribunal for the Far East (IMTFE), or the Tokyo Trials, to prosecute leaders from Japan for war crimes. Twenty-eight Japanese military and political leaders were charged with the most serious crimes (conspiring to wage war) and more than 5,700 Japanese nationals were charged with other war crimes, predominately prisoner abuse. The Nuremberg and Tokyo Tribunals were not free from criticism as they grappled with legitimacy and charges of victors' justice, as the countries that won the war administered justice against those that had lost (Peskin 2005). Despite this, they were a significant development, as they were the first major international courts to prosecute war crimes.

Any momentum in the development of international criminal justice institutions following Nuremberg was constrained by the advent of the Cold War (between approximately 1947 and 1991). After the end of the Cold War, the 1990s saw a sharp increase in human rights movements in international relations and this powerful human rights focus developed 'a victim-oriented discourse that required states to ensure that perpetrators of atrocities were brought to justice' (Schabas 2006, p. 422). These human rights and victim-oriented discourses caused the UN Security Council to react to the atrocities in the Balkans by setting up the ad-hoc tribunal known as the International Criminal Tribunal for the Former Yugoslavia (ICTY) in The Hague (Swart et al. 2011). Closely following this tribunal, the 1994 genocide in Rwanda and the failure of international society to react to the horrors as they unfolded, prompted the introduction of another ad-hoc tribunal, the International Criminal Tribunal for Rwanda (ICTR), in Arusha (Cruvellier 2010).

The ICTY and the ICTR are ad-hoc tribunals created by the United Nations to prosecute crimes relating to specific events. The logistics of setting up these two ad-hoc tribunals proved time consuming and resource intensive for the United Nations and a sense of 'tribunal fatigue' coincided with renewed attempts to establish a permanent court to deal with such atrocities in the future (Bassiouni 1995, p. 57). In 1998, following decades of work from the International Law Commission (ILC), the Rome Statute Conference was convened to discuss the establishment of a permanent International Criminal Court. The historic Rome Conference was attended by thousands of individuals and groups representing state parties, international bodies, such as the United Nations, and notably many representatives of **'global civil society'** including advocates for human rights and victims' rights and media organizations (Glasius 2006). Over the course of the conference, these actors negotiated the Rome Statute that created the ICC (Kirsch & Holmes 1999; Tallgren 1999). In 2002, when 60 countries ratified the Rome Statute, the ICC was born.

Since then, many more countries have moved to support the Statute. At the time of writing, 123 countries have ratified the Rome Statute of the ICC (CICC 2015). When compared to the 193 member countries of the United Nations, it becomes apparent that although the ICC has considerable support, it is still not a universal institution (UN 2015b). There are several countries who oppose the Court, most notably and vocally the United States, but also the other 'superpowers' of China and Russia (Casey 2002; Goldsmith 2003). There has been limited participation in, and engagement with, the Court from Asian countries (Balais-Serrano 2007), with only nine out of 24 Asian countries having ratified the Rome Statue (CICC 2015). The bid for 'universality' is ongoing with the ICC and supporting organizations, such as the Coalition for the International Criminal Court, rallying countries to sign and ratify the Rome Statute (CICC 2015).

The ICC exists permanently to prosecute the worst crimes known to humankind. In 2015, there are situations under investigation involving: the Democratic Republic of Congo, Uganda, the Central African Republic, Darfur, Sudan, Kenya, Libya, Cote d'Ivoire and Mali. The ICC is also undertaking preliminary investigations (to examine whether or not crimes have occurred that fall under its jurisdiction) in Afghanistan, Colombia, Georgia, Guinea, Honduras, Iraq, Ukraine and Palestine. The cases in each of the official investigations are narrow. For example, in the Democratic Republic of Congo (DRC) the ICC has conducted six trials resulting in:

- two guilty verdicts, one for the war crime of conscripting child soldiers, one for war crimes and crimes against humanity;

- one dismissal as pre-trial chamber declined to confirm the charges;

- one outstanding warrant of arrest;

- one acquittal;

- and one ongoing trial.

The war in the DRC has claimed up to 6 million lives (as both a direct result of fighting and as a result of disease and malnutrition), and is one of the worst emergencies in Africa (BBC News 2015). The prosecution of a few relatively 'small fish' does not adequately capture the vast nature of the atrocities in the DRC. To overcome this, the ICC is positioned as a court of last resort through the principle of 'complementarity'. This means that the ICC must complement local prosecutions, which take precedence over ICC trials. In many ways the ICC aims to catalyse domestic prosecutions as it focuses only on a few symbolic trials, which set a standard for the prosecution of international crimes at a domestic level. This model of standard-setting loosely resembles the idea of encouraging national jurisdictions to align local legislation with international standards. Here, it is the ICC which is demonstrating what the international community deems the correct method of responding to international crimes, defining the appropriate response to atrocity, and shaming countries that do not adhere by labelling them and their regimes criminal.

The narrowness of the trials is just one of the criticisms levelled against the ICC. The Court has also been censured for its focus on African countries, the length of its trials, its removal from the site of atrocities, its reliance on state support and its relationship to the UN Security Council from which it is meant to be independent. In many ways, the ICC is hamstrung as it must work within the constraints of the existing system of states and international bodies. It does not have the resources to conduct in-depth and widespread investigations and prosecutions as it exists to investigate different situations around the world as they appear. In this light, the ICC cannot escape politics, as it operates within a highly political system of international relations in which some cases and countries are prosecuted and others are not.

Considering the limitations of the ICC, other international criminal justice institutions have been developed to respond to international crimes in a more in-depth and localized manner. One way of localizing international courts has been the development of **hybrid courts** which feature a blend of international and local judges. The Extraordinary Chambers in the Courts of Cambodia (ECCC) is one example of a hybrid court. The ECCC was established by an agreement between the government of Cambodia and the United Nations to prosecute crimes committed by the Khmer Rouge between 1975 and 1979, during the Cambodian genocide. The ECCC trials are held in Cambodia using a mix of local and foreign judges and Cambodian and international staff. Other examples of hybrid courts include:

- the Special Court for Sierra Leone, which was the first court to convict a head of state, when it found Charles Taylor, former Liberian President, guilty of war crimes;

- the Special Panels of the Dili District Court (also known as the East Timor Tribunal), which operated between 2000 and 2006;

- the Regulation 64 Panels in the courts of Kosovo; and the Special Tribunal for Lebanon (STL), which is conducting prosecutions under Lebanese criminal law for the assassination of Rafic Hariri, former Lebanese Prime Minister, and the death of 22 others.

These hybrid courts are also referred to as 'internationalized courts' and seek to apply international standards in a manner adapted to local conditions (almost a form of judicial glocalization). The courts deal with one specific situation, as opposed to the ICC, which must respond to many different crimes around the world. This means that localized courts can conduct more widespread and in-depth examinations, which may be conducted in a more culturally appropriate, domestic setting. Because of this, hybrid courts can achieve a greater sense of legitimacy than purely international courts, such as the ICC, the ICTY and the

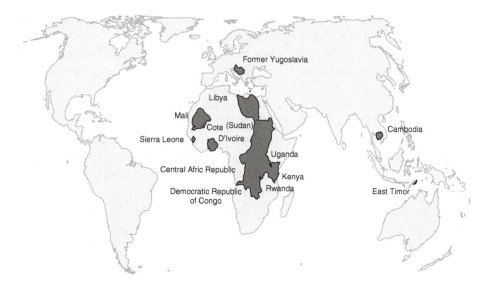

Figure 4.1 Geopolitics of International Courts from the 1990s Onwards

ICTR, as those who have been affected by the crimes have more ownership over, and access to, the trial processes (Nouwen 2006). However, this is not always the case. Hybrid courts bring their own set of unique challenges. Foremost is the cooperation between international and local judges and staff.

To gain legitimacy, courts must be independent, impartial and capable; the mere domestic setting does not guarantee legitimacy and capacity. To have a positive impact on victim communities, hybrid courts must undertake appropriate outreach (Nouwen 2006). The physical locality of a court does not automatically assure victim participation and access to justice. The ICTR, for example, was held in Arusha, Tanzania, as this location was closer to the site of atrocities than the 'capital of justice', The Hague, in the Netherlands. However, for local Rwandans, Arusha could have been considered as far away as The Hague due to difficulty of travel in the region. Thus, the seat of a court does not always equate to more accessible justice.

The location of justice is conceptual as well as physical. As the United Nations often assists in the creation of hybrid courts, and the panels comprise powerful and experienced international judges, hybrid courts can appear very foreign despite their national locale. As international standards are applied, a sense of cultural imperialism can arise. This is a major issue with all forms of international courts; they can be viewed as a form of hegemony whereby power-ful actors enforce justice and punishment on less powerful actors. The crimes of the powerful remain unquestioned by the justice paradigm, and legislation and criminalization legitimate certain acts while demonizing others. For example, some have called for the US war in Iraq to be considered a crime (Kramer et al. 2005); however, it is highly unlikely that an international court would prosecute the United States or that any of its allies would push for prosecution. International courts operate in a political milieu of **geopolitics**.

Examine Figure 4.1, which highlights the countries in which international criminal courts and prosecutions have occurred.

Alternative Justice Mechanisms

Alongside these formal courts and tribunals, sit a raft of different mechanisms that seek to provide justice and repair harm in the wake of mass atrocities and international crimes. **Transitional justice** is the term used for measures taken to redress harm and rebuild communities following violence and conflict. Transitional justice can include criminal prosecutions via international or domestic courts; however, it also encompasses much broader initiatives, such as truth and reconciliation commissions, reparations, capacity building and institutional reforms to develop systems of democratic governance. Whereas prosecutions focus on individual criminal responsibility and a retributive framework, transitional justice mechanisms align more closely with **restorative justice** aims. That is, transnational justice focuses on the needs of victims and communities and seeks to restore balance, redress harm and rebuild society to facilitate the transition from violence and conflict to peace. This may mean seeking truth and acknowledgement from offenders to reach understanding and tolerance, rather than punishing offenders through formal justice systems, which often obscure the story of atrocities, as offenders seek to defend themselves in an adversarial environment. Many examples of transitional justice mechanisms can be seen around the world.

One of the most lauded examples of transitional justice is the South African response to the atrocities of apartheid. The South African Truth and Reconciliation Commission began hearings in 1996 following the Promotion of National Unity and Reconciliation Act, No. 34 of 1995 which sought to reconcile tensions in the country following the devastation caused by apartheid. Apartheid, which began after World War II, involved mandated racial segregation, based on the ideology that different races in South Africa needed to be separated for their own benefit. Segregation was enforced through legislation, politics and violence and resulted in significant poverty, inequality and the forced removal of black South Africans from rural areas. The Truth and Reconciliation Commission invited witnesses and victims of human rights violations to give statements and attend public hearings. Perpetrators could also give testimony and request amnesty from prosecutions. This reconciliatory approach to human rights abuses sought to share history, bear witness, create collective memory, and provide a sense of redress to victims, through the admissions and remorse of perpetrators. Many view the South African

Truth and Reconciliation Commission as a success. Despite this, the effects of apartheid can still be felt in South Africa today, with high crime rates, significant poverty for marginalized groups and ongoing racial inequality (Smith 2012).

Another example of an alternative approach to justice is the Gacaca Courts of Rwanda, which are discussed in Case Study 4.1

Case Study 4.1 – Grassroots Justice

Gacaca trial in Rwanda

© Photo by Scott Chacon from Dublin, CA, USA (Gacaca trial) via Wikimedia Commons

The Gacaca (literally meaning 'grass') Courts were formed in 2001 as part of a response to the 1994 Rwandan Genocide. Following the genocide, the United Nations set up the International Criminal Tribunal for Rwanda, as previously mentioned, and the newly formed Rwandan government also instigated domestic criminal prosecutions of genocide perpetrators. The large numbers of perpetrators made it difficult for these courts to efficiently judge and punish genocidaires. Domestic trials began in December 1996, but only 1,292 suspects had been tried by 1998 (Human Rights Watch 2011). Although this number sounds enormous when compared to the ICC's record of six cases in the situation of the DRC, there were many more Rwandans awaiting trial and by 1998 there were approximately 130,000 prisoners contained in space designed for 12,000. These conditions resulted in thousands of deaths in custody, and the slow progress meant that the trials would have continued for more than a century (Human Rights Watch 2011). Consequently, the Rwandan government established a system of traditional community justice, Gacaca Courts, which were convened in villages across the country. These more informal courts involved locally elected judges. The aim was to give perpetrators the opportunity to confess, show remorse and ask forgiveness, while simultaneously offering victims and witnesses the opportunity to talk openly, hear the truth and move forward together. The Gacaca Courts closed in 2012 after hearing more than 1.2 million cases (12,000 courts were set up to hear these cases). While this grassroots conflict resolution method moved through the backlog of trials and offered a more restorative approach, the courts have left a mixed legacy. There have been criticisms that the Gacaca became politicized, that the trials were flawed and unfair, that not all sides of the genocide were tried, and that the victims did not receive adequate compensation.

The two examples of the Truth and Reconciliation Commission and the Gacaca Courts highlight some important issues in transitional justice. In post-conflict situations, there is a clash between the perceived need for retributive criminal justice and the desire for restoration and healing. Under the restorative paradigm, **amnesty** for offenders means individuals will not receive criminal punishment if they express remorse and give an honest account of their crimes. **Lustration**, a mechanism used in post-communist Europe, is another approach loosely resembling amnesty whereby government officials associated with a **criminogenic** regime are purged and prevented from holding government positions. These approaches stand in stark contrast to the punitive approach of retributive prosecutions. Amnesty is almost the antithesis of international criminal courts, which are founded on the importance of accountability and driven by the aim of 'ending impunity'. How can someone be held accountable and be given amnesty? Which is more important? There have been discussions around how the two should interact; for example, if amnesty is granted in a truth and reconciliation commission does this satisfy the requirements of justice in the eyes of international criminal courts?

This tension is symptomatic of wider disagreements about the role and position of justice in conflict and post-conflict situations, a debate often framed as 'peace versus justice'. Some argue that justice is a necessary precondition of achieving peace and that a rampant lack of accountability and culture of impunity impede peace processes. Others argue that judicial processes can damage peace negotiations, cause perpetrators to commit more crimes to defend their positions, and divert valuable resources from democratization projects, rebuilding communities and protecting civilians. Both positions ask: what is the best way to rebuild society after mass violence, conflict and atrocity? In one version, criminal prosecutions are key; in the other, they are of secondary importance and can be detrimental if pursued too vigorously. Often a mix of judicial and non-judicial mechanisms is required to help rebuild the damage caused by mass atrocities and conflict.

As this discussion highlights, justice is a tool that is used alongside a variety of different mechanisms. Prosecutions do not exist in isolation and other measures are required to achieve a broader sense of justice, particularly for societies in transition. Memorialization is another common response to atrocities. In Rwanda, there are a number of centres and museums to memorialize the genocide, including the Kigali Genocide Memorial Centre and the Murambi Genocide Memorial Centre. Survivors' committees and associations also organize memorials and commemorations in Rwanda, and there is an official national week of mourning and commemoration to mark the genocide. There are also many sites that memorialize the Holocaust and the crimes associated with World War II. For example, some concentration camps in Eastern Europe, such as Auschwitz-Birkenau in Poland, have remained and now exist as museums and memorials that allow individuals to visit as a form of 'dark tourism' (Dalton 2014). These sites fulfil an important role. They create a shared history of atrocities, they allow us to remember the horrors and human stories of conflict, and they create new insight and understanding into the causes of atrocities. It is not always possible to achieve these goals through formal justice institutions, which are bound by strict rules of procedure and process.

Formal justice institutions often 'close off' questions we have about mass atrocities (Shapiro 2015). Trials may close the book on periods of history that are complex, difficult, or painful. In contrast, alternative justice measures and the representation of atrocities through texts, museums, or memorials offer space for open, changeable understandings of conflict and mass atrocity. These forums acknowledge the plurality and complexity of international crimes. As with transnational crimes, the causes of international crime are multiple, meaning justice responses cannot be isolated or narrow. Thus alternative justice mechanisms, as well as international criminal courts and tribunals, and even measures designed to reduce domestic and transnational crime, have a role to play in responding to international crime.

4.5 A Global System of Criminal Justice?

What can we make of these broad and disparate justice responses: from the United Kingdom implementing zero tolerance policing measures, to a Gacaca Court sitting in a tiny Rwandan village; from the United States ranking countries according to their responses to trafficking in persons, to the ICC prosecuting a Congolese warlord for his use of child soldiers; from the implementation of private prisons, to the Nuremberg Trials executing Nazi war criminals? Is there any connection between these measures? Is a global system of justice emerging from this incongruent mass of criminal justice initiatives? Through the **post-modern** lens, we could argue that the multitude of varied criminal justice responses reflects the many different realities and representations of crime in contemporary social life. The reason we have included the varied examples in this chapter is to illustrate the many ways that discourses about crime and justice circulate around the globe, through both formal institution building and informal idea sharing, all of which are shaped by dominant social forces, which define the contemporary, globalized era.

These social forces mean that some trends emerge. Above all, there is a clash between retributive and restorative approaches to justice. The retributive approach prioritizes punitive responses to crime and fosters a culture of incarceration (think of zero tolerance, preventative detentions and criminal justice trials based on individual criminal responsibility for mass atrocities). A restorative approach advocates understanding the causes and impacts of crime, repairing victim communities and rebuilding societies (for example the truth and reconciliation commissions discussed in this chapter, and strategies to minimize the harm of organized crime – as discussed in Chapter 6). The clash between these two paradigms often manifests in contradictory responses to crime, whether at a domestic, transnational, or international level. Australian criminologist Pat O'Malley (1999) has theorized the volatile and contradictory nature of contemporary punishment regimes as stemming from the simultaneous adoption of neoliberal and **neoconservative** ideas. O'Malley (1999) highlights that neoliberalism is concerned with creating fewer constraints on the free market and producing individuals who are responsible for preventing victimization or controlling their behaviour. On the other hand, neoconservativism regards law and order as crucial to remoralize society.

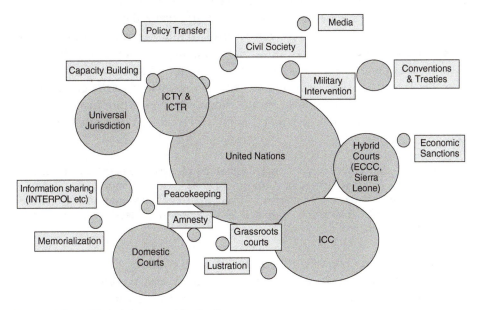

Figure 4.2 A Global System of Justice?

Indeed, since the end of World War II, there has been an increasing turn towards legislation and criminalization as one of the key responses to mass atrocities. The concept that an individual could be prosecuted in an international court for war crimes would have been quite foreign to soldiers at the start of World War I. Now, the lexicon of crime, justice, prosecution and imprisonment features prominently in discussions of war as well as in international interventions. Human rights abuses are now criminalized and we talk about war being 'illegal'. This turn to law and the growing faith in the rule of law as a moralizing force in international society are coupled with the neoliberal premise of the responsibilized subject (individual) making international criminal responsibility the foundation of international criminal justice. The idea of individual responsibility for crime has been transplanted from domestic justice systems, yet this view of crime commission is often incompatible with the reality of transnational and international crimes. Transnational and international crimes are widespread, collective, and are often committed in an environment of great **anomie**. Individual criminal responsibility does not capture the unique nature of mass atrocities, transnational and international crimes. Accordingly, although we may wish for retributive justice in the face of atrocities and human rights abuses, these crimes often shatter the boundaries of criminal justice systems (Arendt 1992) as no punishment appears adequate for such widespread harm.

The prioritizing of law and the reverence of criminal justice as a moralizing force in international society can also be dangerous, for although the law may be presented as impartial and justice is alleged to be 'blind', law and processes of criminalization can be hegemonic and imperial. Legalized discourses of human rights and humanitarianism can serve to justify military or judicial interventions in nation-states and override cultural relativism. Ideas about who constitutes the victims and offenders are often structured by dominant narratives based on race and gender and the West can often see itself as the 'saviour' of the **global south**. Spivak (1994, p. 93) describes this phenomenon as 'the white man saving the brown woman from the brown man'. Bumillier (2008, p. 136) further elucidates this point, stating:

> The human rights model in its global manifestation is a pseudo-criminalized system of surveillance and sanctions. At its most extreme . . . human rights policy can be used to justify military intervention. . . . Thus, it becomes imperative to ask in both a local and global context – how do policies designed to 'protect' women serve to reproduce violence?

The point Bumillier makes is that by focusing on punitive, carceral, options in response to human rights abuses and crimes, countries can obfuscate the conditions, such as extreme poverty, which contribute to the commission of these crimes in the first place.

What is apparent in this discussion of the multitude of criminal justice mechanisms that operate around the world is that no clear or coherent system of justice exists. Instead, norms, ideas, practices and processes are spread through a web-like network of actors, who operate simultaneously at the global, local and transnational level. It is via these actors that norms circulate, are negotiated and transformed into a variety of practices. Dominant and hegemonic tendencies can emerge, such as a current focus on, and belief in, incarceration, punitiveness and retribution. At the same time, these practices are unfixed and can be altered as other perspectives emerge, as is evidenced by the growing transitional and restorative justice paradigms.

4.6 Conclusion

Crime and justice policies, particularly those based on Western understandings of crime and justice, can be considered imperial if they are foisted on other cultures with different traditions. This chapter has examined responses to domestic, transnational and international crime and found some commons threads are woven through the rich tapestry of justice mechanisms. Justice policies are transplanted and diffused through a variety of formal and informal means and in both a horizontal (state to state) and vertical (supranational organization or powerful state onto a less powerful state) manner. Responses to transnational or international crime are rarely framed as forms of policy transfer, but in this chapter we have seen the many ways different ideas, norms and practices flow and disseminate around the world. Keeping the concepts of policy transfer and convergence in mind helps us to uncover the myriad ways that justice norms circulate. The movement of justice norms and policies may be explicit, as is evidenced by direct policy transfer between states, or implicit, such as when norms that are diffused as responses to transnational crime are harmonized or when international criminal courts are established to set the standards for judicial responses to mass atrocities. What is clear is that the machinery of justice is growing, as new mechanisms and approaches are established at local, transnational, international and global levels.

Questions: Revise and Reflect

1. What are some examples of penal populism and punitive justice policies in your country? Do you find parallels to these types of policies in other countries?

2. What role should justice play in responding to mass atrocities?

(Continued)

(Continued)

3. What are the advantages and disadvantages of administering justice through formal justice mechanisms such as the ICC and the ad-hoc tribunals?

4. Can we speak of trends in justice at a global level? What trends do you see emerging? How do these trends circulate and get taken up by local/national jurisdictions?

5. Is there a global 'system' of justice? What would some of the negative consequences be of having a homogeneous global system of justice? (You may want to revisit this question after reading Chapter 9 of this book.)

Further Reading

de Lint, W, Marmo, M & Chazal, N (eds) 2014, *Criminal justice in international society*, Routledge, New York.

Findlay, M & Henham, R 2010, *Beyond punishment: Achieving international criminal justice*, Palgrave Macmillan, New York.

Newburn, T & Jones, T 2007, *Policy transfer and criminal justice: Exploring US influence over British crime control policy*, Open University Press, Maidenhead.

Pratt, J 2007, *Penal populism*, Routledge, Abingdon.

Videos to Watch

Hotel Rwanda (2004) – explores the Rwandan Genocide of 1994 including the causes and repercussions of the violence.

The Reckoning: The Battle for the International Criminal Court (2009) – follows the first ICC Prosecutor, Luis Moreno-Ocampo, as he issues arrest warrants for leaders in Uganda, Congo, and Sudan and navigates complex political terrain while attempting to bring these alleged war criminals to the ICC for prosecution.

Websites to Visit

International Criminal Court (ICC): www.icc-cpi.int/en_menus/icc/Pages/default.aspx

International Criminal Tribunal for the Former Yugoslavia (ICTY): www.icty.org/

International Criminal Tribunal for Rwanda (ICTR): www.unictr.org/

Project on International Criminal Courts and Tribunals: www.pict-pcti.org/index.htm

PART 2
FORMS OF TRANSNATIONAL CRIMES

5

Global Mobility Markets: The Migration of the 'Body' and its Exploitation

This chapter will look at

- Human movement across borders.
- Human trafficking and human smuggling.
- Labour exploitation and labour trafficking.
- The tourism industry.
- The sex tourism industry.
- The medical body, organ trafficking and the global reproductive market.

Keywords

Trafficking	Labour	Organ trafficking
Smuggling	Sexual exploitation	Surrogacy and adoption

5.1 Introduction

A growing number of people are exploited as 'goods' and traded to provide services, in an unprecedented **commodification** process of the human body within global mobility markets. International efforts to fight such exploitation have been often reduced to a discussion about the trafficking and smuggling of human beings, which led to an unparalleled punitive move against traffickers and smugglers at the turn of this century. For the first time, this form of transnational crime was tackled in a top–down action, from international level to national level. International agreements and investment of national governments' human and financial resources have produced an unprecedented law enforcement reaction, although dictated more by the need to fight **organized crime** and border security rather than human rights concerns.

This chapter argues that the movement of people within and across borders has undergone an unparalleled criminalization process, which has enabled the creation and stratification of 'markets' for the exploitation of human beings. These markets go beyond sex and labour exploitation; and this discussion is not limited to the 'full body', but also body parts, which feed a growing 'medical body' market made of organs which may be attached or detached from the full body according to market needs. The human body has become a resource that 'keeps on coming': a commodity that can be used and consumed many times, differently from other goods such as drugs.

These markets are inherently tied to social inequalities associated with the negative impact of globalization. Currently, we are witnessing a more comprehensive socio-economic review of the roots of the problem, as well as a better appreciation of the agency of the so-called victims.

5.2 Human Migration: From Regular to Irregular

In Chapter 2, we discussed the concept of the 'mobile body': who can move across borders and who cannot. The historical and contemporary circumstances that have contributed to the movement of people across borders are often discussed in terms of uneven economic and non-economic developments of regional areas, structural discrimination and corruption, and circumstances created by war or civil unrest. Often, these complex reasons are summarized as pull and push factors.

Push factors
An analysis of push factors attempts to address the reasons why a person chooses to leave their home country and focuses on local circumstances. In this analysis, reasons for leaving are based on economic and non-economic factors, such as a poor and stagnating local economy, lack of growth linked to war or civil conflict, lack of access to resources and employment opportunities, social, gender and caste reasons, economic and social class inequalities, corruption and injustice.

Pull factors

Pull factors are those reasons which would attract someone to move to the destination country. Countries of destination are mostly attractive to those moving because they are generally richer, more stable countries; they project an image of wealth and are perceived as lands of opportunity and future prosperity.

Reverse market

To these push and pull factors, we would need to add the reverse market: when the less developed countries attract attention for their array of opportunities; for example, from an individual viewpoint, that could be the sex tourism market or the medical market; from a corporation's point of view, it could be a cheaper labour market. Common to both cases is an under-legislated or differently legislated environment. Source, transit and destination countries therefore may vary according to the type of markets.

Measuring these mobility markets is problematic, partially due to their invisibility, but also due to their ability, or lack of it, to draw political concern. Some forms of international migration have attracted more attention than others, to the point that a few academics have asked the critical question: 'Who is entitled to move?' (Guild 2005). It is evident that those who are already in an advantageous position, with economic and non-economic opportunities, can move across countries. And yet, the 'desirable' migrants, for example professional and qualified workers, undergo intensive scrutiny to monitor their skills against existing gaps in the labour market of the destination countries. This is especially the case in countries such as Canada and Australia (Hugo 2004). And even then, these workers may experience difficulties in many ways, for example in family reunion visa applications, since the underlying concept is one of economy-driven mobility, in which multinational corporations dictate priorities to the nation-state.

It will not come as a surprise that the international migration of the 'undesirable' migrant, often profiled as an unskilled, under-educated, poor person, has been subjected to a criminalization process in the past few decades. In Hindpal Singh Bhui's words:

> Migrants and asylum seekers are often conflated in the media, in political debate, and in populist rhetoric, with terrorists, criminals, those who are not to be trusted ('bogus'), or the socially unworthy, who place a burden on public services. Such accounts often carry unsubtle racist undertones. (2013, p. 2)

This is especially the case for the type of migration labelled as 'irregular': those travelling without papers such as passports and visas. They are often, and misleadingly so, rounded up in the 'boat arrivals' category in Europe and Australia or as those crossing the US–Mexican border without authorization. This is a different approach from the way 'forced migration' was dealt with after World War II, when the United Nations agreed on the 1951 Refugees Convention, giving rights and safeguards to refugees. Forced migration was understood as a humanitarian and not a criminal concern, with discussions in regard to refugees around safeguarding human rights and ensuring individual and collective protection.

More recent and stringent restrictions on legal migration at a national level have forced people to find alternative ways to move across countries. In fact, the 'production' of irregular migrants is closely linked to the over-regulation and policing of the border. Such border restriction policies – **border securitization** – have gone hand in hand with the criminalization process of the undesirable migrant (Dembour & Kelly 2011; Melossi 2003). This has not helped to clarify the differences between categories of irregular migrants, or to understand better the reasons why people are forced to migrate. This process has commuted de facto the term 'irregular' (as opposed to regular ways of entry) to the term 'illegal' (against laws) (Pickering 2005). Not only have traditional aspects of criminal justice, such as policing and prisons, been shaped to respond to the irregular migrants, but new forms of penalty, for example deportation and detention centres, have been at the forefront of many recent changes (Aas and Bosworth 2013).

5.3 Smuggling and Trafficking in Human Beings

Irregular migration has seen a further diversification of terminology with the introduction in 2000 of the two UN Palermo Protocols supplementing the UN Convention against Transnational Organized Crime (TOC Convention). These are:

- the Protocol to Prevent, Suppress and Punish Trafficking in Persons, especially Women and Children, and

- the Protocol against the Smuggling of Migrants by Land, Sea and Air.

Up until 2000, the meaning, concept and practical consequences of smuggling and trafficking in human beings were governed by similar political objectives, whereby victims were perceived as co-conspirators and a degree of deviancy was attached to them. Although in the 1990s there were attempts to find a common definition of human smuggling and human trafficking, a distinct legal definition for each of these situations was adopted and officialized.

The production of the two protocols on human trafficking and smuggling has been locked to the TOC Convention because, it was argued at the time, human trafficking and smuggling are linked to the activities of organized criminal enterprise, due to its highly profitable, low-risk characteristics, and through the already established channels and connections of criminal gangs across borders. It was later identified that these matters are not necessarily true or easily verifiable, with many cases of smuggling and trafficking being organized informally or ad-hoc, which contravenes the definition of transnational organized crime (see Chapter 7).

The lasting consequence of the protocols 'supplementing' the TOC Convention is a main reason why the protocol instruments did not work as well as anticipated. From a legal point of view, 'supplementing' protocols means that any UN member states who wish to access the instruments adopted by any of the protocols, must first access the TOC Convention, hence the reason why the convention is referred to as the 'parent' instrument (Gallagher 2015). This approach of a parent convention has served the purpose of imposing policy more globally, a point discussed in Chapter 4. By linking the protocols to the convention, the figures of the trafficker and smuggler have been mainly justified through the lens of organized crime and by border-defence rhetoric: a limiting view to a complex situation of social inequality.

Further, the injection of a solid 'organized crime/border control' narrative has also dictated that the two protocols have lived two separate lives for the past 15 years, rather than being seen as a continuation of the same issue of pull–push factors driving the movement of people. The differences between the two definitions and their implications are explained in Figure 5.1. By way of summary, Figure 5.2 lists the main differences between trafficking and smuggling. Thereafter, some shortfalls deriving from crystallizing the two matters separately are addressed.

Definition of trafficking in persons

'Trafficking in persons shall mean the recruitment, transportation, transfer, harbouring or receipt of persons, by means of the threat of the use of force or other forms of coercion, of abduction, of fraud, of deception, of the abuse of power or a position of vulnerability of the giving or receiving of payments to achieve the consent of a person having control over another person, for the purpose of exploitation.'

Art. 3(a), *Protocol to Prevent, Suppress and Punish Trafficking in Persons, especially Women and Children*

Definition of smuggling of migrants

'Smuggling of migrants shall mean the procurement, in order to obtain, directly or indirectly, a financial or other material benefit, of the illegal entry of a person into a State Party of which the person is not a national or permanent resident.'

Art. 3(a) *Protocol against the Smuggling of Migrants by Land, Sea and Air,* supplementing the *UN Convention against Transnational Organized Crime*

Figure 5.1 Definitions of Trafficking and Smuggling

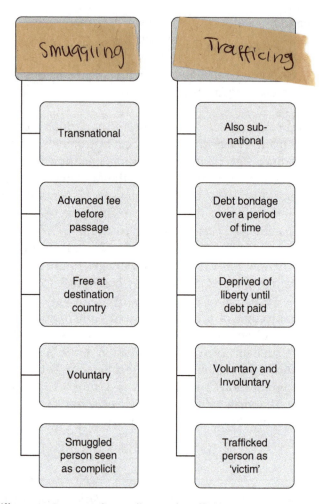

Figure 5.2 Differences Between Smuggling and Trafficking

Adapted from the UN-Toolkit 2006 (UNODC 2006).

It should be noted, however, that the two matters, trafficking and smuggling, are more ambiguous than is presented on paper. For example, people who are smuggled can also be trafficked and vice versa, mostly due to these people's weak economic and non-economic position in the origin, transit and destination countries, which reduces their choices and opportunities. Also, the 'involuntary' character of trafficking has been rather controversial, as discussed further below. Therefore, the distinction between the two areas is much more fluid in reality. However, their legal position is frozen in time as a smuggled or trafficked human being, according to when and where they are caught by law enforcement authorities. Once a status is imposed on them, they are categorized rigidly according to that status, and will consequently be subjected to the national laws under one or the other definition, which would change the support that the criminal justice system can offer to the person.

Looking back at the first 15 years of these protocols, a further criticism has been raised, since the two protocols have artificially created categories of offenders and victims as two distinct and separate matters. In fact, recent UN reports indicate that many offenders were victims themselves, in what is referred to as a 'cycle of abuse' when the status of the victim overlaps with that of the offender.

Human Trafficking

From the turn of this century, trafficking in human beings has been commonly defined as the new slavery within the context of the global economy (Bales 1999). The UN Office on Drugs and Crime (UNODC) defines human trafficking as 'a serious crime and a grave violation of human rights' (UNODC 2015b). For these reasons, a lot of financial and human resources have been poured into this area.

While it is difficult to measure the volume of trafficking, UNODC has been releasing data since 2006: this has allowed monitoring of trends. In their 2012 *Global report on trafficking in persons*, UNODC (p. 10) tells us that the victims of trafficking are mostly women (59%), followed by girls (17%), men (14%) and boys (10%). Trafficking for sexual purposes is reported as more frequent (58%) than for forced labour (36%), followed by other types of trafficking in persons, such as forced marriage (p. 36). Organ removal is a very low percentage at 0.2% (UNODC 2012b, p. 36). Also, UNODC (2012b) registered an increase in the detection of labour trafficking cases compared to previous years. Possibly, this is due to a combination of a better understanding of the labour exploitation market and increased awareness that human trafficking is not solely for the purpose of sex exploitation.

The Human Trafficking Experience

The human trafficking dynamics have been dangerously grouped in one experience of brutality and isolation. For example, in the first few years of the Protocol's life, the victim conditions and relationship with the traffickers have been described as a process of agency stripping, with the victim being physically, psychologically and possibly sexually abused. The violence was explained as necessary 'not only for the development of markets, but also for the "manufacturing" of these "goods", as they contribute to making them "functional" for an industry that requires a constant supply of bodies' (Paulin 2003, p. 40). The examples of victims' recounts of their experiences in official documents were selected to confirm such narratives (see 'Spotlight'). Further, their recounts of fear of retaliation, blackmail and abuses carried out against themselves, and, possibly, even their families back home, have enriched the profile of the victim.

Spotlight – Working Conditions

They said they had invested a lot of money in me, and I had to work to pay them back, because I now belonged to the network. I thought about escaping, but I was afraid of being physically hurt or killed. I worked hard for six months, but they have no mercy on you . . . they're just demeaning. During this time, I was sold many times, and this happened every 10 days – sometimes I just didn't know where I was. You're like a commodity to them. (Maria Fernanda, trafficking victim, interviewed by the UNODC Country Office in Colombia, in UN.Gift 2008, p. 26)

We were trapped by criminals and forced into prostitution in order to pay debts for the trip. We had up to 15 clients per night. (Marcela, trafficking victim, interviewed by the Brazilian NGO Projeto Trama, in UN.Gift 2008, p. 5)

While there is no doubt that severe forms of slavery take place under human trafficking, the reality is more fragmented. The concept and understanding of deception has played a big role in appreciating the complexities surrounding human trafficking. Deception is one of the identifying factors which has led to trafficking and maintains the victim's enslaved status, as explained in the 2000 UN Protocol on Trafficking. Deception was previously understood solely as a lack of knowledge of the activities that the trafficked person would end up engaging in, once in the destination country. More research in the field has revealed that, while cases of absolute violence and isolation have occurred, human trafficking is more nuanced. For example, there are a number of cases where trafficked persons entered the trafficking process voluntarily and/or with awareness of a job, but without full knowledge of its nature or conditions. In these cases, the term 'deception' needs to be better applied to the specific situations.

In other cases, the label of human trafficking has been imposed over a financial arrangement. The work of Sandy (2014) on sex workers in Cambodia offers a good example to help us understand what this means. Here, the sex workers enter a '**debt-bondage**' because they need a loan, an upfront payment, which they would not be able to access using a normal banking system. They will then pay this back by working in the brothel for nothing, or next to nothing, until they pay off the initial debt. These situations tell us a more complex story in which the woman retains agency over her decisions and freely enters into a contract. However, according to the UN Protocol's definition of human trafficking, because of the existence of the debt-bondage, this is considered a textbook case of trafficking for sexual exploitation and the label of human trafficking is imposed in a top–down process (see Chapter 4). In summary, the process of crystallizing various cases as fitting the trafficking definition, for the advancement of a common agenda, could produce more damage than benefits.

Labour Exploitation

Labour trafficking and exploitation is an aspect only recently looked at in detail. It is suspected that labour trafficking is more widespread than trafficking for sex exploitation, with the International Labour Organization (ILO 2015) highlighting that more than 21 million people are victims of forced labour conditions. Human beings are sold for labour in the agricultural or informal economic sectors, or as mercenaries.

The example in Case Study 5.1 allows us to reflect on the links between our request for cheap goods and services and the invisible (to us) labour exploitation that renders our lifestyle possible. The NGO Slavery Footprint has pushed this concept further with their survey titled 'How Many Slaves Work For You?' and it is accessible to everyone at slaveryfootprint.org/: test yourself and find out how many slaves are behind your lifestyle.

Case Study 5.1 – Seafood Slaves

At the Tropicana Hotel on Las Vegas Strip, you can still get a 99 cent shrimp cocktail. It's a great deal for those lucky enough to enjoy the bright lights and decadence that Las Vegas provides 24/7. For those catching and processing the shrimp in Thailand's seafood industry, the deal is far less attractive.

As previously mentioned, it is estimated that 21 million people are in forced labour worldwide, 68% of whom are victims of labour exploitation (ILO 2012a, p. 1). The problem of forced labour is greatest in the Asia-Pacific region, and the fishing industry in Thailand has been particularly highlighted. It suffers from a chronic labour shortage, increasing pressure on profits due to declining fish stocks, and relies heavily on migrant workers. Shrimp is the most valuable fisheries' product in the world and Thailand is the world's largest exporter (EJF 2013a). Ninety per cent of its catch is exported to the United States, Japan and the European Union. It is a highly lucrative industry – shrimp exports alone account for just under 50% of all Thailand's exports (EJF 2013a, p. 4). The 1960s saw a rapid expansion in the fishing industry in Thailand; since then dwindling stocks from overfishing have seen catches reduce by 86%, placing pressure on boat captains to cut costs – and it seems it is the workers who have paid the price (Economist Intelligence Unit 2015).

Ninety per cent of the industry's workers are migrants (EJF 2013a, p. 4). In recent years, reports have emerged that unscrupulous brokers, working on behalf of boat captains, have turned to the poor in neighbouring countries such as Myanmar (Burma), Lao PDR (Laos) and Cambodia to recruit young men (Hodal 2015; Hodal et al. 2014). Many are tricked into leaving their homes under false pretences, and with no means to return home, are forced into exploitative working conditions which they are unable to leave (News.com.au 2015). One such individual was Min Min, a 17-year-old from a poor family in Myanmar. He accepted a job which had been organized by a broker he trusted. Once on board the fishing boat and out at sea, the vulnerability of his situation

(Continued)

became quickly apparent (Potenza 2014). He was under the control of a boat captain who considered him only as a commercial resource to exploit. He was fed little, provided with inadequate clothing and footwear, and subjected to threats. He witnessed workers who were too slow being beaten; and workers who were injured being thrown overboard. According to research conducted by the Environmental Justice Foundation (EJF 2013a, p. 4), more than half of trafficked migrant workers report having seen a fellow worker killed.

Min Min's account is typical. Agents, finding it more and more difficult to recruit workers to the industry, have resorted to ruthless means, such as drugging and kidnapping migrants and recruiting children and the disabled (News.com.au 2015). Recruits are generally then transported over large distances, making them vulnerable and dependent (ILO 2012b). They are 'sold' to boat captains for around US$1000, according to the Thai-based not-for-profit organization Labour Rights Promotion Network Foundation, and are then obliged to work to pay off their 'debt', receiving little or no wages at all for months or years (News.com.au 2015). They are often forced to work 18- to 22-hour shifts without days off in hazardous conditions. The practice of offloading catches at sea onto other boats means that many remain at sea for months or even years on what are, effectively, floating prisons (Cape Argus 2015; News.com.au 2015). If the boats dock at all, it is often only at remote islands where no help is available (IRIN 2012). Abuses are rife; beatings, torture and killings are commonly reported. Aung Naing Win, a 40-year-old father of two from Myanmar, described having to work in the ship's freezer without adequate clothing, in temperatures of 39° Fahrenheit below zero, similar temperatures to the North Pole. Deaths caused by fatigue, illness and unsafe working practices, such as going overboard to untangle nets, are commonplace, as is suicide; many workers simply throw themselves overboard rather than face ongoing abuse (News.com.au 2015).

Workers are disempowered in multiple ways. They are reportedly sold from one captain to another and, with no documents or financial means, are unable to leave or return home. Many workers do not even speak Thai. The police are sometimes corrupt and return runaways if an escape is even attempted (EJF 2013b). Min Min was tortured with fish hooks after attempting to escape and threatened with being tortured to death if he tried again (Potenza 2014). There is no legal recourse: lack of legislation, legal loopholes, corruption and fear of retribution prevent any such action by migrant workers (IRIN 2011, 2012). With the fishing industry reportedly 50,000 workers short, legislation is urgently needed to prevent more migrants becoming victims (Hodal 2015).

In 2014, the United Nations agency ILO adopted a new protocol to ILO Convention 29 on Forced Labour (1930). It was signed by all member countries – except Thailand – whose initial reluctance appeared to stem from a fear about their readiness to implement it. Under pressure from the international community, Thailand amended their vote a few days later (Ganjanakhundee 2014). Article 4 specifically attempts to address the seemingly insurmountable problems victims face in seeking justice, and thereby to address the power imbalance that currently exists (Human Rights Watch 2014). It is hoped that under the new protocol, justice might finally be served for Thailand's seafood workers and others in forced labour.

5.4 More Markets of the Body Trade: Tourism Industry

The market of the body trade refers generally to industries which have boomed in the last few decades, and have occupied a central position within international capitalism. These industries include the exploitation of the young, healthy body, and they can be legal, at the margin of legality, or illegal.

The term *market* is used in this context as it aims to highlight the trade approach: human beings or their parts are bought and sold, are used and consumed in their physical, sexual and reproductive capacity. This market operates in several different ways and in different locations. Common to these situations is the impact of globalization, which has sped up the market's dynamics and fast-forwarded its development. This includes the combined impact of advanced technologies, like telecommunications, the internet, faster and cheaper air travel, and the impact of the flourishing sex and medical industries. In addition, within a capitalist society, some 'privileged' people – the majority of people living in first world countries – can buy items of desire almost instantaneously: this can be a human body for sex or for the purpose of obtaining a child. This view of the market has uncritically been applied to commoditized human beings, exploited to satisfy impellent needs and emotions. This is particularly achievable when the merchandise is cheap and readily available on the market. This market can satisfy specialized and diverse demands, without 'unbearable' delays or costly deals.

These markets are linked to the international tourism industry, which has expanded rapidly during the last 40 years in several geographical areas. While international tourism in first world countries has followed an independent and interdependent process, some other regional areas, like Asia or Africa, were encouraged to expand their tourism and entertainment industries by international organizations like the IMF and the World Bank (Paulin 2003). These external pressures were mainly generated as a result of debt repayment obligations. The IMF and World Bank had lent large amounts of money to promote and initiate the development of local industries. The tourism industry addressed, first, the need for growth of the domestic economy through the spending of valuable foreign currencies, and second, facilitated the hosting of the economically rich, first world visitors, in search of affordable holidays in desirable areas.

Sex Tourism

The substantial number of people involved in the sex industry as a tourist attraction is a side effect of the global expansion of the tourist industry. The combination of the two industries, the sex industry and the tourism industry, has favoured a proliferation of the practices associated with sexual exploitation and abuse. The rise of sex tourism has generated substantial profits within a local and international political, economic and social climate, and can be explored as a form of political economy, whereby the 'trade' in human beings combines with the consumers' mobility. The industry thrives within a truly capitalist model of supply, demand, infrastructure and mobility.

Paulin (2003) refers to this phenomenon of the rise of the sex tourist industry as the 'prostitutionalization' of those societies involved. The Red Light District in Amsterdam is a famous location within Europe for the sex industry. There are other red light districts across Europe, and the exploitation of the conditions created by liberal attitudes, combined with the legalization of prostitution, has favoured the proliferation of sex tourism areas within Europe. In some geographical areas, however, particularly in economically weaker countries, the rapid expansion of the tourism industry coincided with, and contributed to, the development of the prostitutionalization of these societies. In these societies, rules and restrictions on clients and exploiters, which are more effectively and systematically enforced in Europe, or in the United States, Canada and Australia, are either barely developed or not enforced. The exploitation of citizens in poorer or 'less developed' countries can be seen as a form of modern day colonialism. Colonialism in this case can be defined as the exploitation of another country's resources, through an assumption of superiority, or the existence of unchallenged opportunity.

The combination of the internet and the expansion of international travel has also contributed to the proliferation of an interest in the sex tourism industry (Chow-White 2006), reinforcing the assumption that everybody can partake in it, with impunity. The internet has become a reliable tip-sharing resource for many sex tourists. It takes minutes to track down travellers' diaries that are open to a wide audience, with no restrictions or password protection. These diaries give tips about specific locations and places to visit, but they may also offer tips about how to find girls, or boys, for casual sex, and how to operate in those circumstances.

An argument proposed by some (Oppermann & McKinley 1997) is that, in these areas, sexual exploitation is considered to be part of an entertainment industry (the four S's of tourism: sun, sand, sea and sex). Others (Ryan & Hall 2001) and supranational organizations such as the UNODC and EU would be inclined to argue that the level of corruption and organized crime is so intricate and widespread that it is difficult to enforce legislation protecting the victims of the sex industry. It is true to say that in the current political climate all governments publicly denounce sexual exploitation and welcome coordinated international efforts to address and stamp out sex tourism. However, the problem is perpetuated through unequal international distribution of political power: powerful nation-states and powerful persons are in a position to impose practices and dictate behavioural rules upon powerless receivers. Sex tourism is a problem that has emerged as a global concern in recent years, and there is no sign that it is decreasing; in fact all indicators would suggest considerable increases in the frequency and sophistication of operations related to the industry.

Spotlight – The Girlfriend Trade

My Boyfriend, the Sex Tourist is a documentary directed by Monica Garnsey and tele-vized on Channel 4 at the end of December 2007 in the United Kingdom. It features the stories of women on sale to sex tourists and addresses an emerging new form of sex tourism, the 'girlfriend trade'. At some holiday resorts, girls are assigned to – or chosen by – tourists upon arrival, to be their 'girlfriends' for the holiday. These girls are part of the deal; they are part of the holiday package, to entertain the tourists 24 hours a day.

Some of these holiday resorts are easily discoverable on the internet, and are clearly not perceived as illegal by the authorities in the host country. This is a form of exploitation or prostitution, and the clients (the tourists) cannot be placed in the category of sex offenders per se.

Sex industry and international migration are challenging areas in which to col-lect statistical evidence. Despite the difficulties in extrapolating the appropriate data, however, we are now much better placed to identify countries of origin and destination, and to profile 'the sex tourist'.

Sex tourists come from several wealthy countries, such as the United States, Canada, the United Kingdom, Belgium, Sweden, Germany, France, the Netherlands and Italy, as well as Japan, South Korea and China. Their destination countries clearly belong to the group of countries which may be defined as 'third world', 'developing' or 'emerging economies', such as the Dominican Republic, Brazil, Thailand, Cambodia, the Philippines, Kenya and Gambia. These are recognized and established destination countries, but there are other emerging destinations, including Vietnam, Morocco and Russia (see, in general, Oppermann 1999; Oppermann & McKinley 1997). These countries, however, are not necessarily the countries of origin of the sexually exploited people. There is a movement, voluntary or otherwise, of the exploited that is difficult to track down, and in some cases it is also linked to human trafficking orchestrated by organized crime groups. In addi-tion, a lot of human traffic escapes border checks, so not only is it extremely challenging to prevent, but it is also very difficult to calculate the numbers and extent of undeclared, and thus illegal, human movement linked to sex tourists' markets.

The sex tourist is often described as a frequently white, middle aged, wealthy, first world male person. There are of course exceptions, but most research shows that this is an accurate profile. The country of origin varies, but the other char-acteristics remain remarkably consistent (Brungs 2002). Discussions around the reasons for sex tourism revolve around the areas of masculinity and male power, and sense of racial superiority. Nevertheless, women are also exploiters of the sex industry abroad, although fewer cases are recorded. Further research studies have analysed the cases of women who have travelled abroad to engage in sexual relationships with young or younger men (see Sanchez Taylor 2001, 2006). This discourse has also been framed within the emerging masculinization of women within society and the appropriation of power and influence, as well as the decrease in stigmatization of female sexuality. Once the female sex tourist has financial and personal independence at home – traditionally attributed to the male – she can act in a similar fashion. This includes travelling abroad and paying for a timed relationship, thus being the dominant person within the exchange/relationship.

5.5 Organ Trafficking

Medical tourism is a fast-growing tourism industry, whereby a patient travels abroad to receive medical treatment. This industry is closely linked to globalization, trade cooperation and advanced medical technologies and practices, and it includes all aspects of hospitalization, from medical and surgical, to dental and cosmetic. Even if there are no official statistics in this area, scholars such as Horowitz et al. (2007, p. 33) identified references to a growing market of the mobile patient who will travel to less developed countries to obtain healthcare services, while lodged in 'appealing accommodations'. Medical tourism would not occur without health service providers, agents to facilitate the service, governance processes and distribution and promotion of information (Lunt et al. 2015). Most importantly, these services require new or different regulatory spaces to allow for their expansion since they cross several legal and ethical boundaries.

Organ trafficking is a subset of the medical industry. It involves different mobility modes: the patient (the 'broken body') travels abroad to the donor's country or a third country where the operation will take place; the living donor travels to the patient's country or to a third country; or human organs are extracted and transported to the patient.

In 2007, the World Health Organization (WHO) published data suggesting that organ trafficking was estimated to include 5–10% of all the kidney transplants performed annually worldwide. Commercial organ sales, such as kidneys, would come from living donors, usually based in less developed countries, due to a 'gap in supply' in the market (WHO 2007, p. 5), borne out by long transplant waiting lists across the world. This type of donation from vulnerable people is actively promoted by transplant centres and brokers (Budiani-Saberi &

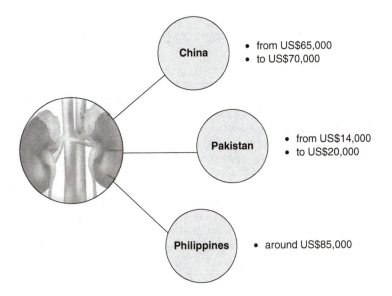

China
- from US$65,000
- to US$70,000

Pakistan
- from US$14,000
- to US$20,000

Philippines
- around US$85,000

Image 5.1 All-inclusive 'transplant packages' for a kidney. Adapted from World Health Organization 2007.

Delmonico 2008). Anecdotally, and as part of investigative journalism, the *Guardian* published in 2012 a story about a Chinese organ broker who advertised his services under the slogan 'Donate a kidney, buy the new iPad!', where he would offer £2,500 for a kidney and reassurances that the operation could be performed within 10 days (Campbell & Davison 2012). As WHO (2007) highlights, there are also potential negative consequences for the donor, which include health issues and psychological trauma.

Even more complex and difficult to measure is the situation of a donor at the end stage of a disease, used for the purpose of a liver, heart, or lung extraction. The WHO (2007) report addresses the pretext of 'saving a life' as a means to justify extraction from an apparently terminally-ill donor, in a situation where the broker and the health facility that provided the organ would gain a remarkable financial advantage. In other cases, it has been reported that body parts have been harvested during post-mortems and sold on to organ donor companies (Louw 2010).

The Global Initiative to Fight Human Trafficking (UN.Gift 2015) has grouped three types of organ trafficking according to the consent and deception of the donor: first, those who are kidnapped, forced, or deceived into giving up a body part; second, those who agree to give up a body part for monetary reward; and third, those treated for an ailment who find out that a body part has been removed without their knowledge. Case Study 5.2 offers an example of voluntary sale.

Case Study 5.2 – Kidneys for Sale

Avoiding all the problems that have grown up around the burgeoning trade in human body parts, Iran decided to legalize the voluntary paid donation of kidneys.

Contrary to generally agreed principles that renal organ donation should only be provided voluntarily and unpaid, in 1988 Iran adopted a system whereby potential donors could choose to legally sell a kidney to unrelated third parties. The scheme was born out of necessity: emerging from the eight-year Iran–Iraq war, there was very little dialysis equipment in the country and nephrologists turned to kidney transplantation as an alternative solution. The government agreed to set up a regulated and compensated system whereby people could elect to sell their kidneys and receive free health insurance, as well as financial compensation. The arrangements are facilitated and overseen by two non-profit organizations and donors are only permitted to sell to other Iranian citizens (Kamali Dehghan 2012). Recipients are offered highly subsidized immunosuppressant therapy. By the end of 2005, more than 15,000 kidneys had been donated in this way (Ghods & Savaj 2006).

In Tehran, there are handmade posters taped up on walls near major hospitals, advertising the availability of kidneys for sale. They contain the briefest details: age of donor, a mobile number, sometimes a blood type or a comment like 'tested healthy' (Kamali Dehghan 2012; Zonnoor 2014). The competition is such that posters are sometimes removed by other sellers (Kamali Dehghan 2012). One such poster has been put up by Marzieh, a widow from northern Iran. She needs money to provide her daughter with the customary dowry for marriage. She has no other means of obtaining the necessary money for her to get married.

Although not the altruistic model we are more used to, the scheme appears to have been successful, at least in addressing the problem of renal failure. Iran currently has no waiting list for renal transplants and the rate of cadaveric and live-related organ donation has also increased since before the introduction of the scheme (Zonnoor 2014). By contrast, in the United States, over 4,000 patients died in 2014 waiting for a transplant. The long-term effects of such a scheme are difficult to assess as donors are generally disproportionately poor and there is limited information as yet about the long-term outcomes for paid donors (Kamali Dehghan 2012).

Elsewhere, other financially desperate people are left with trying to sell their kidneys under unregulated systems, leaving them at the mercy of the unscrupulous. There are many reports of people trying to sell kidneys, for example, in India and Pakistan.

5.6 Commercial Surrogacy and Commissioned Adoption

The reproductive tourism industry is a subset of the medical tourism industry. It aims to provide access to various fertility services and different reproductive technologies under a diverse legislative climate. The new technologies allow people with infertility issues, or single or same-sex people (whose access to these services is restricted) to have biologically related children. In this field, we find cases of 'borrowing' a body for the purpose of surrogacy or for the purpose of 'commissioned' adoption.

Increasingly so, transnational surrogacy has been used by many Western people for a range of reasons at local level, from legal to social restrictions, but also lack of technology or financial power to access available technology. The supply side of reproductive tourism, particularly for eggs and wombs, has allowed access to new possibilities of family formation. Yet, the regulation on commercial surrogacy, whereby the surrogate parent makes a profit out of the contract, remains controversial and is even banned in many nation-states, for example in Canada, the United Kingdom, France, Norway and Italy (Panitch 2013). Those countries which have legalized commercial surrogacy, and do not charge exorbitant fees like in the United States, where the cost is between US$50,000 and $120,000 (Panitch 2013), have seen a steady increase in fertility tourism. The role of brokers and facilitators has been fundamental in steering the market towards certain countries too, as illustrated in Case Study 5.3.

Case Study 5.3 – Surrogacy in India, Mexico and Thailand

Akanksha Fertility Clinic in Anand (India) has been featured in many stories of surrogacy in the United States (Ikemoto 2009, footnote 6) and the United Kingdom (Gupta 2011). Surrogacy in India has been legalized by the Supreme High Court since 2002 and has grown into a big international business, in which it is clear that surrogate mothers would relinquish rights over the baby once the contract is signed. The cost of the operation is US$10,000, making it a fraction of the equivalent cost in the United States (Panitch 2013). The director of the Akanksha Fertility Clinic, Dr Patel, even appeared on *The Oprah Winfrey Show* in 2007; possibly this may account for its international reputation in the United States, Canada and Europe and the fact that the waiting list is 250–300 couples long.

India has enjoyed a dominant share of the market (Panitch 2013) to the extent that the Indian government has introduced new regulation to limit how many pregnancies an Indian woman can go through, including her own children (Gupta 2011). This new regulation includes restricting the service to married, heterosexual couples only (Tuckman 2014). Nevertheless, brokers are advising gay couples, who are now experiencing the Indian system's rigidity, to consider other markets, in particular Mexico and Thailand (Spitz 2014).

In Mexico, surrogacy is allowed only if it is 'altruistic', meaning that the surrogate parent does not benefit from the operation. It costs more than in India (US$35,000–$55,000) but it is still reasonable compared to the US market. However, details are emerging of women undergoing the service for profit (Tuckman 2014).

In Thailand, a similar 'altruistic' rule applies, whereby the surrogate mothers are allowed to receive compensation for expenses. Further, the surrogate mother needs to have a family connection to the potential parents. In fact, the Thai market is a grey area. The case of Baby Gammy has brought this underground market into the light. Born with Down syndrome, Baby Gammy was left behind by an Australian couple, who only took his healthy twin-sister back to Australia. The case was revealed to be even more complex by the revelation that the intended father was a convicted sex offender in Australia (Hawley 2015).

(Continued)

(Continued)

The *Guardian* reports that the reproductive market in Thailand is undergoing a 'crack-down' due to the Baby Gammy scandal, and that the Mexican market is benefiting from this (Tuckman 2014). This suggests that the transnational market is linked and that brokers are playing a central role in directing traffic. It is clear that regulating such a market in a centralized manner should be considered.

The commodification of the female body is central to this analysis, as well as her freedom to make decisions about her body. Consent is a critical legal concept, since it is argued that a woman cannot give consent to something without knowledge of her feelings towards an unborn child – a matter that would become evident only after giving birth (Wilson 2005).

There is also the case of the best interests of the child versus the commercialization of a booming fertility industry (Crawshaw et al. 2014). As an articulation of this, there have been cases in which the child has been born in a legal limbo of statelessness, as the place of birth cannot recognize the child if the intended parents are not citizens of that country, and the intended parents' country cannot offer legal recognition of the baby despite the intended parents' citizenship (Lin 2013). Further, there have been cases of children born with illnesses who have been turned down by the intended parents, as in the case of Baby Gammy (see Case Study 5.3).

There is no international regulation of the reproductive tourism industry. Rather there are obsolete instruments such as the 1993 Transnational Adoption Convention (known as The Hague Convention), which does not fill the gap raised by the newest dimensions of commercial offshore surrogacy. Clearly, the reproductive industry cuts across issues of global inequalities between geopolitical and medical regions (Culley and Hudson 2010). Surrogacy particularly addresses inequalities based on gender, class, race and ethnic hierarchies, since it offers the ability to 'shop to order' and select through advancement in genetic issues.

5.7 Conclusion

This chapter has aimed to show the unprecedented commodification of the human body and its inextricable link to socio-economic conditions of vulnerability. Such exploitation has always attracted a status of denial. Governments have shown resistance in accepting a degree of responsibility for creating an industry of exploitation by producing legal or physical barriers, not just at the border. The criminalization process is part of the problem: the stress is mainly on strengthening the criminal justice response through legislative reform, awareness raising campaigns, local police training programmes, as well as through national and international cooperation.

Yet, it has become clear that these are problems of global significance and scale, and that many nation-states are involved. Further cooperation is urgently needed, and nation-states, rather than denying what is occurring within their territory, should invest more financial resources in researching the problems and combating corruption.

An isolated initiative may be important, but its outcome may not be as effective as strong international collaboration or legislation, which can be enforced and monitored. The work of intergovernmental bodies and non-governmental agencies is important, and should be sustained in terms of human and financial resources. Furthermore, to achieve a better impact, a uniform interpretation and definition of the problem should be attained and implemented. This means discussing the introduction of similar laws and policies; bringing in horizontal and vertical cooperation that goes beyond law enforcement agencies.

Questions: Revise and Reflect

1. What is irregular migration?
2. Consider the difference between trafficking and smuggling in human beings. How are they different, and why do these differences matter?
3. Go to the UNODC website and search for images about smuggling and trafficking. Discuss the similarities/differences.
4. Read again the case of the 'seafood slaves' and discuss your connection to these forms of labour exploitation.
5. How would you explain the existence of the sex tourism industry in three points?
6. What is the 'medical body'? Select and discuss a case of surrogacy or organ trafficking.

Further Reading

Aas, KF & Bosworth, M (eds) 2013, *The borders of punishment: Migration, citizenship, and social exclusion*, Oxford University Press, Oxford.

Ryan, C & Hall, MC 2001, *Sex tourism, marginal people and liminalities*, Routledge, London.

Segrave, M, Milivojecvic, S & Pickering, S (eds) 2013, *Sex trafficking: International context and response*, Willan, Oxon.

(Continued)

(Continued)

Videos to Watch

Jammed – a 2007 movie on the sex slave trade in Melbourne loosely based on official court transcripts.

The Real Sex Traffic – this film was winner of the 2006 Broadcast Award for Best Documentary. It is also available via YouTube.

Lilja 4-Ever – this is a 2002 movie, directed by Lukas Moodysson, about a teenager from the former Soviet Union, who is trafficked to Sweden and forced into prostitution. The 'push factors' – the reasons why Lilja leaves her home country – are highlighted well.

Breeders: A Subclass of Women? – a 2012 documentary on surrogacy laws in India.

Websites to Visit

Council of Europe page on trafficking in human organs, tissues and cells: ec.europa. eu/justice_home/fsj/crime/trafficking/fsj_crime_human_trafficking_en.htm

The UK Human Trafficking Centre, funded in 2006, is a multi-agency centre, which coordinates activities to combat trafficking in the United Kingdom: www.nationalcrimeagency.gov.uk/about-us/what-we-do/specialistcapabilities/uk-human-trafficking-centre

UN Office on Drugs and Crime, and its role in fighting human trafficking: www.unodc.org/unodc/en/human-trafficking/index.html

6

Organized Crime: Threat and Response in the Global Era

This chapter will look at

- A brief history of the concept of organized crime, including recent attempts by governments and international bodies to define the term.
- The nature of the threat from organized crime.
- Two examples of organized crime: illicit drugs and money laundering.
- Responses to the issue through laws, law enforcement approaches and other measures.

Keywords

Organized crime	Risk	Measurement and analysis
Networks	Harm	

6.1 Introduction

This chapter examines **organized crime** mainly as a transnational phenomenon. It also looks at domestic, regional and international responses to the various forms of organized crime, identified by governments and law enforcement authorities as presenting major risks to public safety and national security in the twenty-first century. The various meanings of organized crime are explored, as well as the factors that contribute to the different types of 'organized' crime. The chapter also considers how and why organized crime has come to be seen as an international problem.

6.2 Organized Crime in Context

Our understandings of 'organized crime' have historical roots going back centuries to the criminal activities of bandits, pirates and gangs in rural and maritime as well as urban areas. In common with modern understandings of organized crime, these groups operated as collectives, engaged in acts of plunder and extortion, and displayed a willingness to resort to arbitrary violence and menace to secure their primarily *economic* objectives. Groups such as the Sicilian Mafia offered, for a price, protection from the depredations of others; hence the idea of 'protection rackets', in which those groups or individuals providing and profiting from protection were in reality a source of insecurity themselves (see for example, Gambetta 1996).

Through this historical lens, we can begin to appreciate how organized crime groups and activities often served needs that were not well served by other means, and in particular, by nation-states. Prior to the consolidation of the modern Western state in some parts of Europe in the nineteenth century, many rural areas lacked consistent political authority that was capable of countering the predatory activities of criminal groups. In fact, some historians (e.g. Tilly 1985) have suggested that political authority often emerged from a period of successful organized crime activity. In Western Europe, it was only during the nineteenth century, as police forces got better organized and the justice systems became more effective, that there began to emerge public agencies capable of replacing and challenging private actors engaged in various forms of protection and economic exploitation. In many other parts of the world, this process of state consolidation and pacification occurred later; in some countries (e.g. Somalia) this objective remains unfulfilled.

Today, once again, scholars are referring to the links between organized crime and state development in many developing and post-conflict countries. The predominant view is one of organized crime's dysfunctional contributions in these environments, seeing organized crime activities as threats to peace and good order. In Central America and Mexico, for example, the activities of organized crime groups, both intentionally and unintentionally, have caused large-scale displacement of residents within the borders of those countries as well as cross-border movements (Cantor 2014).

Spotlight – Transnational Crime and Political Turmoil: Libya

The rise of political conflict in parts of the world often coincides with the emergence or resurgence of organized crime in those affected areas. As governments are overthrown or withdraw in the face of strong armed opposition, there can arise opportunities for criminal groups to engage in lucrative illicit activities. As groups fight each other, there is a demand for weapons. As people become victims of these struggles, there is a demand for exit routes, often to other countries in search of safe havens. In order to finance the purchase of weapons or indeed exit routes, drug trafficking, smuggling and kidnapping offer ways of raising money. Organized crime, in other words, can benefit from violence, misery and desperation. The real victims are those who cannot afford to buy protection or their escape (see on this point Chapter 3, Case Study 3.2).

A recent report by the US Institute for Peace (Shaw & Mangan 2015) examined the situation in Libya. The demise of the previous autocratic regime under Gaddafi has led to a period of sustained political conflict, with competing governments and various armed groups fighting over resources and territory. In this environment, a vibrant criminal economy has emerged, engaged in drug trafficking, people smuggling, weapons trading and other forms of smuggling. The proliferation of small arms (mainly assault rifles) has meant that levels of violence have risen as fighting over the spoils of war and organized crime has intensified. Government authority is no longer effective, and therefore is unable to protect the weak and vulnerable. As recent press reports have shown, this has led in part to mass attempts to escape from Libya across the Mediterranean Sea to countries such as Italy, with tragic losses of life.

The term 'organized crime' itself emerged in the United States in the early decades of the twentieth century (Paoli & Fijnaut 2004). It referred essentially to criminal groups operating in urban environments. The Prohibition era of the 1920s, during which American authorities sought to restrict the production and consumption of alcoholic drinks, provided urban-based criminals with fresh opportunities for illicit entrepreneurship. Many residents of cities such as Chicago, Boston and New York were recent immigrants from various parts of Europe. Some found opportunities for personal enrichment through the supply of illicit alcohol and other illegal activities, such as gambling and prostitution. The term 'racketeering' was used to refer to a range of predatory and illicit supply activities by these groups (Paoli & Fijnaut 2004, p. 24).

In the aftermath of World War II, a view of organized crime emerged in the United States as essentially Italian in origin, and linked to Italian criminal groups, in particular the Sicilian Mafia (also known as La Cosa Nostra). This perception of organized crime 'remained the United States' official standpoint for almost three decades' (Paoli & Fijnaut 2004, p. 25). The books and movies of *The Godfather* no doubt helped to cement this image in popular consciousness. As various commentators have noted, this perception founded the **alien conspiracy view** of organized crime, one that remained influential for several decades, and to some extent still has some support. This view proposed that persons from particular migrant groups, in this case Italian, constituted the chief threat in terms of organized crime by bringing their criminal traditions and activities to the United States (Finckenauer 2007, p. 58).

Image 6.1 The Purple Gang, a dominant criminal gang mostly formed by Jewish members and based in Detroit, Michigan (US) during the 1920s. Photo via Wikimedia Commons.

Widespread acceptance of the alien conspiracy view of organized crime in the United States meant that police and law enforcement agencies were inclined to target criminals by reference to their ethnic identity and associations. However, by the 1970s, it was clear that not all organized crime was committed by Italians, that increasingly, in fields such as illicit drug production and supply, there was often intense competition between different criminal groups, so that a different lens was needed if organized crime was to be properly understood. This led some scholars to focus upon markets rather than particular groups, and to advocate an *illicit enterprise* view of organized crime. This furthered an interest in the ways in which these markets were organized and operated (see for example, Paoli et al. 2009).

A growing interest in markets, however, did not signal the end of the study of organized crime through examination of various 'alien' groups; the rise of outlaw motorcycle gangs in the 1960s and 1970s, and the identification of Colombian involvement in cannabis and cocaine trades in North America from the 1970s, ensured that the 'alien' view remained alive. It indeed spread to Europe as well as other parts of the world (Woodiwiss 2003). The end of the Cold War and the changes in Eastern Europe during the 1990s helped make sense of this shift, as people movement from east to west inevitably brought with it criminal activities that were unprecedented in scale, if not always in kind.

The rise of ethnically defined criminal groups from Albania, Romania, Russia, Chechnya and elsewhere in trends in organized crime in Western Europe is widely acknowledged (see Paoli & Fijnaut 2004).

Defining Organized Crime

The term itself, as noted, has a long and varied pedigree. Albanese (2007) sees organized crime in terms of four defining elements: a continuing organizational hierarchy, the pursuit of profit through crime, use of force or threat, and the corruption of public officials to ensure immunity from prosecution. Other definitions abound, and its meaning continues in many ways to be unstable and contested. It has been described as 'a vague and ambiguous catchphrase, the application of which inevitably entails varying – but usually high – degrees of arbitrariness' (Paoli & Fijnaut 2004, p. 41). Some of the flavour of its unsettled meaning will emerge when we look at some specific examples of organized crime below. However, there can be little doubt that the term has achieved considerable political legitimacy in recent years, and has become the topic of legal specification at the international, as well as domestic, level.

A good starting point for seeing this process in action is the 2000 UN Convention against Transnational Organized Crime (TOC Convention). This convention was signed in December 2000. In essence, parties to this convention, drawn from member states of the United Nations, have pledged themselves to tackling a common problem – **transnational organized crime** – through their domestic laws and the activities of their law enforcement agencies and justice systems.

The scope of the TOC Convention is set out in Article 3. Briefly, it applies to offences of participation in an organized criminal group, money laundering, corruption and the obstruction of justice, as well as to 'serious crime' as defined in Article 2 'where the offence is transnational in nature and involves an organized criminal group' (Art. 3.1). 'Serious crime' refers to offences punishable by deprivation of liberty for at least four years or a more serious penalty. 'Transnational' refers to offences committed in more than one state; offences committed in one state but a substantial part of the preparation, planning, direction, or control takes place in another state; offences committed in one state but involving an organized criminal group that engages in criminal activities in more than one state; or offences committed in one state but that have substantial effects in another state.

The TOC Convention (2000) defines 'organized criminal group' in Article 2 to mean:

> A structured group of three or more persons, existing for a period of time and acting in concert with the aim of committing one or more serious crimes or offences established in accordance with this Convention, in order to obtain, directly or indirectly, a financial or other material benefit.

These Articles provide an important insight into the nature of the global threat associated with organized crime in the eyes of most countries as well as the United Nations itself. The *transnational* character of this activity has been key to the emergence of a concerted response from domestic governments around the world. The particular concern about *organized* crime points to the specific threat associated with groups of criminals that have some longevity (i.e. are more than transient in nature) and degree of focused operational capacity in areas of serious crime. The definition of 'structured group' in Article 2 makes it evident that the convention is not limited in its operation to hierarchical criminal organizations, along the lines traditionally associated with Italian Mafia organizations, but also encompasses groups with a more fluid nature, in which particular roles are not necessarily fixed (see Figures 6.1a–6.1c).

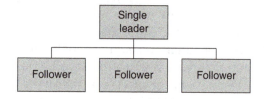

Figure 6.1a   Standard Hierarchy: the godfather is the boss; strict internal discipline; strong social and ethnic identities

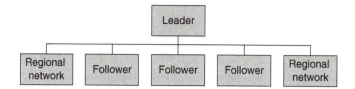

Figure 6.1b   Regional Hierarchy: one leader; regional networks enjoy more autonomy; social and ethnic identities; multiple activities

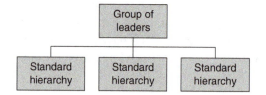

Figure 6.1c   Clustered Hierarchy: a number of criminal groups centrally coordinated by leaders; constituent groups enjoy a degree of autonomy

Reproduced based on: UNODC 2002, *Results of a pilot survey of forty selected organized criminal groups in sixteen countries*, www.unodc.org/pdf/crime/publications/Pilot_survey.pdf

This understanding of the nature of organized crime groups is important for several reasons. First, as noted, it breaks from the traditional Mafia view of organized crime, long held by law enforcement and the media in many Western countries since the early twentieth century. Second, it reflects a growing recognition within law enforcement agencies that globalization has led to the formation of looser networks of criminal personnel (see for example, Morselli 2009), often working in different countries but involved in common activity, for example, the trafficking of heroin from Afghanistan across the Middle East to Western Europe. Such long supply chains almost inevitably depend upon the formation of linkages between distinct criminal groups and individuals that can ensure the secure movement of illicit goods along those chains. Such linkages may not last for long, only existing for as long as it takes for a particular shipment to transit from source to final destination.

Finally, the 'network' view of organized crime carries implications for law enforcement and other crime reduction strategies in response to organized crime activities (see Chapter 3 on networks). Whereas the traditional hierarchical understanding of organized crime groups meant that efforts to deal with them should sensibly be directed to the leadership ('taking out' the godfather, 'cutting off the head' of the organization), the nature of networks (essentially non-hierarchical in many respects, due to their cellular and dispersed nature) implies that, at least in many criminal groups, 'godfathers' do not exist, or are quickly replaced by others. Such resilience makes traditional law enforcement methods less effective, and requires more strategic analysis of the structures of these groups in order to target their more vulnerable elements.

Organized Crime in an Era of World Risk – Transnationality

The post-Cold War environment also can be associated with greater recognition of the *transnational* character of organized crime (Edwards & Gill 2003; Glenny 2008). A loosening of trade barriers, a freeing up of the international finance sector and the greater ability of individuals to travel outside their own countries – all changes witnessed on an unprecedented scale after 1990 – set the scene for organized crime to grow in international significance. In addition to the evidence of substantial levels of transnational trafficking of heroin, cocaine and other drugs, there appeared more signs of substantial levels of small arms trafficking, human trafficking and smuggling. Then, in the aftermath of 11 September 2001, organized crime, particularly in its transnational forms, was linked to modern terrorism, as different modes of financing for terrorist activities came to light.

The growing transnational significance of organized crime has been widely interpreted by many governments and international organizations as a threat to good governance. The US National Security Council, in 2011, issued its Strategy for Combating Transnational Organized Crime, in which it stated that it represented 'a significant and growing threat to national and international security, with dire implications for public safety, public health, democratic institutions, and economic stability across the globe'. Not only are criminal networks expanding, but they also are diversifying their activities, resulting in the convergence of threats that were once distinct and today have explosive and destabilizing effects. In some countries where heroin and cocaine have traditionally been sourced and produced (e.g. Afghanistan, Colombia), criminal groups have become very powerful through the arms they have been able to acquire, the private armies they have been able to employ, and the bribery and intimidation of public officials (including police, prosecutors, judges and politicians).

The transnational dimension of organized crime points to significant political and ideological changes at the international level. Part of these changes is the promotion of a common view of the threat from transnational organized crime in particular. Another is the search for ways of cooperating and coordinating across nation-state identities and structures. For the purposes of this chapter, this new shared reality can be seen as, what Beck has also described as, 'enforced **cosmopolitanism**' (Beck 2006). Recognition of shared global risks 'activate[s] and connect[s] actors across borders, who otherwise don't want to have anything to do with one another' (Beck 2006, p. 13; see also Chapter 3). International police cooperation and international treaties addressing the subject-matter of organized crime have become increasingly important topics for study, as well as matters of practical importance, in the last three decades (see for example, Bronitt et al. 2013).

Is Organized Crime Always Harmful?

Despite the strong negative voices at the international level on this topic, it is important to question more closely the nature of the threat from organized crime and to consider whether there might be logical reasons, as well as clear incentives, for organized crime to emerge, survive and prosper. While there is clear evidence in many cases that it can lead to violence, intimidation and exploitation, this is not universally the case or at least true all the time. On the side of those who supply illicit goods, say drugs, there may be economic opportunities associated with the cultivation and production of those drugs that cannot be met or matched by governments or the private sector. Serious policy on illicit drugs should be attentive to the circumstances around particular illicit markets, in particular the situation of its poorest participants. The ability to look closely leads to a more discriminating view of the effects of organized crime in its different forms. It means that there may be 'good' or at least 'better' forms of organized crime, as well as 'bad' or 'worse' forms (Felbab-Brown 2009). Once this calculation is made, it allows sensible policy to focus on the more harmful forms and to consider how, if at all, the 'better' forms might be replaced rather than destroyed outright.

Differences of interest and values, therefore, can affect the degree of global consensus about the harmfulness of many transnational organized crime forms. Another factor limiting how we can reach a threat assessment of these diverse activities of course lies in their often covert nature. Those engaged in such activities, whether as perpetrators or as 'victims,' are often reluctant to report what they are doing to law enforcement or other government agencies. Consumers of ecstasy in nightclubs in Western cities are unlikely to hand themselves or their dealers over to the police, for example. Those engaged in counterfeiting DVDs or CDs are also not inclined to report themselves to the authorities. So obtaining accurate measurement of the extent of particular organized crimes is necessarily very difficult – 'guesstimations' are often the only option (see Case Study 6.1).

Case Study 6.1 – Calculating the Size and Cost

Given the nature of organized crime, calculating the scale and costs of such activities is not easy. First, one needs to establish how much of it is occurring, and second, one has to measure the impacts it has upon society as well as the economy. Knowing the answer to the first question is difficult, not least because there are few incentives to report it by those involved. So there is likely to be a lot of organized crime that remains unknown, both in terms of its extent and impact. In relation to impact, there is a real question about how it should be, and can be, measured. As noted, not everyone agrees on the actual harms from, say, cannabis consumption. Economists and others have attempted to devise ways of capturing social as well as economic costs, but their methods are inevitably limited by the assumptions they make and how many cost variables they attempt to measure.

The past few years have seen a spate of efforts by national and regional law enforcement agencies to make threat assessments about organized crime, which include estimates on costs. Given the difficulties of coming up with convincing estimates, these assessments often rely on narratives as much as figures, and venture some guesses. For example, according to UNODC in 2009, organized crime was estimated to generate US$870 billion worldwide. In the United Kingdom Threat Assessment of Serious Organized Crime 2006/7, even if it admitted that 'there is still much about serious organised crime which is not known or fully understood'(SOCA 2007, p. 5), it still ventured the view that the 'overall threat to the UK from serious organised crime is high' (SOCA 2007, p. 7). The UKTA report goes on to state: 'Broad estimates put the social and economic costs of serious organised crime, including the costs of combating it, at upwards of 20 billion UK pounds a year'. In 2013, the Australian Crime Commission 'conservative estimates' (sic) a cost of AU$15 billion annually (ACC 2013b, p. 6).

In response to this exercise of 'guesstimate', the Italian research group Transcrime adopted in 2013 a 'Mafia index' to calculate a more accurate estimate with a replicable methodology. This was accomplished by compiling data from Mafia-related organizations, homicides linked to the Mafia, city councils dissolved for Mafia infiltration and goods confiscated from organized crime and other variables. In summary they stated: 'Crime pays a lot less than is commonly thought. The media's belief that criminal organizations have revenues equal to 10% of the GDP needs to be debunked' (Transcrime 2014, p. 20).

However, the vagueness of such assessments is sometimes obscured in the policy judgements drawn and acted upon in relation to them. In this regard, they might be said to resemble other forms of 'intelligence' assessments – they are never complete in terms of the data needed for highly accurate assessment. In an area like money laundering, for example, there are all sorts of obstacles to assessing how much 'dirty money' is laundered by organized crime groups. Relying upon such estimates, therefore, is fraught with risk.

Studying Organized Crime: Actors, Activities and Networks

As noted already, the phenomenon does not lend itself readily to study through direct observation or other empirical methods. This explains the relative lack of academic work in this area, compared to other areas of criminology. Much of the void has been filled in the past by journalistic investigations (see for example, Glenny 2008) as well as by historical accounts (sometimes in the form of biographies or autobiographies of former organized crime participants, e.g. Maas, *The Valachi Papers*). Television series such as *The Sopranos* and *Breaking Bad*, as well as a host of British and American movies (*The Godfather*, *The Long Good Friday*, *The French Connection*), have also contributed to public perceptions of organized crime in recent decades. Newer scholars in the field have mined the transcripts of major investigatory commissions and criminal trials of alleged Mafia members in order to develop an understanding of how organized crime groups operate internally as well as externally (e.g. Paoli 2003).

There are clearly several major ways of approaching this subject-matter analytically. One is to focus upon the *actors* involved in organized crime. This leads, in many instances, to a study of the key individuals or groups involved. The groups studied have previously been seen in traditional organizational terms, as discrete, hierarchically structured organizations (e.g. the Mafia). Now, scholars recognize a wider range of organizational forms being used by organized crime groups, in particular the formation of networks of individuals and groups.

One advantage of focusing on the particular actors is that it enables scholars to study the variety of forms of organized crime engaged in by particular actors. It is widely accepted (for instance, in the Europol 2013 report) that organized crime groups tend not to confine themselves to one form of criminal activity, but in fact often engage in several forms at the same time (e.g. drug trafficking *and* extortion). The significant element for analysis here is the common one – the actor engaged in various organized crimes. Given the patterns of migration of people from countries such as Italy, China, Colombia and various Eastern European countries over the past 50 years (or even longer in some cases) to other parts of the world, in particular Western Europe, North America and Australia, many organized crime analysts have recently noted the links between particular organized crime groups in source (supply) countries and groups in market (demand) countries. The impact of ethnic diaspora upon the spread and effectiveness of organized crime activities is widely noted in relation to activities such as drug trafficking and people smuggling (see for example, Zaitch 2002).

Another approach is to focus upon particular *criminal activities*, say, drug trafficking, in order to understand the phenomenon more broadly than a focus upon a particular actor involved in drug trafficking would allow. Such an approach allows for an examination of the markets that typically develop around illicit goods and services, including the processes of competition that go on between different criminal actors in these areas. An example in this category is Paoli and colleagues' study of the world heroin market (Paoli et al. 2009). A more dynamic, as well as broader, view of major categories of organized crime is thus obtained through this approach.

A third approach to the field, increasingly reflected in the kinds of threat assessments provide by Europol and UKTA, is a focus upon the *networked character* of organized crime. Seeing organized crime in terms of networks permits the complexities of globalized forms of organized crime to be better captured. Supply chains for many illicit goods and services require the cooperation of different actors across geographical space, and/or with complementary skill sets. These functional requirements increasingly cannot be found within single organized crime organizations of the traditional kind. Hence, it makes sense to look at how these activities are networked across groups, as well as between key individuals, and how these networks adjust to attacks upon their activities by law enforcement or their competitors (see for example, Kenny 2007; Morselli 2009). The highly profitable nature of organized crime means that assistance will often be needed from legitimate business services to assist in money laundering. Also, the unlawful connections that inevitably emerge in many circumstances between powerful organized crime groups and government and business officials that facilitate further criminal activity, mean that the links between the 'dark' networks of organized crime and the 'bright' networks of the supposedly 'legitimate' world of business and government need to be understood (Raab & Milward 2003; see also the discussion of shadow networks in Chapter 3). The study of corruption, as well as money laundering, within organized crime studies inevitably requires a grasp of the relevant networks involved. The same can probably now be said of all other areas of organized crime in the transnational arena, given the logistical and organizational challenges presented by the globalization of organized crime.

In the end, the study of organized crime probably requires a combination of each of these approaches. Understanding the motivations of key organized crime actors will not emerge from a study of networks alone, nor from the study of just one form of organized crime activity, as many groups engage in more than one illicit activity. Similarly, so long as government policy continues in part to reflect preoccupations with particular organized crime forms, the study of, say, drug trafficking will continue to be looked at, largely separately, from other forms of organized crime. As noted, the recent interest in a network analysis of organized crime reflects the changing character of organized crime in terms of how it organizes transnationally; the more dispersed, horizontal character of the participants lends itself to the study of key hubs, nodes and links, in order not just to understand what is going on, but also to facilitate more targeted, efficient and effective responses to counter these activities.

6.3 Species of Organized Crime

National threat assessments, such as those undertaken by the United Kingdom National Crime Agency (NCA 2014) and Europol (Europol 2013), identify those areas of organized crime of particular concern to law enforcement authorities in the current climate. The latest Europol assessment identifies eight areas:

- drugs,
- counterfeiting,
- crimes against persons,
- organized property crime,
- economic crime,
- cybercrime,
- environmental crime,
- and weapons trafficking.

The latest UK assessment list is similar in nature, but includes child exploitation and abuse. The particular threat from transnational crime groups is emphasized in both assessments, noting the increased mobility and cross-border reach of these groups.

Here, we examine two kinds of serious organized crime widely viewed as posing a transnational threat: illicit drug trafficking and money laundering. Other examples will not be addressed here. These include small arms dealing, environmental crime (examined in Chapter 8), human trafficking and people smuggling (see Chapter 5), cybercrime and copyright piracy. The issue of terrorism is dealt with separately in Chapter 7.

Drug Production and Trafficking

While new concerns, such as cybercrime, are seen as posing increasing threats, drug production and trafficking remains at the forefront of most threat assessment exercises and law enforcement agency priorities (see Europol 2013, p. 19). Its highly profitable and relatively visible nature makes it an ongoing threat and challenge for law enforcement agencies around the world. Fraud and money laundering, or for that matter people smuggling, tend to have a lower profile and hence attract less attention. The highly competitive and often spectacularly violent activities of groups such as Mexican drug trafficking organizations (e.g. Los Zetas, Sinaloa Cartel) ensure a lot of publicity and public concern, leading commonly to significant investment in enforcement activities.

There is considerable dynamism in this field of illicit activity. As countries vary their enforcement activities or as certain regions become politically unstable, new production areas, players and trafficking routes can emerge to challenge or replace those that previously dominated this illegal trade. For example, since Colombia stepped up its action against drug producers in 2000, a lot of the production of cocaine has moved to Peru and Bolivia. Moreover, as Colombian traffickers came under pressure at home from government actions, their ability to operate internationally became weaker, creating opportunities for other criminal groups, in particular from Mexico, to take over and control large sections of the global cocaine trafficking networks. Dynamism can also stem from changes in domestic demand. Drug users in many countries are turning to synthetic drugs (such as amphetamines), meaning that new groups, often based in other parts of the world from those serving the long-established markets for heroin and cocaine, can play a more significant role in drug trafficking and production.

While much of the focus of the study of drug markets is upon those in charge and the obscene levels of profit extracted by those running the major trafficking groups, there is another side to the problem. In many areas where drugs are sourced and produced (for example Afghanistan, which produces opium poppies for heroin production, and Colombia, which produces coca plants for making cocaine), there are often few legitimate alternative financial opportunities for those involved in actual cultivation of crops and production of the drugs for trafficking. Those tending the crops receive very small salaries by Western standards, but often these payments represent a decent, reliable income by local standards, making their participation in illicit activities attractive, compared to the often limited and far less profitable alternatives.

Another driver of drug trafficking is the law itself, in combination with efforts by countries and international organizations, such as the United Nations and the International Narcotics Control Board, to criminalize and penalize those engaging in certain forms of drug production and trafficking. An historical view of drug laws in many Western countries reveals that these laws have not always existed. At one time or other, many drugs currently prohibited under national laws and international conventions were not illegal or the subject of law enforcement activity. For example, Coca-Cola, the famous American soft drink, once contained ingredients from the coca plant, the same plant used to produce cocaine (hence its name). Cocaine was removed from the drink in 1903, a few years ahead of legislation banning its use (Durlacher 2000).

Similarly, we are now witnessing not just the decriminalization of so-called soft drugs, such as cannabis in many places, but even the legalization of cannabis in a small but growing number of US states. After more than a century of prohibition, legitimate American businesses are being given the opportunity to produce and sell cannabis products for recreational as well as medical uses. Two reasons can be provided for this dramatic shift in policy. One is the widespread public demand in recent years for the product for both medical and recreational purposes. The other is growing public awareness of the enormous costs associated with trying to police the drug markets. In addition to the expense of mounting law enforcement operations, there are the costs arising from the criminalization of persons who often otherwise had no criminal propensities or posed no real threat to anyone else.

In the past, a lot of drug trafficking has been attributed to criminal groups with particular ethnic identities – the Sicilian Mafia, the Colombian cartels and the Mexican cartels, to mention just a few. To a great extent, their ability to operate effectively has been linked to the familiarity and trust within those groups. For example, as Colombians came to migrate to the United States, Spain and other countries, Colombian drug trafficking organizations were able to call upon their diaspora (the migrants, in this case, from Colombia) in those countries to participate in the transnational operations of those groups.

The globalization of drug markets, however, has meant that a wider range of participants has come to work together, involving participants from different ethnicities and backgrounds. Increasingly, law enforcement authorities deal with crime groups consisting of different nationalities or at least networks of groups made up of smaller ethnically defined groups that are working together in some particular trafficking trade. As the most recent Europol threat assessment points out, increasingly drug trafficking groups are poly-drug as well as poly-crime focused (Europol 2013). In other words, these groups are diversifying into other crimes and other types of drugs. The breakdown of the previously strong ethnic divisions is consistent with the expanded range of economic opportunities arising from diversification; cross-ethnic cooperation, in other words, has led to more crime opportunities for many groups.

Money Laundering

Money laundering has been described as the 'common denominator of almost all serious and organized crime' (AUSTRAC 2014, p. 22). Given the profitability of many forms of transnational crime, in particular drug trafficking, many criminal actors have had to deal with a very practical challenge – how to deal with the proceeds of crime. Given the highly cash-oriented nature of much organized crime, successful drug traffickers in particular often face difficulties counting, storing and disposing of large volumes of cash. In the 1980s, the cocaine trafficking activities of Pablo Escobar's organization were reportedly so profitable that he needed to spend US$2500 every month on rubber bands alone to package the money (Escobar 2009, p. 76). Finding ways of safely handling and converting such large amounts of cash became a priority. As one might predict, given the money at stake and potentially to be made by those assisting crime groups to manage their cash, a range of services quickly emerged to meet that need – the services of so-called money launderers.

While attempts have been made to estimate the amount of illicit money laundered, there are obvious practical difficulties associated with such an undertaking. Even the principal global regulator in this field, the Financial Action Task Force (FATF), has conceded on its website that it is 'absolutely impossible to produce a reliable estimate of the amount of money laundered'. UNODC (2015a) has stated, 'The estimated amount of money laundered globally in one year is 2–5% of global GDP, or $800 billion – $2 trillion in current US dollars'. While there are many deficiencies in these estimates, there can be little doubt that the illicit proceeds from crime are significant in size and involve the movement of money across jurisdictions in order to conceal it. Only some of the proceeds of organized crime get laundered, it must be noted. A lot of money historically gets spent on 'conspicuous consumption' – cars, alcohol, prostitutes, drugs, restaurants and holidays. Cash is also necessary to pay off officials, who might otherwise report illicit activities, and to pay the salaries of those working within the crime groups.

Traditionally, money laundering is seen as a three-step process (Figure 6.2). The first step is *placement* – moving the money into the legitimate financial system. This involves breaking up large sums into small amounts and depositing them over time, often into a number of different bank accounts or financial institutions. The second step is *layering*. This involves movement of these funds from location to location, rendering the trail harder to follow for anyone trying to investigate the source of the funds. This may involve wiring money from one country to another, or disguising transfers as payments for goods or services. As money has become increasingly digitalized, it has become easier to move and also to disguise, often through numerous rapid transactions between banks and companies in different jurisdictions. Often these banks are located in other countries and have been selected on the basis of the absence of close regulation of financial transactions in those countries. Countries that also have strict confidentiality regimes for bank customers are popular with those who do not wish to attract the attention of government authorities with regard to their financial dealings. The third and final step is called *integration*. At this point the funds re-enter the legitimate economy, as money invested in real estate, legitimate business undertakings, or the purchase of luxury items.

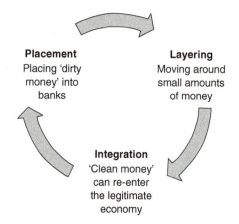

Placement
Placing 'dirty
money' into
banks

Layering
Moving around
small amounts
of money

Integration
'Clean money'
can re-enter
the legitimate
economy

Figure 6.2   Money Laundering

Tackling money laundering is a priority established within the TOC Convention 2000, in Articles 6 and 7. Article 6 requires states to criminalize activities intended to conceal or disguise the proceeds of crime, while Article 7 requires states to implement a 'comprehensive domestic regulatory and supervisory regime for bank and non-bank financial institutions and, where appropriate, other bodies particularly susceptible to money-laundering'. Apart from any moral objective, the aim of criminalizing money laundering is a practical one – the removal of incentives for participation in various forms of organized crime. The attention given to money laundering has increased further in the post-September 11 climate, as authorities have turned their attention more to the ways in which terrorist activities can be financed through participation in various forms of transnational organized crime, including drug production and trafficking and illegal (stolen) oil sales.

Money laundering provides us with a useful reminder of the close links between organized crime and many spheres of legitimate activity. The various stages of money laundering make it often inevitable, but also desirable, that criminal actors rely upon bankers, financial advisers, accountants, lawyers, real estate agents and others to achieve the goals of 'laundering' illicitly obtained funds. Some participants from the 'legitimate' world will be cognizant accomplices in this task, while others may be wilfully blind or even naïve to what is going on. By 'cleaning' their funds though, these professionals not only contribute to their own enrichment, they also enable organized crime figures to participate more fully in 'respectable' society.

Money laundering clearly has benefited from the international liberalization of the banking and financial sectors. Offshore banks and other financial institutions have long been recognized as key contributors to the trade in 'dirty money', and have therefore been targeted by national and international policies, including the monitoring of country laws by the FATF. The shaming or praising of countries (similar to the tier system adopted by the United States on human trafficking, as discussed in Chapter 4) is part of the imposed legacy of money laundering policy. Money laundering is also a good example of how improvements in technology have benefited organized crime, along with legitimate business. The creation of instantaneous payment systems has meant that financial transactions can be conducted online in an instant, avoiding face-to-face dealings and enabling participants to remain anonymous. The speed of these transactions, and their ability to benefit from the liberalization of currency exchange controls, make them easier to carry out, yet often harder to trace.

An emerging phenomenon within the study of money laundering is the part played by various digital currencies (for example, Bitcoin) and so-called new payment systems that are not managed through mainstream financial institutions or regulated by national governments. In 2012, Australia's financial intelligence unit, AUSTRAC, commented that the 'extent of their use by organised crime groups is unknown'. AUSTRAC did note, however, a likelihood of greater risk in the future from these new approaches as measures against 'traditional' methods of countering money laundering become more effective (AUSTRAC 2012, p. 16).

6.4 Responses to Organized Crime

As noted earlier, there has been, and remains, considerable international as well as regional, national and local interest in finding ways to combat organized crime. Much of the attention has been on the *supply* side, rather than the *demand* side. As a consequence, there has been much more focus and investment in law enforcement and other measures to disrupt those producing and trafficking illicit goods and services. The transnational element of organized crime, by presenting a common or shared threat to individual states, has led governments and law enforcement agencies to explore ways in which cooperation is possible between states and their law enforcement agencies in preventing and disrupting the different forms. In large measure, this world-view of organized crime, and the development of common, transnational approaches to countering its various forms, have been facilitated by international and regional governance institutions such as UNODC and the EU.

Securing a consensus on organized crime at the international level is by no means straightforward. One of the key challenges is overcoming the differences of laws and procedures, as well as of cultures and politics, for the purposes of acting decisively against criminal groups. The 'Global Prohibition' regime around certain drugs, in particular heroin, cocaine and cannabis, in place since the early twentieth century, was largely a creature of certain Western countries, in particular the United States (see Nadelmann 1993; Woodiwiss 2003). This has meant that getting cooperation for such ventures as the 'war on drugs' has required that countries such as the USA persuade, by various means, other countries and their law enforcement agencies to pursue the crime agendas of the USA and other Western countries. This process has been described as the 'Americanization' of criminal justice by scholars such as Nadelmann (1993) and Woodiwiss (2003). It is part of the 'package' of legal mechanisms imposed on other countries, discussed in Chapter 4. This process, to put it bluntly, has not been easy or particularly effective in many instances (Goldsmith & Sheptycki 2007), and has even contributed to increased levels of violence and other social harms in those countries in which these agendas have been pursued. As one cynical observer said about the USA's attempts to co-opt Colombians into fighting against cocaine production and trafficking in that country, 'In the war against drugs, the US is ready to fight to the last Colombian' (Kline 1999, p. 121).

On the supply side, there are some fundamental difficulties facing law enforcement and prosecutors. One is that there is no apparent shortage of people attracted to being involved in these highly profitable activities. A college degree is not a prerequisite for participating in, and profiting from, these activities.

The fact that some organized crime groups provide employment, protection and social services to those in their areas of operation has been all too often overlooked by those seeking to bring such activities to an end. Similarly, many government officials, including police, prosecutors and judges, will be bribed *not* to act, or have financial interests that will be threatened if they take action against organized crime. In order to get national governments and law enforcement agencies to participate in these international agendas, agencies such as the United Nations and foreign governments have often provided various forms of inducement in the form of law enforcement technical assistance, judicial and prosecutor training, the building of courthouses and prisons and development assistance (as discussed in Chapter 4). Development assistance has taken the form, in countries such as Colombia and Afghanistan, of measures to support local farmers to cultivate legal rather than illegal crops.

On the demand side, it is often noted that there is comparatively little investment or emphasis by the same governments and authorities that are heavily investing in supply side law enforcement. For commodities such as cocaine or methamphetamine ('ice'), there is clearly ongoing strong demand in the destination countries in Western Europe, Australia and North America (UNODC 2012a). In many countries with significant addiction problems, there are insufficient treatment facilities to support people to get off their drug habits. Until a few years ago, the prioritization of supply reduction over demand reduction was not widely criticized, as overwhelming political support at the international level for the 'war on drugs' continued. However this is starting to change, as more countries and political leaders are calling into question the effectiveness of law enforcement measures in dealing with illicit drug issues. Bodies such as the International Narcotics Control Board and UNODC are now recognizing that the past focus on supply side issues in relation to illicit drugs has not worked. The UNODC's World Drug Report 2012 has called for '[r]ebalancing drug control policy through alternative development, prevention, treatment and fundamental human rights' (UNODC 2012a, p. iii).

Case Study 6.2 – Are Things Getting Worse?

Changes in the global drug trade in heroin and cocaine provide the most telling examples of the limits of transnational law enforcement efforts. In relation to heroin, the news is not good. After nearly a century now of multilateral cooperation in the fight against the illicit cultivation of opium, Professor Hamid Ghodse, President of the International Narcotics Control Board, could only note in a speech on 24 July 2008 that, 'Whatever problems remain, they dwarf the problems that the international community faced almost one hundred years ago'. In other words, things during this period went from bad to worse. After a century of unsuccessful targeting of this species of organized crime, many see the need for a re-examination of approaches to tackling such issues, one that looks at prevention as well as punishment, and addresses demand as well as supply.

In Portugal in 2000, the government decided to change its approach to illicit drugs. Rather than abandoning completely the old ways, it decided to give greater emphasis to prevention measures than it had adopted previously, by putting many more resources into addiction treatment facilities. It also decided to tone down the reliance on the criminal law, instead treating drug use under administrative regulations. In the past 15 years, in line with growing doubts about the effectiveness of the prohibitionist approach, there has been much interest from other countries in how the Portuguese programme is working. One fear many observers had about the Portuguese model was that it would lead to more people trying drugs. A recent evaluation of the social costs concluded several things. One was that there was now more money being spent on addiction-related services, but this needed to be seen alongside the reduction in other costs associated with law enforcement, imprisonment and drug-related deaths. On balance, the authors concluded, there was a 12% reduction in social costs up to 2004, rising to 18% between 2004 and 2010 (see Goncalves et al. 2015).

Changes to Domestic Arrangements

A couple of changes within the policing of organized can be noted: the first being a move towards *centralization and specialization*. In a country such as the United Kingdom, with 43 separate police forces, responding nationally to organized crime has led to a number of changes. In particular, it has meant finding better ways of sharing and storing criminal intelligence so that individual police forces have the ability to access intelligence from other police forces.

This led, in 2006, to the establishment of specialized agencies intended to complement the powers and resources of traditional law enforcement agencies. The United Kingdom developed the Serious Organized Crime Agency (SOCA), a national body focused upon intelligence collection, dissemination and analysis (this body was replaced in 2013 by the National Crime Agency) (Harfield 2006). It also meant finding the capacity to carry out joint operations between separate law enforcement agencies.

Similar challenges have arisen in federally organized countries, such as Germany and Australia, as well as within regional associations such as the EU. In Australia, for example, the fact that criminal law and law enforcement are principally organized and to be found at the state/territory level has resulted in the formation of national-level specialist agencies. The Australian Crime Commission, in particular, focuses on criminal intelligence collection and sharing in order to deal with organized crime. Additionally, AUSTRAC, mentioned earlier, serves as the national financial intelligence unit. As in many other countries, many of the innovations in domestic law enforcement regarding organized crime have been driven by experiences principally with the illicit drug trade, particularly the difficulties of effectively targeting the 'Mr (and sometimes Ms) Bigs' – in other words, the leadership of the criminal groups.

A second observation relates to the development of *special investigative measures* for the purposes of combating organized crime. There has been a marked shift in many jurisdictions towards more intrusiveness in the methods permitted for use against suspected organized crime groups. These measures may take the form of permitting covert surveillance of various kinds, the conducting of 'sting operations' and holding special inquisitorial hearings at which failing to answer questions may result in a penalty. Measures of this kind can be seen widely within the EU as well as in other countries. In Australia, the Australian Crime Commission and other law enforcement agencies can call upon the services of Examiners, who conduct special investigatory hearings in serious and organized crime matters. They can compel witnesses to answer questions and produce documents. One of the key concerns held by civil liberties groups about these domestic responses to the threat of organized crime is that the categories of crime to which they are applied are often not tightly defined, and that their extraordinary investigative powers can end up being used against 'small fry' criminals as well as supposed 'big fish'. These law enforcement powers, once ceded by governments to law enforcement agencies, can be very difficult to get back.

Recent concerns about organized crime, and particularly its transnational forms, have contributed to a visible shift in Western policy from reactive law enforcement to preventive law enforcement. For example, the emergence of SOCA in the UK in 2006 reflected a significant shift in government policy towards preventing and reducing the harm caused by serious organized crime

(Harfield 2006), a view which remains current today. A greater emphasis upon detection and disruption of criminal planning and preparatory acts, and upon dismantling crime groups, is evident in policy prescriptions. This is in place of, or rather in addition to, a prevailing focus on after-the-fact criminal investigations and prosecutions. While enhanced means for traditional law enforcement remain important, the picture is now more complex and varied. Part of the philosophical shift towards prevention and disruption, before serious harm can occur, is reflected in new criminal law provisions as well as new police powers. Within Europe as well as elsewhere, there has been a commitment to making membership of criminal organizations an offence in its own right (similar developments in counter-terrorism have also been seen post-9/11) (Levi 2004; see Chapter 3 section 3.3). Offences of this kind are intended to prevent serious harm from emerging, by attacking the group formations associated with organized criminal activity themselves.

6.5 Conclusion

Responses to organized crime, as one might predict, tend to reflect dominant analyses of the nature of the issue. Historically, and still, many leading analyses of the phenomenon have focused upon the threat from particular criminal organizations. Initially, these were Mafia-type bodies, led by godfather figures, while more recently, a networked structure has been recognized and is becoming the new orthodoxy within analysis of organized crime. Efforts to target identified organizations (enhanced legal powers, new operational tactics, etc.) have not lost their relevance or currency, and are continuing to evolve, usually in the direction of more draconian powers. At the same time, certain illicit activities have themselves become the focus of policy development. While initially this could be seen most visibly with respect to illicit drugs, it has since been extended to people smuggling and human trafficking, in part reflecting community-based concerns about these activities and not just the operational preoccupations of law enforcement agencies. It also is a logical development given the evidence that particular illicit activities such as drug trafficking attract a seemingly ceaseless supply of participants. The globalized nature of the threat from these activities is a relatively recent addition to organized crime analysis, linking matters of domestic law enforcement strongly to matters of national security and foreign policy.

More than 10 years ago, Levi and Maguire observed, '[F]ew [countries] appeared to be looking beyond immediate operational goals towards a lasting reduction in organised criminal activity' (2004, p. 457). This is arguably still the case. As we have noted, longer term solutions require more lateral thinking.

As we have seen, the harms from organized crime arise not just from the activities themselves but can be linked to the absence of viable alternatives in terms of jobs and safety in some cases, as well as shortages in demand reduction facilities such as treatment centres for drug addicts. As the Latin American Commission on Drugs and Democracy noted in 2008, the 'war on drugs' fought on Latin American soil comes at a high price for those countries directly involved, including governmental corruption and widespread violence. With respect to most if not all forms of organized crime, there is a need for greater contextual appreciation of the drivers of supply, a proper understanding of the full range of harm associated with existing supply methods and efforts to counter them, and more critical engagement with the sources of demand and the factors generating that demand.

Questions: Revise and Reflect

1. What are the key features of globalization? How has globalization affected organized crime?

2. What are the major threats associated with organized crime at present? How are these threats assessed or calculated?

3. What is the 'alien conspiracy' view of organized crime? Is it still relevant? What alternative perspectives of organized crime exist? How do these perspectives differ from each other?

4. What has been the main way in the past of tackling organized crime? Critique the limitations of existing approaches to tackling organized crime. What other considerations should apply to the analysis of, and responses to, this problem?

5. How can political factors (including corruption of public officials) impact upon organized crime and its ability to evade law enforcement?

6. If you have watched the AMC series *Breaking Bad*, consider the strengths and weaknesses of their money laundering 'structuring' method (a method of placement by breaking down the amount of cash into smaller deposits of money).

Further Reading

Edwards, A & Gill, P (eds) 2003, *Transnational organised crime: Perspectives on global security*, Routledge, London.

Martin, J 2014, *Drugs on the dark net: How cryptomarkets are transforming the global trade in illicit drugs*, Palgrave Macmillan, Basingstoke.

Saviano, R 2007, *Gomorrah: Italy's other mafia*, Pan Books, London.

Videos to Watch

Maria, Full of Grace – story of young Colombian woman drawn into transnational cocaine trafficking network operating between Colombia and the USA.

Blood Diamond – an account of the 'blood diamond' trade in Sierra Leone, showing how the pursuit of precious minerals can lead to extreme violence and destabilize entire countries. Stars Leonardo di Caprio.

Lord of War – a film based on the life of Yuri Orlov, a global arms trader, showing the intersection between the ruthless pursuit of profit (the arms trade) and ongoing political chaos in developing countries. Stars Nicolas Cage.

Traffic – a film about drug trafficking across the Mexico–US borders. Stars Michael Douglas.

Websites to Visit

European Union's website on Fight against Organized Crime: ec.europa.eu/justice_home/fsj/crime/fsj_crime_intro_en.htm

Financial Action Task Force, the world's leading international organization monitoring money laundering and terrorist financing activities and efforts to counter them: www.fatf-gafi.org/

United Kingdom's National Crime Agency: www.nationalcrimeagency.gov.uk/

UN Office on Drugs and Crime's website dealing with organized crime: www.unodc.org/unodc/en/organized-crime/index.html

7

Terrorism in a Networked World

This chapter will look at

- Terrorism as a transnational phenomenon, its structure and motivation.
- Jihad terrorist groups, home-grown terrorism and cyber-terrorism.
- The risk of developing tough responses considering the 'causes' of terrorism.
- Public fear and policy choices in the 'war on terror'.

Keywords

Terrorism

Networks

Home-grown
terrorism

Suicide terrorism

War on terror

7.1 Introduction

In this chapter, we consider the phenomenon of modern transnational **terrorism**. The events of 11 September 2001 (New York), 12 October 2002 (Bali), 11 March 2004 (Madrid) and 7 July 2005 (London), as well as countless other examples over the past couple of decades, point to a kind of terrorism with which Western societies have not been familiar, yet which seems to target them in particular though not exclusively by any means. We will focus on ways of explaining its nature and significance, and how it has been responded to by individual nation-states and the broader international community. In this context, the 'war on terror' will be examined as a particular response to a perceived threat.

7.2 Modern Terrorism: Networked, Transnational Groups

At the heart of our discussion of both the 'problem' and the 'responses' is the *transnational* dimension of both aspects – in other words, the 'spilling over' of national borders of both the phenomenon itself and the organized responses to it. Beck highlighted that:

> The perceived risk of global terrorism has had exactly the opposite effect than that which was intended by the terrorists. It has pushed us into a new phase of globalisation, the globalisation of politics, the moulding of states into transnational cooperative networks. (Beck 2002, p. 46)

As Beck's comment indicates, threats such as terrorism (but also ecological threats and global financial crises) are no longer confined by political borders, and thus require responses that are also transnational in character. The concept of networks is a principal theme in our discussion. It helps us to think about the connections made between different persons and groups in different countries that can lead to a September 11 attack on the one hand, and on the other, the formation of multinational and international coalitions of military, security and law enforcement officials to take action against modern terrorist groups. As we shall also consider in this chapter, the responses to modern terrorism tend to assume particular understandings of the nature of the problem. Perceptions of catastrophic risk, uncertainty and even dread have been visible in various policy prescriptions for how to reduce or eliminate the threat posed. Who defines the 'problem' thus will heavily influence the responses taken up, a point we shall return to when discussing the 'war on terror.'

Defining Terrorism

While this chapter does not attempt to look at terrorism in general, a general grasp of what the term means is critical to the remaining discussion of one particular form of it, transnational jihadist terrorism, which is the main concern of the chapter. There are many definitions of the term, and little agreement within international policy circles as to a common meaning of the word. The saying 'one person's terrorist is another person's freedom fighter' points to the different perspectives possible in terms of the motives for, and moral appropriateness of, certain acts that some people, at least, would call terrorist.

A common definition used in the United Kingdom is 'the use or threat, for the purpose of advancing a political, religious, or ideological course of action, of serious violence against any person or property' (Townsend 2002, p. 3).

Contemporary violent jihadist terrorist groups such as al-Qaeda and its affiliates present analysts with a paradox. They appear to contain within them the elements of religious traditionalism of a fundamentalist kind, including a rejection of secularism and **modernity** more generally, yet also embrace the technologies of the twenty-first century, including the internet, modern military weaponry, mobile phones and transcontinental travel. They are in this sense both opponents, and practitioners, of globalization. As Louise Richardson has noted:

> The ideology of militant Islamist movements is, of course, radically anti-globalisation. They want to remove external influence and return to the rule of traditional Islamic law, called *sharia*. These are the very groups, however, which have most creatively exploited the attributes of globalisation to their own advantage. While articulating a vision of a pre-modern future they seek to achieve it by ultra-modern means. (2006, p. 83)

One clear implication we can draw from their transnational practice of globalization is their distancing from nation-states. While some states may be willing to tolerate their presence within their borders, or even to support or sponsor their activities, those activities are not dependent upon particular states, and are certainly not limited operationally to the borders of particular states. As responders to the threat they pose, states are equally obliged to forge relationships with other states, being unable within their own borders to act alone to deal effectively with the perceived threat.

7.3 Understanding Jihadist Terrorist Groups

In the aftermath of September 11, 2001, a renewed academic as well as political and public interest in the nature of modern terrorism occurred. The al-Qaeda 'model' of modern terrorism became the subject of much analysis. How was it possible that a group of men of Middle Eastern (mainly Saudi) origin, inspired and assisted by others located in Afghanistan, could train and prepare in Europe as well as the United States, to launch a series of attacks upon American targets, using civilian devices for military purposes? As noted in Chapter 6, traditional organized crime analysis has focused upon criminal groups as organizations, typically geographically centred in one country or part of a country and with a hierarchical, closed structure. A more recent focus upon markets in crime has taken as its basis the coming together of often disparate groups and individuals to trade in illicit goods and services, united by a common interest in profiting from the trade concerned. This has occurred transnationally as well as within particular countries, but profit has been the unifying motive for those involved.

In contrast to much opinion about the drivers of transnational crime, the profit motivation does not characterize what is known about modern jihadist terrorist motivations. While religion is used as a central justification for most jihadist acts, the jihadists' claim to formal training and standing in religious matters is typically very limited or non-existent. French scholar of Islamic affairs Olivier Roy has characterized the violent Islamic militants of recent years as 'part of the de-territorialized, supranational Islamic networks that operate in the West and at the periphery of the Middle East' (Roy 2006, p. 159). Moreover, he observes:

> ... they are all far more a product of a Westernized Islam than of traditional Middle East politics. However 'old time' their theology may sound to Westerners, and whatever they may think of themselves, they are clearly more a postmodern phenomenon than a pre-modern one. (2006, p. 161)

Nor can we describe these groups in terms of 'markets for terror' or as resembling hierarchical, bureaucratic organizations. Their more fluid, adaptive and resilient natures have required another way of conceptualizing how they work. It is against this background that the idea of network analysis arises. Before exploring this concept further, it should be noted that there are other dimensions of modern terrorism that may not be reducible to the network idea.

The significance of ideological inspiration for jihadist terrorist involvement reflects the **post-modern** take on traditional religion described by Roy, and replaces the profit motive behind most forms of transnational crime, or the national liberation, nation-state specific political objectives of many earlier terrorist groups (e.g. ETA in the Basque region of Spain, the IRA in Northern Ireland). The description of it as a movement rather than a group is suggestive of the blurring that can occur between those highly active in modern terrorism and those who support and sympathize with their tactics and objectives, with the effect that efforts to eliminate or incapacitate particular members of the active groups can often spawn the replacement of those removed by other members of the broader movement.

However, ideology, while widely seen by experts as essential to the justification of terrorist acts, and hence a fundamental ingredient of jihadist terrorism, does not fully explain the decision by individuals to get involved. Sageman (2004) has strongly argued that the formation of social bonds between small groups of (almost always) young men precedes the ideological commitment to terrorist involvement, commenting somewhat flippantly, 'It may be more accurate to blame global Salafi terrorist activity on in-group love than out-group hate' (2004, p. 135).

The study of terrorism through the tool of network analysis causes us to look at the relationships (links) between individual actors, between individuals and groups and between groups involved in terrorism. A network, it has been suggested, can be readily understood as 'a series of nodes that are connected through links of communication and/or exchange of resources', those nodes being 'individuals, organisations, firms, or even computers' (Eilstrup-Sangiovanni 2005, p. 8). By focusing on these links or connections between different elements, one can begin to identify networks involved in particular activities, and indeed connections between, in this case, terrorist networks and other sectors of the society in which they operate. Networks in short are mechanisms for collaboration, just as markets and bureaucracies are, but rather 'seen as horizontally structured systems of production and exchange with a predominance of informal ties and loosely coupled relations in contrast to tightly coupled, rigid, hierarchical organizations' (Raab & Milward 2003, p. 418). This account seems to fit better with collective understandings of the nature of al-Qaeda-type jihadist groups as decentralized, loosely linked cells (see 'Spotlight') that often take their direction from generalist Islamist literature encouraging jihad or websites making available information useful for the conduct of local-level, small-scale terrorist activities.

Spotlight – The Structure of Networks

Raab and Milward (2003) have coined the term 'dark networks' to refer to networks of individuals and groups involved in covert and illegal acts. Here, they envision transnational terrorist as well as criminal groups as falling within this category. In this and more recent work (Milward & Raab 2006), they recognize that there is considerable variation within this category. Some dark networks remain partly hierarchical with a few key individuals coordinating many of the activities (e.g. the original al-Qaeda model), while others are radically decentralized and only indirectly (often virtually) connected to others engaged in such activities. One of the features of networks that makes them difficult for law enforcement to deal with is their *resilience*. Like a web, a network can often survive the removal of part of its initial structure, and undergo subsequent repair through the substitution of other actors or groups for those 'links' broken or removed through law enforcement or other tactics.

Undoubtedly, there is also a relationship between terrorist networks and the environments in which they exist and operate. Those environments can be virtual, of course (the internet), but real territorial bases remain pertinent for many forms of transnational terrorism. For example, the Taliban government of Afghanistan in the mid/late 1990s provided a congenial environment in which Osama bin Laden and his associates could continue their training and planning of terrorist actions. This observation, as we shall see later, has led to many policy prescriptions in relation to dealing with weak, failing and failed states, on the assumption that these environments are criminogenic or **terror-genic**, and hence a security threat to other states. Milward and Raab (2006) have taken the view that territory should be considered simply one resource among others (technology, finances, weapons, law) for the commission of terrorist acts. Another scholar, Hehir (2007) has argued that there is no causal link between failed states and international terrorism, commenting that 'the factors that give rise to terrorism are not exclusive to failed states and that the capacity of democratic governance to eliminate terrorism is far from proven' (Hehir 2007, p. 328).

Other terms used by social scientists to capture the terrorist threat associated with weak or failed states include 'zones of turmoil' (Mann 2001) and 'wild zones' (Urry 2002). Urry has observed, 'In these zones charismatic leaders with alternative armies provide plausible solutions to . . . massive inequalities, especially those that seem to result from American domination over Islamic societies' (2002, p. 62). Such 'wild zones' are not confined to far-removed, unstable countries however. Through processes of mass migration, social exclusion and feelings of alienation and humiliation among recent arrivals, 'wild' and 'safe' zones can exist in close proximity and even overlap – as the New York attacks showed, 'wild zones are now only a telephone call, an Internet connection or a plane-ride away' (Urry 2002, p. 63). Such 'chaotic juxtapositions' contribute to the sense of growing insecurity that many in Western countries have felt over the past couple of decades, and to the measures called for to deal with the perceived dangers.

Home-grown and Suicide Terrorism

The July 2005 London bombing attacks, it was quickly established, were not committed by foreign 'sleeper cells', like the September 11 attacks in New York were, but rather by radicalized, second-generation British Muslims. Journalists tracked the origins of the bombers to the bleak streets of suburban Leeds in northern England, and identified some of the locations and participants in the apparent radicalization of these young men. Many of the apparent supports and inspirations for their suicide bombings were local (see 'Spotlight' below).

Spotlight – Comparing Western European and American Radicalized Young Muslims

The emergence of radicalized young Muslims within Western countries, especially in Western Europe, has now become a target for social interventions, designed to encourage more moderate thinking and discourage further movement towards joining jihadist groups. By contrast, some observers see little similarity with the

(Continued)

(Continued)

situation of American Muslims in terms of their likelihood of being radicalized. Marc Sageman comments:

> For most American Muslims, the terrorist message does not become a catalyst to action as it does for their European counterparts, since it does not resonate with their beliefs or personal circumstances. For the United States, pursuing policies of political, social, and economic inclusion rather than exclusion has paid an enormous dividend. (Sageman 2008, p. 108)

Husain reiterates this point from a British point of view, adding 'What the white majority in Britain take for granted, their sense of belonging, is not so easy for ethnic minorities' (2007, p. 283). In the US context, Vidino (2009) has suggested that the United States may need to do more in future to avoid replicating the problems seen in Western Europe, noting that American law enforcement agencies have recently stepped up their surveillance of radical Muslim groups out of an apparent concern that similar risks exist in that country to those already demonstrated in London, Madrid and Paris.

In the aftermath of the Iraqi occupation, there was a significant incidence in the use of suicide terrorism as a tactic of jihadist groups. Atrans (2006) reports that in 2004, 'there were more suicide attacks than in the entire world in any previous year of contemporary history, involving "martyrs" from fourteen other Arab countries, as well as volunteers from all over Europe' (2006, p. 130). Efforts to explain this apparently irrational behaviour in terms of individual psychopathology or structural deprivation (poverty, alienation, etc.) have proved either misleading or inadequate. Many suicide terrorists, for instance the September 11 attackers, were highly educated, middle-class men. Political motives, in particular the US occupation of traditional Muslim territory and the persistence of Israeli domination of Palestine, have been correlated by Pape (2005) with resorting to this tactic. However, recent work by Atrans (2006) has pointed to the importance of small-group dynamics and an emotional commitment to particular faith-based beliefs in understanding why young men, and women, get drawn into this kind of tactic. As noted earlier, Sageman (2004, 2008) has also highlighted the powerful effect of small cliques of young men (mainly). Many scholars have commented on the frequency of themes of humiliation and injustice in interviews conducted with survivor-perpetrators of such attacks, again pointing to the influence of particular globalized ideologies about mistreatment of Muslims around the world in the thinking of these terrorists.

Overall, while the structure, function and scope of terrorist networks remain important in terms of understanding how these networks operate, it is important also to look to the contexts or circumstances in which the members of these networks live and understand how they perceive their surroundings. While there remains controversy within policy and academic circles about whether certain environments 'cause' terrorism (e.g. poverty, social alienation, failed states), it is clear that certain environments can predispose or facilitate some persons to be drawn into jihadist activities.

New Media Technologies, Network Warfare and Cyber-terrorism

There can be little doubt that the internet, above perhaps all other modern communication technologies, has played a significant role in the radicalization and recruitment of young Muslims to jihadist activities. It *deterritorializes* relevant aspects of the recruitment, planning and execution processes by making available information and channels of communication widely, if not globally, to potentially large audiences that are integral to the effectiveness of those processes. Along with television, it provides a means whereby events can be presented to potentially mass audiences in a very short time-frame, contributing to the sense of an immediate threat from terrorism. However, unlike television or other media, the internet provides terrorists with much greater control over the content, and indeed allows them to provide far more background information (Anderson 2003, p. 25). As was seen in the aftermath of the Iraqi occupation in 2004 and 2005, internet-uploaded images of improvised explosive devices blowing up Coalition vehicles and videoed beheadings of Western journalists and aid workers were in some instances played on television to mass audiences, or reported on by television news reports, magnifying the awareness about disturbing terrorist activities and contributing to public fear. James Der Derian has referred to this kind of media-driven tactic as 'network warfare': 'With information as the lifeblood and speed as the killer variable of networks, getting inside the decision making of the opponent became the central strategy of network warfare' (Der Derian 2002, p. 111).

Despite efforts to close down such sites, much of the material placed on pro-terrorist websites can easily resurface on new websites, thus allowing ongoing access to material as well as providing an archive of older materials. Al-Qaeda and other jihadist groups and their affiliates have constructed and run websites of their own that promote and facilitate jihadist activities. Sageman (2008) has observed the role played by internet chatrooms in terms of connecting would-be jihadists and drawing others into processes of recruitment. He argues that as the physical environment for would-be terrorists and terrorists has become tougher in the post-September 11 environment, the internet has offered 'new safe methods of interaction by thousands of terrorist sympathizers' (Sageman 2004, p. 121).

Cyber-terrorism has been defined as 'the use of computer network tools to harm or shut down critical national infrastructures (such as energy, transportation, government operations)' (Weimann 2005, p. 130). Unlike the reasons behind most other misuses of cyber-technologies, the goal of cyber-terrorism is political and social. There is little doubt that this terrorist tactic could potentially have very serious repercussions were it, for example, to cause metropolitan transport systems to malfunction or fail, or corrupt the databases of major banks or government agencies. However, to date there has been little evidence of it happening (Anderson 2003; Weimann 2005). Certainly, jihadist groups so far seem to prefer bombs and beheadings to email viruses, web blockades, or computer hacking, not because they lack the ability or the technology to do these things, but perhaps because their impacts are not always as apparent and, thus, may not provide the critical publicity most terrorists seek. A television camera can record the destruction of a bomb in a busy marketplace, but would struggle to capture a computer virus. While computer nerds and other groups may seek to create havoc or achieve notoriety in the cyber-realm through their illicit activities, their motives tend to be personal and thus distinguishable from those of jihadists. However, many security policy analysts, as well as some academics, are not ready to dismiss this form of networked terrorism. Weimann has commented, 'The challenge is to assess what needs to be done to address the ambiguous but potential threat of cyber-terrorism – but to do so without inflating its real significance and manipulating the fear it inspires' (2005, p. 146).

7.4 Responding to Jihadist Terrorism

As the quote from Beck at the beginning of this chapter reminds us, the identification of certain challenges as presenting global problems has been accompanied by a series of pressures to respond globally to those problems. Thus, there has been a 'global response' to terrorism of an unprecedented kind and degree since the events of September 2001. As jihadist terrorists have disregarded national borders and directed attacks against a variety of targets in Western and other countries, those countries, and the peoples who have been targeted, have a common status through a shared victimization. That shared status forms the basis for common action against the perpetrators. Counter-terrorist measures, traditionally the preserve of national governments, have become issues of transnational and international policy. Ways of preventing, and disrupting, the activities of jihadist terrorists are the subject of international agreements and policies. However, as we shall see below, there are real limits to the degree to which countries can be brought to cooperate in practical ways in response to the terrorism threat. Some definitional differences around the meaning of terrorism, as well as analytical differences about the nature and extent of the threat, underpin some of the difficulties; many more prosaic obstacles lie in the challenges nation-states face in cooperating with each other on transnational and international issues. While it is widely accepted that networked problems such as modern jihadist terrorism require networked responses by law enforcement (e.g. Arquilla & Ronfeldt 2001, p. 15), other government agencies and civil society, it is much harder for nation-states to move quickly and with agility in this direction than it is for small, semi-autonomous terrorist cells to wage a jihadist campaign against their declared enemies. The adaptiveness of modern terrorist groups has been most evident in terms of its adjustments to particular counter-terrorism measures, making those groups harder to trace and tackle for counter-terrorist agencies.

In terms of counter-terrorism responses, the first point to be made is that there is no single response but rather there are many (see Table 7.1). Choices among the array of options will largely reflect differences of resources and perceptions of the nature of the problem among those choosing or required to respond. The sudden, dramatic nature of September 11 clearly had a powerful effect not just upon the millions who watched the events unfold on their television screens, but also upon the political leaders of countries such as the United States and their allies. The images of what was promised by way of counter-terrorist responses were equally dramatic and threatening. The very concept of a 'war on terror' presupposes an understanding of terrorists as a military-type group that requires to be defeated in the way enemy armies typically are beaten, i.e. through destruction and/or surrender. The construction by the US administration of al-Qaeda and its supporters as the 'enemy' certainly fits well with military-type measures. Of course, a key problem in pursuing this analogy is to find an enemy to fight; the elusive nature of modern jihadist terrorists makes them a difficult military target, one which, given their methods of operation, raises the prospects of innocent persons being caught up in broadly conceived counter-terrorist operations. The examples of Abu Ghraib prison and Guantanamo Bay serve as reminders of the 'false positive' problem in dealing with such a diffuse phenomenon – under conditions of great uncertainty regarding who is 'the enemy', it becomes necessary, in order to lock up the 'real terrorists', to lock up a lot more persons, many or most of whom are entirely innocent of involvement in terrorist activities (the 'false positives').

The second point is that counter-terrorist responses will reflect the distinction between 'near' and 'far' enemies. For those located in remote regions of weak or failing states, *international* and *transnational strategies*, often with a military component, have usually had appeal. Destroying al-Qaeda's bases in Afghanistan in late 2001 is a good example. However, different measures are required in so-called 'home-grown' terrorism cases. Destroying the suburb of Beeston, Leeds (where two of the four London bombers had lived), was hardly an option in the aftermath of the 7 July 2005 attacks. Where the problem is seen to have a *local* source, often a 'softer', more socially nuanced approach is required. In the case of attacks in Western countries carried out by citizens of those countries, programmes for the deradicalization of potential jihadists, and generally making greater efforts towards the social inclusion of those living vulnerable, marginal lives, make a lot of sense. As we have seen in recent times in a number of Western countries as well as in a country such as Indonesia, such approaches will still be accompanied by resort to law enforcement measures against those linked to the commission of terrorist acts, resulting in punishment of various kinds (including capital punishment in the Indonesian example).

One can look to the response by major Western countries and international bodies, such as the United Nations Security Council (UNSC), in the aftermath of the September 11, 2001 attacks. The UNSC passed Resolution 1373 on 28 September 2001, giving member states of the United Nations 90 days in which to report upon concrete actions taken to implement the terms of the resolution. The resolution serves as an international interpretation of the events of September 11, in terms of the threat to be addressed, as well as requiring a series of steps to be taken. The theme of cooperation is strong in the terms of this document. It calls 'on States to work together urgently to prevent and

Table 7.1 Responses to Transnational Terrorism

Levels of response/agency responding	Type of response (examples)
International	
Multinational, e.g. United Nations	Political, e.g. peacekeeping
Multinational	Legal, e.g. UN Security Council resolutions, conventions relating to terrorist financing
European Union	Nation-building programmes (pre-EU accession targets)
Transnational	
Bilateral, e.g. US Department of Justice	Technical assistance, e.g. counter-terrorism capacity building, rule of law programmes
Coalition, bilateral	Military measures
Coalition, bilateral	Intelligence sharing, activities by security agencies
Coalition, bilateral	Civil-military relations, e.g. provincial reconstruction teams in Afghanistan
Coalition, bilateral, regional	Development aid and assistance
Bilateral, regional	Law enforcement cooperation, e.g. intelligence, extradition, mutual assistance
National/local	
Government	Law enforcement (prosecutions)
Government	Disruption of networks
Government	Social integration/inclusion programmes
Civil society, e.g. religious groups	Social integration/inclusion programmes

suppress terrorist acts, including through increased cooperation and full implementation of the relevant international conventions relating to terrorism'. The UNSC also established a committee under the resolution to monitor its implementation. The key aim of the resolution was the prevention and suppression of financing of terrorist acts, as well as of other forms of support for such acts. A largely unarticulated, yet dominant assumption behind the tactics of the United Nations, when a new convention is established or a Security Council resolution is passed, is that there are 'rogue' states within the international arena that do not play by common rules, and that need to be socialized into the normative universe of international society. One such rogue state in late 2001 was the country of Afghanistan, whose Taliban government was seen as a legitimate target for its support for and tolerance of the activities of al-Qaeda.

The War on Terror

It is nearly eight years since the **war on terror** was declared by the Bush administration. It has been an enormously expensive exercise. A recent research report to the US Congress (October 2008) put the cumulative cost of the US war on terror operations, since September 2001, at US$864 billion. This estimate was for Departments of Defense, State, USAid and Veterans Affairs costs (Belasco 2008). Evaluating its effectiveness is difficult and inevitably controversial. One can point to the absence of repeat events like the September 11 attacks on US soil as evidence of successful prevention efforts by the FBI and other security agencies. On the other hand, it is possible to look at the outbreak of jihadist (including suicide) terrorism in Iraq in 2004 and 2005, and see the Coalition occupation as a provocation to further terrorist recruitment and targeting of Coalition and other targets inside Iraq. One of the obvious difficulties is the limits of the war metaphor in relation to terrorism. Terrorism is a means, rather than an end, in the hands of irregular agents of violence, so that achieving a clear victory over such elements by conventional military means is probably impossible. The lack of clarity of objectives, despite the huge investment of resources in it, has resulted in some pretty harsh criticism. It has been described by Jonathan Raban as a 'cripplingly expensive, meagerly productive effort to locate, catch and kill bad guys around the globe' (Raban 2005, p. 25). Efforts to combine local-level civilian with military programmes more recently in countries such as Iraq and Afghanistan point to recognition within Coalition ranks that a broader, in some ways softer, approach is needed if the conditions that encourage terrorism are to be ameliorated.

More generally, nation building and state building agendas have been advanced as ways of addressing terrorism in so-called 'failed' and 'fragile' states. The incorporation of development considerations into security agendas (the 'securitization of development') reflects in part the recognition by many Western countries and commentators that military measures are not sufficient to the challenge. Mark Duffield has written that the 'new found concern over fragile states' indicates that the 'war' is primarily not a military issue, but rather an 'indefinite and globalized counter insurgency campaign that utilizes the civilian petty sovereignty of aid agencies to engage with questions of poverty and political instability' (Duffield 2007, p. 127).

Law Enforcement Measures

The passage of domestic laws dealing with terrorist activity has been a primary response to transnational terrorism. While introducing new laws can be seen as a way whereby politicians can demonstrate they are taking action on a particular problem, it should be reiterated that, as part of the globalized response to September 11, 2001, there was significant pressure from the international level, on this occasion the United Nations, to bring about more comprehensive and harmonized criminal laws dealing with terrorism and related offences. While the criminal law of countries affected has typically contained offences that cover most of what terrorists do that is harmful (murder, destruction of property, intimidation, etc.), the repertoire of criminal offences has been expanded in most Western countries in the post-September 11 response. While new substantive offences of terrorism have sometimes been introduced that effectively name differently criminal acts that are already covered by the criminal law, new offences have also been created that expand the scope of the criminal law and, in the eyes of some critics, undermine fundamental principles of criminal law. The criminalization of membership of a terrorist organization, for instance, punishes *status* rather than *conduct*, something which Western criminal law has been reluctant to do, yet is seen by many counter-terrorism officials as necessary in the battle against terrorism. One of the key questions to be asked in this context is what kinds of laws are needed to deal with the problem effectively. While assertions about their necessity, or, oppositely, their redundancy and even sinister nature, are common, there is a need for a more systematic look at the threat and the appropriateness of the measures proposed (Goldsmith 2007, 2008).

Similar issues also arise regarding changes to procedural laws affecting search, seizure, arrest of suspects, and more broadly, the investigation of alleged terrorism activities. In the recent 'war on terror,' preventive detention and control orders have been seriously debated and, in some jurisdictions, introduced. Exceptional powers to fight terrorism have a long history in this regard (the abolition of jury trials in Northern Ireland in the 1970s being just one example). Inevitably, concerns arise concerning the abuse of these unusual powers, especially as they can easily impact upon innocent persons and deprive innocent and guilty persons alike of their usual legal rights when facing investigation and charges. However, the level of public fear on the issue of terrorism has seemingly contributed to a tendency within criminal law and law enforcement circles towards a more preventive approach to terrorism and serious crime. The risks and harms from such activity occurring are seen as sufficiently high to place a *premium on prevention*. The nub of the challenge lies in being able to predict, and thus prevent, terrorist activities. This is not easily done, with the result that over-prediction is inevitable if there is to be a preventive effect. However, this approach disregards the rights of those wrongly suspected of being potential terrorists, and can cause alienation and hostility towards the government and law enforcement officials. As these measures particularly affect a country's own citizens, there is a real risk of counterproductive outcomes.

Case Study 7.1 – United Kingdom's New Strategy (Compared to the EU's Strategy)

In March 2009, the United Kingdom government released a new strategy document for countering international terrorism. Entitled *Pursue Prevent Protect Prepare*, the report cites the ongoing threat to domestic and international security from al-Qaeda, its affiliates and imitators. The strategy focuses on pursuit (stopping terrorist attacks), prevention (stopping people from becoming terrorists or supporting terrorists), protection (strengthening protections against terrorist attacks) and preparation (mitigating the impacts of attacks). In a speech foreshadowing the release of the strategy document, Prime Minister Gordon Brown stated that the UK response must be international, national and local in character, and that investment in the national counter-terrorist framework was to rise from £1 billion to £3.5 billion in 2011 (Brown 2009). PM Brown noted that 'Britain is at the forefront of international cooperation – from helping Pakistan investigate the murder of Benazir Bhutto to the work of our armed forces in Afghanistan and, in the longer term, our aid programme and our support for conflict prevention and stabilisation' (Brown 2009).

The new UK strategy in many respects resembles the EU's Counter-terrorism Strategy which came two years earlier. The EU strategy also commits to: prevention, protection, pursuit and response. A greater willingness to share information among law enforcement and security agencies has been identified as important. The strategy also stresses the need for greater international cooperation outside the EU.

Police in many Western countries have learned some hard lessons in this regard. Saturation-type policing and resort to particular racially based profiles have not proven particularly effective, and indeed arguably have proven counterproductive as the de Menezes shooting in London has shown (see Case Study 7.2).

Case Study 7.2 – The de Menezes Case

The shooting by police of Jean Charles de Menezes, a young Brazilian electrician, in Stockwell subway station, South London, on 22 July 2005, in the aftermath of the London bombing attacks two weeks earlier, has had many ramifications. These are instructive in terms of the challenges faced by governments in dealing with terrorist threats and the associated public fear of such attacks. Identified wrongly as a terrorist suspect, the swiftness and lethality of the police response raise some fundamental questions about how governments and their agents can respond adequately and appropriately to public concern about further terrorist attacks.

The fact that there had been an unprecedented terrorist attack in London shortly before was inevitably in the minds of those police officers working to prevent further attacks. As can occur in the case of major unsolved crimes, there is often significant public pressure felt by governments and law enforcement officials to take quick and decisive action so as to reduce the risk of future harm. However, 'getting it wrong' impacts not just on the innocent person targeted but also upon the credibility of the agency directly involved – in this case, the London Metropolitan Police. More broadly, it has been suggested, 'the security practices adopted by Britain in the context of the war on terror are serving to undermine societal trust and exacerbate fear and tension within society' (O'Driscoll 2008, p. 359). It seems clear that such events do undermine confidence in the police, especially among members of minority groups.

More recently, there have been efforts to engage particular ethnic and religious communities residing within Western countries where there has been an association between those communities and certain radicalization activities linked to recruitment and support for jihadist-type activities. Efforts at social inclusion and integration have increased in some areas, as well as the trialling of specific anti-radicalization measures (see for example, Lambert 2008).

7.5 Conclusion

The study of modern jihadist terrorism and responses by governments and other agencies to the threats associated with it provides a useful introduction to the phenomenon of globalization, and to the nature of transnational threats. The kind of terrorism examined in this chapter can be distinguished from other kinds of modern terrorism (such as seen recently with the splinter IRA groups in Northern Ireland, or ETA in Spain) by reason of its profession of religious justification and its focus on global, rather than local, issues. Its decentralized nature through networks and channels for imitation (websites, television, email, etc.) also serves to differentiate it from earlier forms of terrorism which relied more on hierarchical structures, localized issues and personal knowledge of other participants.

The other side of globalization in this regard is the way in which countries, agencies and the international community respond to this challenge. More than ever, the talk of the importance of international cooperation is heard, and more effort and resources are going into structures, mechanisms and tools that can operate transnationally against jihadist groups. New domestic laws harmonizing with the laws of other countries, new joint task forces linking up agencies within countries and across national borders, and greater emphasis upon building the capacity of 'fragile' or 'weak' states, linked as havens or facilitators of terrorist activities, provide evidence of this growing international cooperation in practice.

Despite various inroads into the problem (arrests, prosecutions, convictions, military actions, etc.) jihadist terrorism is not about to disappear. It will continue to evolve over time, partly in response to how it is policed and tackled in other ways by governments and government agencies. How long the public is willing to accept some of the new counter-terrorist strategies, at home as well as abroad, is an open question. Military casualties in zones such as Afghanistan undoubtedly impact upon public acceptance of military strategies in countries such as the United Kingdom, Canada and Australia, whose military personnel are involved in counter-terrorism activities. Similarly, the wrongful arrest, charging, or even shooting of terrorism suspects in one's own country can also reflect badly on security agencies and government policies. Governments will need to negotiate their strategies carefully in this regard, at home and abroad, if some of their measures are not to exacerbate existing difficulties or cause new problems.

Questions: Revise and Reflect

1. How do modern jihadist terrorists differ in their goals and methods from other kinds of terrorists?

2. What role has technology played in the evolution of this kind of terrorism?

3. How might the jihadist terrorist phenomenon be explained or understood?

4. How significant is public fear of future attacks in terms of explaining the responses provided by Western governments to September 11 and other terrorist events since that time?

5. Which counter-terrorist methods have been most prominent since 2001? Are there risks associated with these methods, and if so, what are they?

Further Reading

Stern, J & Berger, JM 2015, *ISIS: The state of terror*, HarperCollins, New York.
Storm, M 2014, *Agent Storm: My life inside Al Qaeda*, Penguin Viking, London.

Videos to Watch

Munich (2006) – film directed by Steven Spielberg. Looks at the events around the attack on Israeli Olympic athletes in Munich in 1972.

Body of Lies (2008) – film directed by Ridley Scott.

United 93 (2006) – film directed by Paul Greengrass. An enactment of the events on United flight 93 on September 11, 2001.

24 – television series that deals with fictitious events of the Los Angeles Counter-Terrorism Unit.

Sleeper Cell – television series that looks at terrorist cells operating within the United States.

Spooks – UK counter-terrorism TV series involving the UK security intelligence agency, MI5.

Websites to Visit

The European Police Office (European Law Enforcement Organization) publishes a Report on Terrorism (EU Terrorism Situation and Trend Report) called TE-SAT: www.europol.europa.eu/

This website contains news from the Office for Security and Counter Terrorism in the UK: security.homeoffice.gov.uk/

Website of the UN Action to Counter Terrorism: www.un.org/terrorism/

8

Crimes against the Environment

This chapter will look at

- Environmental harm and its definition through a critical-human rights lens.
- New environmental risks.
- The geopolitics dimension of environmental issues.
- The central role of the nation-state in the push for transnational cooperation.

Keywords

Green criminology   Neoliberalism   Environmental harm

8.1 Introduction

The topics broadly discussed until now have been the subject of international conventions of clear-cut criminal justice, or the subject of clear international advocacy for defining the problem according to criminal justice standards, whereby the culprits are often identified as evil others (traffickers, smugglers, terrorists, members of organized criminal gangs). In this chapter and Chapter 9 on **state crime**, we enter into areas where the crime itself is not always defined according to international conventions with legal powers, and at times not even included in national laws.

In recent years, discussions around environmental concerns have increased and developed at both national and international levels. Environmental issues, perhaps, offer the best example of a transnational issue affecting human beings in different regional areas and to differing degrees. For instance, the right to access clean air and water, or the effects of deforestation, can be seen as 'local' problems as well as 'open' problems, with consequences and repercussions involving human beings globally, and extending beyond our lifetime, to affect and implicate future generations.

This chapter embraces the view that environmental issues can be harmful, even if they are not always considered, in a statutory sense, as a 'crime'. From a critical viewpoint, crime can be defined not only in strict legal terms but also in consideration of the harm caused to others and/or damage to the environment (**social harm** definition). Therefore, the proposed view is that environmental harm is a form of transnational crime. As such, it provides an opportunity to discuss the local, national and international responsibilities of individuals, companies and states in the global economy.

8.2 Towards a Definition of Transnational Environmental Crimes: Legal-procedural and Criminological Approaches

A typological approach of determining 'environmental crimes' and environmental rights is challenging; producing a list of environmental 'crimes' can be difficult, due to the nature of and disciplinary context in which these activities are classified. A legal-procedural analysis of whether environmental issues are 'crimes' is still an evolving matter and highly debated (Brack 2002; Hall 2014; Williams 1996a). This is particularly relevant when placed in an international context, in which laws may vary from country to country, determining whether or not they lie within a criminal law framework.

Obviously, there are areas that are more contained and better defined as environmental criminal activities: for instance, the involvement of organized crime in the illegal movement of hazardous waste (D'Amato et al. 2015; Massari & Monzini 2004); the removing, killing and trading of endangered species of flora and fauna (Brack 2002); or the black market trade in illicit antiquities (Mackenzie 2011). These areas have attracted some relevant attention and regulation, both at a national and international level (Brack 2002). In these areas, there is a more established awareness which helps to clarify some of the legal-procedural definitions, at both a national or regional level, in order to establish or elucidate criminal liability. However, to approach environmental harm from a strictly legal-procedural viewpoint raises problematic issues, as pointed out by some criminologists (see for instance the work of White 2008, 2011).

The primary reason for such criticisms is that the legal-procedural approach is limited, as most environmental issues cannot be framed as 'crimes'. For instance, it is now more evident that deforestation and stratospheric ozone depletion constitute problematic areas, but it is difficult to frame these problems as crimes in traditional terms (that is, as a crime described by criminal law in a given territory). In fact, traditional criminal law cannot help us in understanding this subject at this point in time.

A second reason for criticizing a strict legal-procedural interpretation of environmental crimes is because the *right to use* (for instance to use clean air or water) can also have a more idiomorphic interpretation. This can be seen by approaching the area in two different ways:

1. Using one approach, we can say that the damage and impact of environmental activities may not affect contemporary society or existing individuals, but may produce consequences for future generations, who have or will have suffered from a deteriorating environment. In a strict legal approach, this is an incalculable problem, because it relates to somebody who does not exist now but potentially in the future. Whereas this prediction of the future is against legal principles, the harmful effects for future generations are criminologically framed, understood and discussed as real harm.

2. Using another – and less speculative – approach, this is an area that can be broadly defined as anthropocentric (human-centred) environmental law – which is legal-procedural law directly related to specific physical human needs or rights. However, the analysis of environmental impact and damage with an anthropocentric perspective is not the only possible lens through which we look at these matters. While there may be damaging effects upon us as human beings, we can also incorporate a wider vision of the whole of the ecological system, including flora and fauna (Beirne & South 2007). Therefore, an anthropocentric interpretation of what environmental 'crime' is in respect to specific human beings may also be at a transitional point. The ecocentric approach may be a way of interpreting a harm that can affect several people, or indeed be dangerous for several generations, as well as having a permanent impact on the planet's ecosystem.

These points are explained further in the following sections.

Criminological Approach and Transnational Impact

A strict legal-procedural analysis is very limiting and fails to emphasize the direct and indirect impact of environmental activities. A criminological approach would allow us to be more multidisciplinary and embrace more areas in an attempt to understand what is happening in our global society. Nevertheless, the concept of 'environmental crime' within criminological studies is still evolving, as the area under discussion is relatively new. Different authors have explored different problematic areas around the limits of defining ecological harm as a 'crime'. For instance, from a criminological point of view, the debate around these themes has been initially framed in terms of environmental hazards (Lynch 1990), rather than 'crimes'. The central argument is that certain hazards, those hazards created by humans, are 'a subset of crime' (Lynch 1990). This means that environmental hazards can be linked to some human responsibility, rather than other natural consequences of these processes; therefore, we have a degree of direct involvement in the creation of the problem as well as the solution, leading to an essential re-evaluation of the distribution of human, financial and technological resources. More recently, this interpretation has moved to more cogent terms, as this approach may limit 'crimes' to a short chain of cause and effect, or one action being directly linked to the creation of a particular hazard.

This does not cover the larger changes exacerbated by human intervention, but not attributable to humans in the first instance (e.g. climate change). It is to be noted, in this more recent context, that the word 'environment' is now more inclusive and over-reaching. It incorporates a range of risk issues (Macnaghten 2006), from nuclear radiation to climate change, from the pollution of fresh water to genetically modified food, and from the production and dumping of toxic waste to trafficking in engendered species.

Another problem highlighted around the loose concept of environmental 'crime' is that 'crime' is usually defined by the state (see Chapter 9). Therefore, the definition of what an environmental crime is, its regulation and punishment, is decided by the national government. So while the involvement of organized crime in dumping waste is tackled as an 'environmental crime' almost unilaterally by the nation-states, there are other forms of environmental crimes that have produced harms, but are yet to be *officially* classified as 'crimes' because it does not serve a purpose for the state. It is argued that some practices may be permitted by law, but may cause damage to the environment, and are maintained and perpetuated because of their intrinsic legal value; legality is decided by the state, with its interests, networks and policy objectives in mind (Passas 2005).

Some developing countries may not have the institutions or the means to create, develop or defend further domestic legal definitions to protect the environment, and are subjected to severe pressure to respond to the requests, needs and rules of other, more powerful nation-states. In these cases, the 'need' to improve the environment and living conditions is established somewhere else, and external plans are developed and imposed ruthlessly on developing countries, creating a new layer of environmental and social problems (see Chapter 2).

In this context, it should be duly noted that the framing of environmental criminogenic activities by the 'state' is in an evolving process, whereby the 'state' as rule-generator can be understood in broader terms. Through the decentralization of state authority (see Chapter 2), other agencies, for instance international bodies (such as the World Bank) or non-state actors (multinational companies), can suggest or impose a regulatory framework on more fragile or weaker nation-states. This framework can produce negative – even criminogenic – impacts on the local environment and population, even if not intended (see the 'Spotlight' below).

Spotlight – World Bank: Forced Resettlement of People

Caufield (1996, pp. 262–263) highlights that the World Bank, by its admission in the 1994 *World Development Report: Infrastructure for development*, approved nearly 200 projects (building dams, roads, pipelines, canals, plantations and urban renewal) with the open intent of improving the socio-environmental conditions of weaker nation-states. These projects, however, resulted in the resettlement of around 2.5 million people.

This practice has been heavily criticized as 'the worst thing you can do to a people, next to killing them' (Scudder, quoted in Caufield 1996, p. 262). Even the World Bank had recognized earlier on, in 1986, that forced resettlement is a disastrous system with negative consequences. In light of this, it had promised to avoid, minimize, or compensate the displaced people, and restore their living and earning standards. However, later reviews have shown that the World Bank 'violated its own standards'.

Caufield claims that only half of the projects had a resettlement plan, with the other half basing their resettlement plans on estimates rather than in-depth studies.

For these reasons, the interference over 'ecological' national sovereignty has been a further matter explored recently. Ecological sovereignty is invoked when some powerful countries have had (and used) the power to manipulate the sovereignty of less powerful states' internal environmental policy. This ecological principle has been stated in the 1972 United Nations Environmental Programme (UNEP) Stockholm Declaration, principle 21, and reconfirmed in the 1992 UNEP Rio Declaration, principle 2. These two principles require nation-states to manage their ecological sovereign powers in a way that will not damage the environments of other states. They are, in theory, trying to address the need to reformulate transboundary responsibility – responsibility that is left to a vague self-compliance system. These principles, in effect, have become more *customary international law* (Elliott 2004), which is based on rules of law centred in the belief that some conducts of nation-states are, or should be, accepted practice.

Another problem with the definition of environmental crimes is about how inclusive it is required to be. In recent years, there has been a tendency to frame it more in terms of 'developing awareness' and 'taking responsibility', rather than criminal or criminogenic activities, favouring a regulatory approach. Mostly, this is due to the focus on (past, present and future) environmental catastrophes, like radiation and nuclear power issues or the effects of global warming. Environmental damage and impact on human beings, as well as ecosystems, are embedded in our new perception of being surrounded by uncertainties: we can be the victims of new forms of risk (see Chapter 3). The regulatory approach has been criticized by many criminologists, as it leaves industry to self-monitor progress, while it is industry which in many cases is causing or contributing to natural disasters.

8.3 From Micro to Macro Responsibility

The fragmented approach to environmental harms certainly does not facilitate the emergence of a coherent and unified discussion and analysis of their criminal aspects, with unclear consequences in the regulatory area. As a result of this, the struggle to apply a wider approach to environmental crimes is far from being achieved, especially due to the transnationality of the harm and the uncertainty over responsibility. Attempts towards cooperation and supranational agreements are hampered by territoriality and priority factors determined by key nation-states and powerful corporations.

To analyse this further, environmental harms can be broadly grouped into two areas according to a micro–macro approach linked to whether a legal definition of crime exists. The more we are removed from a micro analysis of environmental harm the less we can make use of criminal law. The looser the casual chain is, the less we can refer to environmental issues as 'crime'. In these cases, we see the predominant input and presence of corporations, national and international agencies. Paradoxically, in the macro analysis we can identify examples of 'legally' perpetrated crimes (Mackenzie and Green 2008; Passas 2005).

If we take this in stages, in the first group there are those activities defined and accepted as environmental crimes, generally committed by identifiable *deviant others*, for example individuals, organized criminal groups or fragile or enemy nation-states. This makes use of the traditional interpretation of criminal conduct and individual responsibility. In the second group, the environmental harm is construed or perceived as occurring without a causal chain of events linkable to an individual. In this case, the responsibility is either attributable to no one or, in a latest development pushed for by UNEP, is – or should be at least – collectively shared.

However, the case of the Dancing Shiva (Case Study 8.1) attests to the complexity of the matter; where does individual responsibility on the illegal trade in antiquities end and where does the national government's responsibility for the protection of cultural artefacts begin?

Case Study 8.1 – Return of the Dancing Shiva

In 2008, the National Gallery of Australia purchased a 900-year-old bronze statue for AU$5 million from New York art dealer Subhash Kapoor (ABC News 2015). The statue of Shiva, as Nataraja, Lord of the Dance, was one of 21 items the gallery purchased from Kapoor over several years. In total it spent AU$11 million on these transactions (Kleinman & Dhillon 2014). It was not alone. The Art Gallery of New South Wales, as well as many museums around the world, such as the Metropolitan Museum, New York, and the Museum of Fine Arts in Boston, also purchased items from Kapoor (Kleinman & Dhillon 2014).

Subhash Kapoor was an established and well-known figure on the international art scene. His gallery, 'Art of the Past', with its prestigious Manhattan address, opened in 1974 and he was familiar on the New York social scene as a connoisseur of Indian art (Kleinman & Dhillon 2014). It is alleged, however, that he was also the mastermind behind an art smuggling empire, which dealt in stolen and fake artefacts, and sold them through his gallery, alongside legitimate pieces of art (Kleinman & Dhillon 2014; Pohlman 2014). Ninety million dollars' worth of stolen antiquities were found in his New York warehouse.

US authorities described Kapoor as one of the most prolific art smugglers in the world, who had managed to create a 'black-market Sotheby's' (Kleinman & Dhillon 2014; March 2014). His operation allegedly raided archaeological sites in India, Pakistan and Cambodia (Pohlman 2014). Some treasures were looted during excavation, before they were even catalogued; others came from remote sites and unguarded temples (Kleinman & Dhillon 2014; Pohlman 2014). Often their removal was not noticed until much later, if at all. Multiple replicas were made to disguise the original during transportation and false documents and histories were created to fool customs and museum officials (Kleinman & Dhillon 2014). Kapoor is currently awaiting trial in Chennai, charged with looting millions of dollars' worth of cultural artefacts from temples in the southern Indian state of Tamil Nadu (March 2014). Indian authorities refuse to put an exact figure on the treasures which they maintain are 'priceless' (Pohlman 2014).

The illegality of this trade goes far beyond mere theft, for it also represents the loss of cultural artefacts (Lenzner 1994). This issue has come to greater prominence in the last 50 years, as former colonies begin to recover their cultural identities and assert their rights to their historic heritage (Franzen 2013). Proving cultural ownership, however, can be tricky. The Archaeological Institute of America, a non-profit group which represents American archaeologists, estimates that 80–90% of artefacts on the market have no documented provenance (Franzen 2013). This, despite the introduction of the UNESCO Convention on the Means of Prohibiting the Illicit Import, Export and Transfer of Ownership of Cultural Property in 1970, to which 123 countries are signatories (UNESCO 2014).

Australia ratified the convention with legislation of its own in 1986 (Protection of Movable Cultural Heritage Act) and Australian government guidelines on purchasing antiquities place responsibility on purchasers to ensure that the objects they intend to buy have been legally acquired and exported (Pryor 2015). The expectation is that museums and art galleries will exercise all due diligence in establishing the provenance of items before purchase (Reed 2012). In the case of the Dancing Shiva, the gallery was falsely assured the statue had been out of India since 1971, the year before India banned the export of antiquities (ABC 2014). Attorney General George Brandis described the decision as 'incautious' (ABC 2014).

The National Gallery agreed to return the statue to India in 2014 without expectation of financial compensation (Boland 2015). It also announced it would take steps to review the provenance and legal status of other recently acquired items in its collection: 72 items are currently being investigated. A refund has since been negotiated for a 2,000-year-old stone 'Seated Buddha' statue, purchased in 2007 from a different dealer, after doubts were raised about the authenticity of its provenance (Boland 2015; Pryor 2015). The gallery has placed a temporary moratorium on purchasing further Asian antiquities (Pryor 2015).

Individual Responsibility

The most accomplished area of environmental crimes is the one that identifies individual responsibility. In this case, the individual identifiable as the perpetrator is dealt with through the traditional criminal justice system; if the case is transnational, cooperation by the police and at prosecutorial level is sought. Transnational cooperation is possible because there is a shared willingness to define the wrongdoing as illegal. This can lead to a shared legal definition for which civil or criminal sanctions apply, such as those cases in the EU (see 'Spotlight').

Spotlight – The EU and Environmental Criminal Laws

The movement towards cooperation and possible harmonization of national environmental criminal laws and penalties at EU level has been impressive. The push for common minimum EU-wide standards on criminalization of serious breaches of EU environmental legislation (for instance, maritime pollution) found also the contribution of the European Court of Justice (Case C-176/03 *Commission* v. *Council* [2005] and Case C-440/05 *Commission* v. *Council* [2007]).

The EU is committed to set a unique example of supranational collaboration and legally binding provisions in this area, although this is more the beginning of a process, crystallized in the 2008 Directive 2008/99/EC on the protection of the environment through the criminal law.

A good example is the protection of biodiversity and the legislation against the trade of endangered species. The regulations in this area can be found in different nation-states and at international level. From time to time, we may have seen images of smuggled snakes or parrots hidden in plastic bottles or other creative mechanisms to avoid detection at the border. Countries such as Australia enforce a strict quarantine policy with severe sanctions for the individual (on the spot fine and imprisonment) in such cases.

Another example of individual responsibility we may witness in our everyday life is the (light) form of punishment meted out to those who do not separate their waste for recycling purposes. In these cases, the regulation is seen as having educational purposes, to teach us how to protect the environment.

The regulatory regime becomes stricter when organized criminal groups are recognized as the deviant others. Transnational environmental crime perpetrated by organized criminal enterprises has generated a lot of attention over the last decade, with the inclusion of organized wildlife smuggling and timber trafficking on the list of criminal activities recognized by the UN Congress on Crime

Prevention and Criminal Justice in 2007 (see Chapter 1 for the original 1995 list). As Elliott (2012, p. 88) points out, criminal groups engaging in environmental crimes are estimated to earn 'from $31 billion to $40 billion a year' in profits, rendering the area appealing and a growth area.

By way of example, the narrative around the transnational toxic waste trade, and the dumping of waste or hazards into waters or land, would suggest a tough law enforcement approach. Organized criminal groups are involved in the 'garbage trade' because it has proven to be a lucrative business. This includes urban waste, which comes with legal public contracts and high demand for the service. Southern Italian cities are often discussed as a case study on this matter (see D'Amato et al. 2015 and the reference to the 'Land of Fire' in the book and movie titled *Gomorra*); however this is an issue in common with other cities as well. In 2006, the Interpol Pollution Crime Working Group estimated that the laundering of waste between Canada and the United States generated CAD$2.48 million a year (Interpol 2006). Illegal dumping of toxic, industrial waste and e-waste trade (referring to discarded electronic products) is also a matter of concern. In 2013, the Interpol Pollution Crime Working Group highlighted their continuing efforts in mapping out the illegal export of e-waste to developing countries, which focuses on targeting legislative and law enforcement loopholes (Interpol 2013).

Elliott (2012) explains that organized criminal groups are open to new forms of environmental exploitation to expand profits and combine different illicit activities (parallel trafficking) to pursue financial interests. The case of the illicit trade in cultural artefacts, especially in conflict situations, is an emergent but symbolic example of market adaptability. It also lends itself as a good case study to see the expansion of deviant others to terrorism. The involvement of the Islamic State in the looting of antiquities for the purpose of generating profit has been the subject of a recent UN resolution on 'Saving the cultural heritage of Iraq' (2015). The aim is to avoid or minimize the impact of **cultural cleansing**, a strategy used to erase the heritage of civilizations.

Linked to the above point, politically weak or enemy states are 'named and shamed' by other nation-states or the international community as acting against a green culture. The explosion of the nuclear reactor in Chernobyl, in 1984, was not only one of the worse environmental disasters in history, but also one event that was used to blame the lack of rigour and protection of human life and the environment practised by the Soviet Union, and its aggressively managed nuclear agenda. The classic scenario of the national or international government protecting human beings is reiterated, and the search for deviant others – people, organized criminal groups, or disengaged and non-collaborative states – is perpetuated.

Corporations and Nation-states

There are intergovernmental agreements which play an important role in the area of environmental protection, such as the 1973 Convention on International Trade and Endangered Species and Wild Fauna and Flora, the 1887 Protocol on Substances that Deplete the Ozone Layer, and the 1989 Convention on the Control of Transboundary Movement of Hazardous Waste and their Disposal.

However, intergovernmental agreements in environmental matters do not work as well as some would hope. This is because of the artificial disaggregation between the deviant others (individuals and organized criminal networks) and the legitimate society (corporations, national and international governmental agencies). A wide spectrum of activities that negatively affect the environment have minimal or hidden causal-chains that link them to perpetrators. This means that some activities cannot be easily linked to a one specific group of people or a nation-state, mostly because of the aforementioned legal-procedural limits.

The role of corporations has been pinpointed in those situations whereby forms of direct or indirect responsibility for damage to the environment or harm to individuals have been identified as either the negligent or intentional outcome of a company's actions or inaction. Environmental harm can also be a by-product of the company as it achieves its targets. But the causal-chain of events is difficult to prove in court. This could be because the actual polluter is a firm based in one country, but with satellite companies in other countries. Choosing to have a satellite company in another country can serve a variety of purposes. For instance, the labour costs may be cheap, or the chosen country may have a less regulated or developed and sophisticated legal environment. These foreign companies can exploit such 'weaknesses' without dealing with the consequences. Thus a company's responsibility for misconduct or wrongdoing can be easily misplaced in a series of forum shopping or diversion activities (see for instance the case of Bhopal in India). As Martin (2003, p. 379) indicates, these projects 'contribute to the creation of "pollution havens" – areas where companies can relocate to, in order to take advantage of less stringent environmental regulations'. These investments are legitimate, and are supported, openly or not, by local and/or foreign governments or international bodies, such as the IMF and the World Bank, through sponsoring or protecting the activity of the company. Globalized trade regulations and free market politics are other reasons why companies have activities in selected third world or semi-industrialized countries. Bisschop (2015) refers to the role of corporations as facilitators of green crimes, highlighting again the criminogenic aspect; this point is echoed by Elliott (2012), who mentions as facilitators, but also as organizers and beneficiaries, members of the government and law enforcement agencies.

Timber logging and trafficking is a useful case study to appreciate the complexities of these situations. The process of deforestation is a demand-driven issue where corporate profits are a compromise between cheap harvesting and management of specific types of wood in the country of origin for a quick turnover of final product at the destination country (Tacconi 2007). This includes a range of illegal activities of which the forestry industry often claims to have no knowledge and which are often framed as an organized criminal issue (Banks et al. 2008). It also requires governmental intervention for harvesting regulation and other forest activities, which in essence have visible consequences (a log is not a matchstick!). Timber logging is a complex activity in which many parties are involved, despite the fact that the area has been the subject of some international regulation and monitoring.

The case of timber logging is also closely associated to other aspects of concern: depletion of forest and damage to biological diversity, violation of indigenous peoples' rights, increased poverty and a lack of opportunities for local people due to the loss of resources and impact on regional conflicts in the fight for resources (Tacconi 2007). The environment is not seen anymore as an isolated issue, but interconnected with other social issues, as well as justice issues. It is now made more explicit in recent discourses, at all levels, that there is a link between problems of the environment, the global context of environmental inequalities and geopolitics. Therefore, environmental issues, global economics and effects on human rights and social justice are all connected.

It is not only the damage to the environment and environmental consequences of economic activities that are at the core, but also the direct and lateral effect on the lives of human beings among the local population, especially those populations already living in disadvantageous conditions. Even if broadly speaking, victims of environmental harm cut across certain status and social conditions (Williams 1996b), there is a concentration of detrimental impact in certain geographical areas. Zarsky (2002, p. 1) argues that 'the allocation of environmental resources, like political and economic resources, is typically skewed towards the rich and powerful'. The rights of economically weaker people or countries to gain access to political discourse, or any viable vehicle for political recognition, have been unprotected, and as a result these groups are often the least able to press for compensation or for meaningful policy changes. In many regional areas, an unequal distribution of costs and benefits has created increased poverty and vulnerability, or the over-exploitation of natural resources without a long-term plan, such as acute deforestation.

The impact of environmental harm goes beyond human beings: the flora and fauna are also defenceless victims. Those harms against non-human species are sometimes referred to as **speciesism**, which is based on a hegemonic view of animals' inferiority, which renders them exploitable. This includes experimenting on animals for human benefit or any other form of mistreatment of non-human species (see Nurse 2013; Wyatt 2013). The fisheries depletion is an interesting example to consider. Overfishing is causing the depletion of global fish stocks, habitat pollution and destruction, as well as human-introduced invasive species, which have been highlighted as added causes to the depletion. There are other points to consider: the huge improvement in fishing technologies and the capacity to stay at sea for longer time periods than in the past, to mention only a few.

The negative impact and consequences of these activities, therefore, go beyond human beings, yet are mainly human-made. **Ecocide** or **geocide**, understood as the systemic destruction of the ecosystem, refers to the unprecedented anthropogenic impact on the earth. It is also referred to as the 'missing fifth Crimes against Peace' in the Rome Statute, which established the ICC (see Chapter 1). This means that ecocide would have been included with genocide, crimes against humanity, war crimes and crimes of aggression (Gauger et al. 2012). It is usually considered a by-product of war or conflict situations where the environment is destroyed, which causes long-term crisis, due to insecurity and mobility. However, Agnew (2013) underlines how the ordinary acts of everyday life, dictated by consumerism and a culture of disposal, have a profound effect on the environment. These acts of everyday ecocide are promoted by marketing companies and the media. Further, in reference to ecocide, Banks et al. (2008) focus on the need to cap the numbers of companies around the globe (from 3,000 to 300) to reduce environmental foot-printing on the earth.

Linked to ecocide is the case of natural disasters, such as earthquakes and flooding. These are considered environmental harms when their causes or effects are shaped by humans. Examples are building in an area known to be prone to natural disasters or building against regulations specifically put in place for an emergency, such as a volcanic eruption (consider the narrative of the disaster-to-be when Vesuvius erupts in southern Italy; Solana et al. 2008). Here, there is the possibility of proving a causal-chain: how a disaster could be avoided or limited by implementing more rigorous planning. South (2014) also mentions the impact a natural disaster may have on primary resources, for example food and clean water, which in turn creates a new level of insecurity and mobility. Klein (2007) considers how a crisis following a natural disaster is exploited by national and international governmental institutions, together with corporations, who push for unpopular policies when people are most vulnerable and unable to display any significant form of resistance.

The uncertainties and damage created by these activities are widely discussed, and yet in this area the traditional role of criminal justice agencies has had a small or non-existent role (see however the use of the restorative justice process in Case Study 8.2).

Case Study 8.2 – Restorative Justice and Environmental Crimes

An innovative way to respond to environmental crime has been the use of key principles of restorative justice. Brian J Preston, chief judge of the Land and Environment Court of New South Wales (Australia), refers to the central role of the victim in the environmental restorative justice process. He identifies specific individuals and classes of people as victims (Preston 2011). His reflections are based on an Australian court case, chaired by him, on environmental offences caused by a mining company on Aboriginal land, which also caused the destruction of Aboriginal artefacts (*Garrett* v. *Williams* 2007).

The judge offered the prosecution and defence lawyers the chance to hold a restorative justice conference before the sentencing stage, which included Aboriginal people: this opportunity had never been given before (McDonald 2008). The owner of the mining company offered an apology, which was accepted by the representative of the Aboriginal community, with the owner commenting: 'I have [also] realised how both Aboriginal objects and the Aboriginal place are more important to Aboriginal people than I previously appreciated. I am seriously remorseful about what has occurred' (McDonald 2008, p. 44).

An attempt to redress the lack of individual responsibility is by linking those environmental harms to those who are supposed to act and protect, for example national or international governmental bodies: this would create a new layer of responsibility. This approach is described by several authors (Elliott 2004; Simon 2000) as transnational in scope. South (2014) asks whether the environment can be afforded rights. The purpose of this question is to aim for the protection of all. Can a discipline of earth jurisprudence be conceived in a manner that offers rights to other components, such as biological and geological?

It is undeniable that this area has attracted much political attention, and 'going green' is deemed a way of gaining consensus and popularity. However, there are areas where nation-states, NGOs and the international community raise the profile of important issues but responsibility and remedies do not follow as promptly as needed. A typical example of this is the combination of population growth, urbanization and industrialization, which have had a major impact on the environment. Downie and Chasek (2013) talk about the unintended consequences of actions as the 'tragedy of the commons': we cannot readily protect air, water and other environmental resources because they are not owned privately.

8.4 Conclusion

National and international governmental bodies have seen multiplying discussions and roundtable meetings about how to protect the environment: environmental issues are incorporated in geopolitical discussions about the late modernity society, where *risks* and *fear* are becoming overt iconic themes, exploited by a media-rich global boom, defining 'our' reality and speculating about an apocalyptic future.

Lynch (1990) refers to the uncertainties of the twenty-first century and considers the global community within the new economy. He insists that environmental crimes should be contextualized in a broader reality, and argues that 'we must look towards this global community and beyond crime, as commonly constructed, to discover the pervasive political and economic powers that negatively affect all life on this planet each and every day' (1990: 166). In particular, he refers to powerful political and economic elites who can rule and dictate decisions that affect the environment and, ultimately, the global community.

Some topics in these areas have reached centre stage. Climate change, for instance, is now a keenly discussed issue at global level, and has attracted wide attention, from non-governmental agencies to national and international governmental bodies, from mainstream media to a vast and well-informed public. As highlighted more than 20 years ago by Giddens (1991), climate change and global warming have been perhaps the 'new' most discussed forms of risk within contemporary society. Climate change can damage the ecosystem, as well as human beings, and therefore is global in its effects as all communities are vulnerable. This has brought, or in some cases reinforced, the idea of the globalized world being a *single* 'fragile' and interdependent community.

As Giddens argues (1991), differently from other areas of transnational criminal activities, like terrorism, there is only a 'we' – not 'we' and the 'other', the enemy – as 'we' face the problem, even if the single episode occurs thousands of miles away. We will pay the consequences of exploiting our fresh waters or polluting the soil. In this discourse there are no 'others', even if we act as if we do not pay the fine or are immediately affected by any consequences.

In this global network society, the 'risk and environment' debate is framed as a geopolitical topic. Alliances are forged to compete and reach objectives rather than solely relating to the environment. National governments can be major players, but the power is distributed unevenly, or alliances are formed to defend or challenge cases of national interest.

However, it should be noted that riskiness in the area of global environmental harm has been dealt with, with a double-standard approach: either it has been minimized by those in power at both a national and international level (Walters 2004), or public reaction to this form of anxiety has been exploited by national governmental bodies to gain or maintain popular consensus. In both cases, legal actions and law enforcement have marginal consequences. In fact, although the monitoring and management of environmental issues have now reached an international dimension and have caught the public's attention, possible interventions are still discussed in terms of self-compliance and moderate degrees of responsibility.

Climate change, deforestation, overfishing, fresh water depletion, toxic chemical contamination and the extinction of certain species are some of the environmental problems common to many geographical areas. There exists a lack of adequate response to these problems, in terms of the responsibility of companies, nation-states and international bodies, as well as a lack of sufficient understanding of the impact of such activities, and their definition as 'crimes' that violate human rights.

This implies that, in order to achieve policy objectives in the area of environmental crimes, national and international governments must share a responsibility at different levels for the promotion of social and economic equity, as well as for environmental protection, when considering their overall investment policies. Cooney and Lang (2007) propose a model of adaptive governance, whereby we respond to uncertainty via a multiple approach, composed of knowledge acquisition, low impact on the environment and monitoring of progress.

Questions: Revise and Reflect

1. How do the negative aspects of globalization contribute to the problem of environmental crime?

2. Do we live in a 'riskier' society? Discuss the link between risk and environmental harm.

3. Watch the film *Gomorra*. Discuss the role of organized crime in the area of environmental crime, and the role of the nation-state in addressing this problem.

4. Read the case of the Dancing Shiva and discuss who is responsible for the events.

5. Consider the role of the international community and geopolitics in the area of environmental crime, and discuss its benefits and limitations.

Further Reading

South, N and Brisman, A (eds) 2013, *The Routledge international handbook of green criminology*, Routledge, London.

Videos to Watch

An Inconvenient Truth – a video-documentary about global warming, presented by former United States Vice President Al Gore.

Gomorra – this feature film, adapted from Roberto Saviano's best-selling book, is based on the activities of the Camorra, an organized criminal syndicate around Naples, and the exploitation of new environmental policies to dispose of toxic substances.

The Day After Tomorrow – a movie about sudden global climate changes based loosely on the theory of 'abrupt climate change'.

9

State Crime, Human Rights and Crimes of Globalization

This chapter will look at

- The definitions of state crime and the increasing visibility of criminogenic activities of the state.

- The broadening of the label 'state crime' now applicable to international governmental bodies which represent multiple states.

- The emergence of a culture of state accountability through peer pressure, international community pressure, civil society and supranational judicial assessment.

Keywords

State crime   Accountability   Crimes of globalization

9.1 Introduction

Now more than ever, the conduct of states and supranational bodies is discussed beyond national borders. In this chapter we discuss the role of the state and its degree of criminal responsibility for its own actions. The state can be involved in criminogenic activities and can be responsible for criminal acts or omissions that cause significant harm to people and territories. The activities of national and supranational bodies also have the potential to cause harm, and the actions of these bodies are becoming more visible through monitoring and scrutiny by governmental and non-governmental players (including the media, NGOs, academic scholars and individuals). The growing awareness of universal human rights has offered a framework through which to consider the behaviour of states as criminal. This is because human rights give a language that we can use to assert that states have a responsibility to their citizens to uphold universal rights.

In this chapter we demonstrate how the framing of global forms of crime and their monitoring at international level have given new impetus to the dialectic proposition of the existence and analysis of state crime. The chapter highlights that the increased awareness of universal values as well as the growing impact and significance of human rights have contributed to the emerging opinion that the state can commit crimes. However, the concept of state crime is not without its contradictory elements and in this chapter we explore some of the theoretical and practical difficulties in viewing the state and international institutions as criminal actors.

9.2 Defining State Crime: A Global Criminological Perspective

The state is expected to deliver justice. It is not expected to oppress and kill people or destroy the environment. The state is meant to be the guarantor of basic human rights and standards of living for its citizens. It is not meant to be the body that undermines individual and group rights for its own benefit, advancement or agenda. Of course these expectations are idealist and throughout this book we have seen many examples that demonstrate situations where states have both directly and indirectly contributed to widespread harm and destruction.

But can we consider states' role in causing or facilitating harm as criminal? Normally states are the arbiters of criminal justice; they are the bodies that define which acts are considered crimes and determine how these crimes should be dealt with. They are the organizations that formulate and implement systems of criminal justice to respond to crimes within defined territories. How can states be criminal? We can start talking about state actions as criminal when the state does not protect – systematically – its citizens according to universal human rights standards. Furthermore, the state can be actively engaged in producing harm or in contravening domestic or international rules in order to achieve or maintain positions of strength. While pursuing these objectives or failing to protect people, the state causes intended and unintended effects. State crimes have been recently described as the 'most devastating and costly types of crime' (Rothe & Ross 2008, p. 741). Some of these consequences are very visible and quantifiable, for instance mass atrocities, genocide, **gendercide**, ethnic cleansings (see Chapter 1 and the Glossary for definitions of these crimes). The 'Spotlight' below gives a snapshot of some of the harm caused to victims of various state crimes committed around the world.

Spotlight – The Victims of State Crime: Examples from Around the Globe from the 1970s to the 1990s

The killing of 1.3 million people in Pol Pot's Cambodia in 1975–79;

The politically inspired 'disappearance' of 90,000 Argentinians in the late 1970s;

The killing of over 250,000 Ugandans by Idi Amin's government;

The murder of tens of thousands of Kurds by Iraqi forces during the 1980s, including the use of poison gas supplied, ironically, by the US Government;

The deaths of 250,000 East Timorese at the hands of Indonesian military forces in 1978;

The murder of over 1 million Hutus in Burundi (now Rwanda) in two waves of genocidal violence (1988 and 1994);

The widespread process of 'ethnic cleansing', involving the systematic rape, torture, starvation and murder by Serbian security forces of Muslim Bosnians after 1992 and of Albanians in Kosovo in 1998–99. (Extract from list in Watts et al. 2008, pp. 214–215)

Illegal, criminal, or criminogenic state activities are more noticeable nowadays in the presence of an international layer of agencies. In the **new world order** it is easier to draw attention to the illegal activities or omissions of one state and their negative consequences on people. Slaughter (2004) describes the new world order as defined by a complex web of government networks that include state actors (presidents, prime ministers, foreign ministers), the United Nations, international organizations and bodies and NGOs. This new world order means that there are many different levels and layers of power and multiple actors who can call attention to harmful state practices. Throughout this book (particularly in Chapters 1 and 4) we have seen how many different groups, organizations, individuals and states now operate via fluid, dispersed networks that constitute a complex global order. Through the growth in the number of state-activities watchers, the harm caused by the state is more under scrutiny, and states are more likely to be held accountable in different ways. International standards of values and rights crystallized in conventions, treaties and national and supranational courts' rulings have contributed to form a new conscience towards the role and functions of the state.

Definition

While there is no single and accepted definition of state crimes (Matthews & Kauzlarich 2007), we can consider, for the purposes of this chapter, the working definition offered by Kramer and Michalowski (2005, pp. 447–448):

State crime is any action that violates public international law, international criminal law, or domestic law when these actions are committed by individuals acting in official or covert capacity as agents of the state pursuant to expressed or implied orders of the state; or resulting from state failure to exercise due diligence over the actions of its agents.

The advantage of embracing this definition is that it complies with a general model of criminal liability: the responsibility for criminal offences is personal rather than collective. In fact, the 'state' is a rather abstract concept; who is the 'state'? The answer may vary, to include the government, parliament and state police as a collective entity, but also the prime minister or president as individuals although acting officially to address a function of the state. The statutory individuality of criminal liability is insufficient to embrace the several forms of collective criminal responsibility and, particularly, to apply and enforce this responsibility to the state. That is why Kramer and Michalowski's (2005) definition refers to individuals or agents: this definition engages with the legal-procedural concept of criminal liability.

The other advantage of a definition that locates state crimes within an international criminal justice context is that universal values contained in international treaties are the benchmark against which the state's actions can be held accountable. We have overcome the borders of domestic legal frameworks though the development of international criminal law, and have accepted that states face obligations of conduct and can be held liable for their actions or omissions.

It should be emphasized, however, that state crime, to put it simply, does not exist in national or international criminal law statutes at this point in time. There are a number of offences correlated to activities that can be broadly grouped under the state crime label, such as corruption, corporate or political crimes and forms of collective homicides, genocide and torture. However, the legal definition of state crime does not appear in domestic laws or in international documents. This has pushed many criminologists to be cautious when discussing the idea of the state being criminally liable (see, in particular, Cohen 1990). Green and Ward (2004) suggest that it would be difficult to relate some forms of state harm to existing international laws, arguing that a less legalistic definition of state crimes would help us appreciate the link between state conduct and damage caused.

The crucial aspect of criminal liability becomes even more complex when, under the label of state crime, we start considering that sometimes more than one state is liable for the same conduct, or when we are responding to transnational or international forms of crime. Only recently, new approaches to the study of the discipline of state crime have highlighted that there are cases when more than a single state is causing harm. This raises the questions: How many states are responsible? Should all of them be held accountable for a criminogenic conduct? And who could hold these states responsible?

The matter becomes even more complex when we refer to the state as a group of states forming an officially recognized supranational body. Conventionally, so far, the state is the national governmental body, but what happens if an international governmental body displays criminogenic conduct? We can define state crimes as those illegal activities or omissions committed not only by the nation-state, but also by the supranational state or its governmental bodies, in their public functions. This new approach to the above definition can produce a more detailed analysis of the criminogenic conduct of national or supranational bodies, which would coincide with the interaction among agencies in the globalized world.

Given the complexity of this area, the chapter will proceed with a brief contemporary overview of the genesis of discussions around state crimes. Later, we discuss the international recognition that the state can commit an offence, and consider the fragmentation of state power within the new world order of webs of governance and supranational power.

Contemporary Overview: Crimes of the Powerful and State Crime

The idea that the state can commit crime comes from a tradition of critical theoretical criminology that has developed since the 1960s. This strand of criminology argues that the fact that criminal behaviour is identified and articulated by the state means that the state has a monopoly on determining if an action or omission is illegal and criminal or not. Essentially, it is the state that decides the content of law (see Muncie & McLaughlin 2001 for a general overview). There are crimes that are conventionally described as criminal by the state, tackled by the criminal justice system, and openly recognized by society as deviant behaviour for opportunistic reasons. For instance, think of the state and societal attitudes towards street crimes such as youth offending, drug-related offences or murder. These are behaviours that we readily recognize as being against the law and therefore criminal offences. These ordinary forms of crime are classifiable as 'conventional' as society has accepted them as criminal and it is conventional that these acts are against criminal law. These forms of crimes are also 'opportunistic', in that the state could choose what to define as criminal conduct according to its perceived needs and interests. An example of this is the drug-related activities that are constructed as a problem that needs to be addressed. The state criminalizes these activities to respond to a need by society to please the electorate. Furthermore, targeting these forms of crime is not interfering with the state's goal of maintaining power; rather it is complementing such a target. Therefore, conventional crimes offer an opportunity for the state to respond to a societal need while maintaining consensus and power.

But who is the state? Who decides the content of law? Radical criminologists highlight that it is the powerful groups within a society that can decide or influence decisions regarding law and crime. These groups can obtain and maintain the monopoly of power. Law, in essence, is described as 'bourgeois law' (see Valier 2002, p. 114), law proposed and accepted by powerful groups within societies. The consequence of the influence of powerful groups on the construction of law and criminalization of conduct is twofold. First, human and financial resources are devoted to pursuing crimes that already exist and are clearly identified and labelled as wrongdoing and therefore accepted by the collective (or society) as criminal. Second, often conventional crimes have in common the fact that they are committed by powerless people, diverting the attention and resources to one sphere of criminal activities. Just think of the difference between a street crime such as theft which may result in the loss of $100 and the act of corporate fraud which could cause millions of dollars of damage.

Powerful groups remain mostly sheltered by external controls because the judiciary, police and academics do not receive the legal instruments, assistance and financial resources to investigate the (legal or illegal) activities of the elite. This means that the power of the elite remains unchallenged and unchallengeable. Gramsci (1971) described this as the legitimization of certain activities, to include illegal and criminogenic conducts through a process of hegemony rather than collective consensus, as certain activities are constructed as normal and acceptable even if they cause harm. This process includes the indisputable belief that the state is serving the interests of all, and therefore should go unchallenged. It is a common sense and shared conviction that the state operates to serve its people in the best possible way; yet, this assumption allows the state to avoid the scrutiny of citizens and formal institutions. This is a **hegemonic** way of assuming consensus.

The analysis of the dichotomy of powerless crimes versus powerful crimes reveals that those cases processed by the criminal justice system relate to certain offences generally committed by those who have no power in the decision making process. Differently, those illegal (and criminal) activities committed by the powerful are *under-detected*, *under-processed* and *under-discussed*. Mostly, they are overlooked altogether, while attention is focused and maintained on powerless and conventional forms of crimes. To appreciate these reflections, one would only need to think about the emphasis put on those street crimes rather than white collar or corporate crimes.

These ideas of resisting the state and the powerful began to grow in the 1960s (**Marxist criminologists**) and then proceeded in several different ways, including critical criminology, feminist criminology, green criminology (discussed in Chapter 8), and now constitutive criminology (see 'Spotlight'). Alongside these strands of criminology, a state crime approach and analysis also took root, slowly and with difficulties (see Barack 1991; Ross 1995, 2000). It was Chambliss's 1988 presidential address at the American Society of Criminology on state-organized crime that shone more light on this area (see Chambliss 1989; Rothe &

Friedrichs 2006). Now, as Ross (2000, p. 1) points out, the state is recognized not solely as 'a victim, a punisher or a mediator, but it is also identified as a perpetrator of crime'.

Spotlight – Constitutive Criminology: A Post-modernist Theory

Unlike so many theories on which the study of criminology is based, post-modernist theories of criminology do not look at the causes of offending but take a different approach. In the words of Gibbons (1994), they are based on *'a different set of assumptions about reality, inquiry and criminality than those that guide mainstream criminology'* (p. 152, emphasis in original). Post-modernist theories are concerned with power relations within society, such as race, gender and social class, looking to these to explain differences and a sense of 'otherness' that may be related to crime. Specifically, it is the power relations that are expressed and reflected in criminological discourse that frame how different members of society are regarded and, thereby, advantaged or disadvantaged. It asserts that dominance and privilege are concepts constructed through the criminal law, which does not take into account the diversity of individuals and the specific social context in which they act.

Radical criminology, a movement which developed in the early 1970s, started to consider the social context of crime, looking to locate it with reference to contexts of class, culture, race, gender and history (Halsey 2006). Most attention was given to class and its associations with a capitalist society. Critical criminology developed as a branch of radical criminology towards the end of the decade. It looked more broadly at how the environment shapes individuals and their actions and, conversely, how individual actions, in turn, influence the environment (Halsey 2006). Critical criminology posited that no act by itself was criminal, only those that were proscribed by criminal law in space and time. Consequently, crime and justice issues should be considered within a narrative of power structures and social inequality; one in which the poor, ethnic minorities and women are disadvantaged by social relations, infused by negative assumptions based on class, race and gender. When viewed through a critical criminology lens, transnational crime may be analysed in terms of global power divisions, for example the dominance of the West, and how those power differences inform the discourse on world justice.

The theory of constitutive criminology was subsequently developed as a sub-field of critical criminology by Stuart Henry and Dragan Milovanovic in 1991. It theorized that each individual has power which he or she exercises within a particular social context. That power can be utilized to the detriment of others, causing pain, conflict, harm or injury. Offenders are those who expend energy to negatively affect others who are unable to affect them in return. Conversely, victims are described as individuals who 'suffer the pain of being denied their own humanity, the power to make a difference' (Henry & Milovanovic 1996, p. 116). Their theory describes a concept of harm that goes beyond the law and can be considered in terms of two harm types: reduction and repression. Harms of reduction represent a 'loss of some quality relative to their present standing' (Henry & Milovanovic 1996, p. 103). Harms of repression prevent the offended party from attaining something they desire: a denial of position or standing. These harms (losses or denials) can be construed in terms of different criteria, such as economic, social, psychological, physical, or related to human rights (Henry & Milovanovic 1996). Thus, the offender may be any entity that uses its power to cause a loss or denial to others: a trafficker, a multinational corporation, an organized criminal syndicate, or the state. What unites them in this broad definition of criminal harm is the overuse of power which reduces others from what they are (reduction) or prevents them from becoming what they might be (repression) (Henry & Milovanovic 1996).

9.3 Visibility and Accountability in the 'New World Order'

The combination of more sophisticated international standards and the **fragmentation of state power** helped the discipline of state crime to develop further. International standards have offered a new lens through which state crimes can be identified and analysed. A violation of international law and principles, even if it does not imply a direct violation of domestic law, still offers a high standard against which state activities should be compared.

By using international standards as a benchmark, new forms of state harm have been analysed as criminal, for instance crimes against humanity and global forms of crimes that affect large populations, such as gendercide and mass killing.

Spotlight – Parallels between Conventional Crime and State Crime

Global forms of crimes – as opposed to ordinary and conventional forms of crimes – have become the core concern of the discipline of state crime. With more international instruments and human rights conventions, global forms of crime have found parameters and benchmarks against which they can be discussed. Cohen (1993) was already considering parameters for global crimes by adopting a parallel approach to domestic forms of crimes. Murder, for instance, is against domestic criminal law. Why does genocide or mass killing not count as multiple murder? These concepts operate in tandem and have helped criminologists to move beyond domestic legal instruments and disentangle the discourse around global forms of crimes.

Cohen's contribution has been particularly important for at least three reasons.

1. He has mapped out state crime using accepted and legalistic terminology and concepts, but approached it from a human rights standard. This is, in a way, a transformative process, to help us understand and connect with otherwise alien or unusual situations, above all in a territorially confined legal dimension.

(Continued)

(Continued)

2. He denounced the existence of a culture of denial of state crime: if we cannot see and discuss these crimes, we cannot connect with these realities. Large-scale human suffering has no technical language that allows us to discuss it adequately in terms of state responsibility. Criticizing this culture of denial of state crime Cohen favours more focus and debate over the fact that state crimes occur and occur rather often.

3. By focusing on human rights, Cohen anticipated the current global climate and order. Cohen's intervention was pointing, indirectly, towards new dynamics whereby different national, international and non-national agencies would pay attention to socio-political interests and human rights conditions beyond an individualist as well as nationalistic approach.

The 'old' ideology of the Westphalian state order – as described in Chapter 1 – can be positioned against the new world order. The decentring and redistribution of state power and relative responsibilities to supranational and subnational levels have allowed certain crimes that were already occurring to be more visible than before. This has been the case for state crime. The globalization process has brought a wider and more uniform understanding of human rights issues and socio-legal responsibilities. The pressure on states to be part of a global network and accept rules decided outside their national space has become greater than before, alongside the pressure to be seen as performing well and according to accepted standards (think back to the US tiered ranking system for countries according to their response to human trafficking, as discussed in Chapter 4).

By way of example, the war and related ethnic cleansings in the 1990s in the former Yugoslavia were highly visible and discussed. The mounting pressure from states and people alike to 'deliver justice' for the mass atrocities pushed the United Nations to form the International Criminal Tribunal for the Former Yugoslavia (ICTY) to prosecute those people, common soldiers, generals and state leaders such as the former president of Serbia Milošević for crimes against humanity.

Globalization has also brought innovative means and mechanisms to share more independent information in a rapid manner, contributing to denouncing, and possibly, fighting crimes committed by the state. NGOs, media and individuals have become more networked, better organized and more capable of submitting case studies and data on crimes committed by states. In 2015 the International Bar Association (IBA) launched a new mobile application that can be used to record and widely distribute footage and evidence of mass atrocities around the world. As the IBA proclaimed, 'now anyone with an

Android-enabled smart phone – including human right defenders, journalists, and investigators – can download the Eyewitness to Atrocities app and help hold accountable perpetrators of atrocity crimes, such as genocide, crimes against humanity, torture and war crimes' (IBA 2015). This initiative adds to other instruments designed to shine the spotlight of attention on state crimes and mass atrocities, for example websites that track the actions of particular states or leaders accused of international crimes. Another example is the NGO Amnesty International, which runs campaigns aimed to protect people from gross violations of human rights. One campaign, to offer an example, concerns the people of the Democratic Republic of the Congo, where government forces have continued to torture, rape and kill civilians and use child soldiers. In the last 10 years, the internal conflicts in Congo caused the death of 5 million people, including war-related causes such as malnutrition and disease. The ICC decided to open an investigation in 2004 and trials against identified former state members started in 2009.

This new world order sees the introduction of players other than the state who have become fairly visible and demanding watchers, for instance the United Nations or the European Court of Human Rights. These new powers monitor states' actions and omissions, and can be vocal, and at times incisive, in their assessment of human rights conditions. Other times, international financial institutions, like the World Bank and the IMF, have the opportunity to push local initiatives by allocating or withholding grants, affecting internal dynamics positively and acting as controller of state crimes, especially more fragile states in need of economic capital (Rothe et al. 2006, p. 163). The combination and intersection of these three elements have contributed to a greater level of visibility of state crimes in a shrinking world.

Also, the **defragmentation of state power** and the fortification of the presence of an international community or **global civil society** have meant that states have less power to under- or over-criminalize certain behaviours – or at least it means that states have to justify their position to a number of interlocutors that before were inexistent. For instance, in the case of the United Kingdom, there are now supranational layers of power to which the British government is accountable. Sometimes this accountability is quite loose (for instance the interconnection with the United Nations) and other times it is closer, for example the supremacy of EU law and its Court's rulings, as well as the Council of Europe's European Court of Human Rights.

The concurrent development of the discipline of **victimology** has also contributed to this trend of better visibility of victims of all forms of crime. The idea that the victim needs more protection and attention has been gaining momentum since the 1960s. Traditionally, though, the concept of victim protection has been linked to the idea that it is the state that protects the victim. The framework of state crime has now highlighted that victims also need to be protected from the actions or omissions of the state (Jamieson & McEvoy 2005; Kauzlarich 2008; Kauzlarich et al. 2001).

Is there an evil, immoral or malicious state? In 2001, Stanley Cohen published a critical work on human rights and crimes of the state titled *States of denial: Knowing about atrocities and suffering.* In this work Cohen discusses how the state can be a perpetrator or collusive bystander both during times of atrocities (for instance, political massacres, disappearances or torture) and later, when perpetrators have to justify, deny or minimize their actions. He demonstrates how the state uses techniques of neutralization to deny harmful events occurred or to deny direct involvement or even knowledge of the facts (Cohen 2001). This theory explains how the state can 'get away with' committing crimes, and not be held accountable for their actions. Further, Jamieson and McEvoy (2005) discuss how states take advantage of the limits of jurisdiction and territoriality when *othering* both perpetrators and victims. These othering strategies in the case of perpetrators (state crime by proxy) aim to:

- ensure that individuals who cause harm while pursuing state goals (such as specialist, private or paramilitary forces) do not get caught;

- distance the state from the illegal actions committed by perpetrators in the event that they are caught; and

- put in place political measures to ensure that criminal investigations are deviated or terminated before they can prove the involvement of critical state agents.

Case Study 9.1 – Abu Ghraib Prison During the Iraq War

Jamieson and McEvoy (2005) provide several examples of othering strategies by proxy. One example is the case of private military companies employed by the American CIA accused, alongside the US Army, of abusing prisoners at Abu Ghraib prison outside Baghdad. This case came to public attention via photographs showing public and private military personnel abusing prisoners in 2004. This example proves that the state, in this case the United States, distances itself from the perpetrators by denying knowledge of the abuses and proceeding to prosecute those accused.

While the American soldiers accused of these facts were prosecuted through a US Army's internal discipline procedure, the civilian contractors were more difficult to bring to justice (which jurisdiction? The Iraqi or the US court system? Did they act as individuals or was it the responsibility of the firm which signed the contract? Does a private company's action fall under the jurisdiction of the ICC?). Jamieson and McEvoy (2005) argue that this case highlights the benefits of outsourcing military and intelligence operations to private companies to bypass any further investigation that can link illegal actions to the state.

Image 9.1 One of the most iconic images of prisoner abuse that took place at the Abu Ghraib Prison is the one above. Photo via Wikimedia Commons.

When it comes to othering victims, classified by the state as enemy individuals, jurisdiction and territory are also exploited to hold enemies as detainees. These individuals are transferred or held outside national territories, with the collaboration of third-party nations, a process known as **extraordinary rendition**. These enemies are forcibly imprisoned to minimize their movements and are often tortured during interrogations to extract information. Jamieson and

McEvoy (2005, p. 516) cite a former covert agent who worked for the CIA across the Middle East during the 1990s who stated that enemies of the US state were sent to the Middle East in order to obtain information from them via dubious means (i.e. torture):

> If you want a serious interrogation, you send a prisoner to Jordan. If you want them to be tortured you send them to Syria. If you want someone to disappear – never see them again – you send them to Egypt. (Bob Baer, quoted in Grey 2004, p. 25, extracted from Jamieson & McEvoy 2005, p. 516)

One of the questions posed by the practice of extraordinary rendition and torture is whether these enemies of the state themselves become victims of the state as their rights are abused. After the 9/11 terrorism attacks, the case of rendition flights (extra-judicial transfer of prisoners to locations where it is common knowledge they will be abused) exploded at international level, hence the current level of visibility.

Degrees and levels of visibility and accountability for state crime vary enormously. Often accountability is dependent on the position of the state in question within the global geopolitical hierarchy. Scrutinizing past actions of problematic, fragile or enemy states (for instance, Nazi Germany or the death squads in Latin American countries during the 1960s and 1970s) is less complex than monitoring or intervening in the current affairs of powerful contemporary states. Some states are more open to global scrutiny than others, some others commit more *open* violations (visible to external groups), or violations there are clearly recognizable as such by international criminal laws (such as genocide). This is demonstrated in the record of the ICC, which has disproportionately investigated and prosecuted African states. As this demonstrates, in the new world order some states have lost power while others have gained or reinforced their power (Rothe et al. 2009). Does this demonstrate that powerful actors at a global level are able to define crimes and manipulate legality (or hide beneath a cloak of legality) to achieve their strategic interests and realpolitik aims? This highlights a replication of the link between hegemonic power and law described by radical criminologists at a domestic level (discussed earlier). Certainly, processes of accountability for state crime are partial, uneven and biased, demonstrating that a radical criminological approach to international law and accountability is needed.

9.4 International Institutions and Crimes of Globalization

The fact that some institutions and states hold much more power than others in the new world order highlights that the premise behind state crime, that powerful actors must be criminalized and held accountable for the harm they cause, needs to be taken to a supranational level. It is important to recognize that powerful global institutions also hold the potential to become criminal actors and facilitate or cause widespread harm by their actions and omissions. For this reason, it is flawed to argue only in favour of a better distribution of the traditional state power, compared to the past. Just because there are powers above the state does not mean that harm stops. Wherever there is power there is the possibility for abuse of power. New international institutions have brought new levels of economic and non-economic wealth and openness to dialogue to the world; yet they have brought new layers of problems. This is why critical criminologists Dawn Rothe and David Friedrichs have shifted from using the terminology of state crime to adopting the terminology of crimes of globalization (Rothe & Friedrichs 2015). The work of these two eminent authors lists a new series of cases that can be grouped into two categories: international institutions of justice and crimes of globalization.

As highlighted by Rothe and Friedrichs (2006), only recently have criminologists attempted to look at international institutions of justice and social control within the context of state crime. International bodies and tribunals should be analysed considering the over-reaching extension of their actions (or non-actions). There are numerous examples of international institutions acting in ways that cause harm. There are even many examples of the United Nations causing damage and acting criminally. Some examples include: corruption within the United Nations and the Oil for Food Programme; the UN's role in Iraq; and instances of rape, violence and use of prostitution by UN military personnel, including peacekeepers.

From these examples we can see the need to construct criminality at a higher level. This is where the use of a framework of crimes of globalization comes in. Rothe and Friedrichs (2015, p. 26) state that 'Crimes of globalization are those demonstrably harmful policies and practices of institutions and entities that are specifically a product of the forces of globalization, and that by their very nature occur within a global context'. Alongside the positive outcomes and benefits of the globalization process there are also many negative effects. We explored some of these negative effects in Chapter 2 when we looked at anti-globalization movements which protest against the large-scale crimes and harm caused in the name of globalization. Many scholars have also examined the negative effects of globalization (Friedrichs 2007a; Friedrichs & Friedrichs 2002; Rothe et al. 2006). In particular, the global dominance of powerful organizations over poorer regional areas and local governments has pushed some scholars to view globalization as generating significant criminogenic tendencies (see Friedrichs & Friedrichs 2002). According to Friedrichs (2007a, p. 168), 'governments are increasingly puppets of corporations and financial special interests'. The proliferation and success of transnational corporations have created yet another *player* in the global scene, in addition to nation-states, the international agencies and non-governmental agencies. These corporations are part of high-level decision making processes, and are able to impose such decisions upon government agencies and national markets. The ability to be so powerful and efficient is also due to new technology and levels of rapid and secure exchange of communication as well as monetary transactions.

Alongside the harm caused by transnational corporations, crimes of globalization also cover the intended and unintended negative outcomes of the activities of international financial institutions. The actions of international financial institutions like the World Bank or IMF can have the impact of draining local and regional power. Some financial investments are either externally imposed or decided with local authorities with no real power to oppose resistance. These investments have, in some instances, caused damage and human suffering to local populations. In addition, actions by the global financial institutions such as the World Bank and the IMF have been accused of supporting the interests of Western governments and corporations rather than privileging the development of poorer countries (Friedrichs 2007a). In a globalized economy, power struggles are even more evident and have been highlighted by scholars and NGO representatives. It has been highlighted (for instance by Rothe & Friedrichs 2006) that rich, powerful and industrialized countries (G7) along with international financial institutions operate in a top–down approach, pursuing transnational corporate interests rather than local economic and social improvements. This is exemplified in Case Study 9.2. Multinational corporations and financial institutions are responsible for the consequences of policy decisions. They are often, perhaps, attempting to realize positive outcomes and there is no specific intent to cause harm – but the consequences of their decisions can have devastating financial, human and environmental consequences.

Case Study 9.2 – The Sinking of *Le Joola*

Rothe et al. (2006) suggested that the 2002 sinking of the Senegalese state-run ferry boat *Le Joola*, and consequent death of more than 1,800 people, represented more than just an example of a single state's crime. In the *Le Joola* case, these authors argue that pointing the finger to those state agencies who failed to enforce traffic regulations (as a crime of omission) is not sufficient to explain thoroughly what happened. The external pressure put on the Senegalese state which has modified the internal socio-political and economic structure must also be analysed. Decisions taken by external supranational governmental organizations, in this case primarily the World Bank, produce devastating criminogenic effects on more fragile countries that can contribute to the context in which tragedies, such as the sinking of *Le Joola*, occur.

9.5 State Crime and Transnational Crime

Faust and Kauzlarich (2008) have argued that state crime can include harm towards state citizens, other states, or citizens of other states' jurisdiction. Considering this overarching form of state responsibility which extends to individuals outside a state's direct jurisdiction and emphasizes a human rights standard approach in place of a legalistic approach to crime, the concept of state crime can be applied to both international and transnational forms of crime. We explored the difference between international and transnational crime in Chapter 1, and in Chapter 4 demonstrated the differences between responses to transnational and international crimes. As these chapters highlighted, international crimes are more defined since the introduction of the Rome Statue of the International Criminal Court created a specific list of crimes, which includes genocide, war crimes and crimes against humanity. With the formalization of discussions around crimes against humanity, the field of international criminal law has been enriched by a clearer legal understanding of international crimes and their consequences in terms of state responsibility.

However, as we have seen throughout this book, although the codification of international crimes makes some state crime inadmissible it also makes some state crimes admissible. Just think of the debates and controversy surrounding the definition and inclusion of the crime of aggression in the Rome Statute (see Chapter 1 for a review). Justice organizations focus on bringing attention to and prosecuting the codified crimes, such as crimes against humanity, and other crimes, such as the crime of aggression, fall into the background as they are not easy to prosecute and are not clearly defined as crimes. This means certain states are labelled as criminal while others are constructed as 'saviours' (Mutua 2001) and champions of justice. For example, the ICC has investigated and prosecuted cases in African countries including Sudan, Uganda, the Democratic Republic of Congo, the Central African Republic, Kenya, the Cote D'Ivoire and Mali. Crimes against humanity have occurred in these countries – countries that are comparatively weak in global geopolitical terms. The ICC has not pursued any powerful countries, meaning states such as the United States, France, the United Kingdom and Australia. The continuing impunity of states such as the US and the UK is highlighted by the inability of the ICC to investigate the crime of aggression. The United States and the United Kingdom could be considered criminal for their invasion of Iraq and Afghanistan, acts that could be defined as aggression.

In addition to state responsibility for international crimes, states can also be considered responsible for transnational crimes, particularly if we view state responsibility as illegal activities or omissions that are harmful. Through this lens, the state has the *responsibility* to act or refrain from acting and abstain from direct and indirect *involvement* in behaviour that could cause harm. This responsibility or involvement may not be specifically codified in law but it constitutes harm to a number of people and groups and is outside the boundaries of human rights. Transnational crimes should be included in the framing of state crime.

The state can be directly complicit in transnational crimes, or it can indirectly contribute to an environment in which transnational crime flourishes. Part of the issue is the framing of the problem of transnational crime, and this is where a critical criminological approach of questioning ingrained assumptions about which acts constitute crimes and which actors are criminalized becomes useful. By framing transnational crime as something committed by external, enemy others, the state effectively minimizes its role in facilitating transnational crimes and diverts attention away from its responsibility to prevent transnational crimes. Prevention in this case means focusing on core conditions and contexts which enable and facilitate crime.

A prominent example of how the process of othering and criminalization is used to divert attention from state complicity, involvement and responsibility for transnational crimes is the case of irregular immigration. Irregular immigration, that is immigration cases where individuals have not sought asylum through official means – often referred to as illegal migration or 'queue jumping' – is often constructed by destination states as a threat to national security and integrity. The enemy other is the asylum seeker and the smuggler. Here national governments divert the attention from their responsibility to support asylum seekers and their failure to contribute to conditions of safety in other parts of the world (as part of the discourse of globalization), as explored in the 'Spotlight' below.

Spotlight – Refugees and State Crime

After World War II the countries of the world signed a convention giving rights and safeguards to refugees (Refugee Convention). Forced migration was to be a humanitarian and not a criminal concern, with discussions in regard to refugees to involve human rights and protection. As Pickering (2005) highlights, the law and order approach of the receiving states has labelled refugees not only as irregular but also as illegal. The rhetoric built around this topic is that refugees are not following internal rules on regular entrance into the receiving country, and therefore they are in breach of the usual regulations that other people would follow. The refugees who enter a country irregularly are consequently deemed as breaking the internal rules of nation-states and having no respect for these states. This construction reinforces the idea that irregular migrants are outsiders – essentially, it is a 'method of social, political, racial and cultural exclusion' (Pickering 2005, p. 8). The receiving state, rather than having a humanitarian obligation to help out on a large scale, has shaped a role for itself as defender of the internal community from outsiders. This is certainly a common theme when it comes to transnational crimes.

In the case of transnational crime, states direct public attention to the criminal actions of organized groups that trade in weapons and drugs, smuggle in counterfeit medicines or branded products, or traffic human beings or body parts. First world countries exploit the second and the third worlds for their own strategic advantage and economic advancement. This exploitation impacts on the deterioration of the second and third worlds' economic and non-economic conditions (see Friedrichs 2007b), creating an environment where crime is one of the only viable options for vulnerable groups. Trafficking in human beings, in weapons, in drugs, the prostitutionalization of certain areas for sex tourists, ecological devastation, the offshore investment banks and complexification of money laundering, are all linked to the refusal of first world countries to take responsibility for their actions and their failure to consider the broader circumstances of their policies. The culture of denial of the harm caused by states includes the omission to look further into the exploitation of legal gaps, the absence of more sophisticated rules, the acceptance and misuse of corruption, and the lack of willingness to cooperate at all levels.

While all this occurs, transnational crime is used by first world countries as an alibi, as a political tool to generate fear and anxiety. The 'us' versus 'them' culture is fortified by national governments as a political and electoral campaign: the organized criminal gangs are smuggling in drugs and illegal foreigners or asylum seekers; the terrorists are bombing our territory. The idea of the national territory being invaded is sold without highlighting the underpinning responsibility of the state or the harm caused by the state in a direct or indirect form, like the lack of a routine monitoring system. The threat of transnational crime serves as a method for achieving internal (national) consensus, and foreign policy has become an instrument used to obtain and maintain a respectful position within international networks and/or agencies. In this climate a punitive stance on crime (as explored in Chapter 4) becomes a powerful political tool for governments to ensure election or re-election and maintain a good external image.

9.6 Conclusion

The labelling of particular acts as crimes and individuals as criminals is a process of picking and choosing – some acts are crimes, others are acceptable even if they cause harm, some actors are illegal, other are legitimate even if they are immoral. A state crime and crimes of globalization approach highlights the harm that is caused by actors that we may not necessarily define as criminal. The creation of harm through acts of commission and acts of omission is the key paradigm upon which state crime and crimes of globalization are built.

Human rights standards provide a strong framework that can criminalize the role of states and organizations. The core point that arises from state crime and crimes of globalization literature is that we must look at crime in a broader manner to encapsulate harms and human rights abuses that are facilitated both directly and indirectly by different organizations, including both states and international organizations.

Questions: Revise and Reflect

1. Should the state be considered criminal? What are some of the ways states could be punished or sanctioned for their criminal behaviour?

2. Write a list of acts you think should be defined as crimes of globalization.

3. How could a more even international order be created?

4. Visit the Bashir Watch website: bashirwatch.org/. What role do you think NGOs and everyday citizens or online 'activists' should play in drawing attention to, tracking down and helping prosecute state leaders and offenders?

Further Reading

Chambliss, WJ, Michalowski, R & Kramer, RC 2010, *State crime in the global age*, Willan, Portland, OR.

Cohen, S 2001, *States of denial: Knowing about atrocities and suffering*, Polity Press, Cambridge.

De Feyter, K, Parmentier, S, Bossuyt, M & Lemmens, P 2005, *Out of the ashes: Reparation for victims of gross and systematic human rights violations*, Intersentia Publishing, Antwerp and Oxford.

Green, P & Ward, T 2005, *State crime: Governments, violence and corruption*, Pluto Press, London.

Rothe, D 2009, *State criminality: The crime of all crimes*, Lexington Books, Lanham, MD.

Rothe, D & Friedrichs, D 2015, *Crimes of globalisation*, Routledge, Abingdon.

Videos to Watch

Extraordinary Rendition (2007) – an action thriller dramatizing the secret transfer, detention and torture of a US resident from Egypt who becomes a terror suspect following an attack on US interests in North Africa. The film depicts the controversial US practice of 'extraordinary rendition'.

The Whistle Blower (2010) – a drama based on the true story of Kathryn Bolkovac, a US policewoman who served as a UN peacekeeper in post-war Bosnia. In the course of her work Kathryn uncovers a large-scale sexual slavery ring used by international personnel (including Americans).

Websites to Visit

International State Crime Research Center: www.statecrimecenter.com/
International State Crime Initiative: statecrime.org/

10

Towards a Global Criminal Justice?

This chapter will look at

Future directions in transnational criminal justice.

Keywords

Global criminal
justice

Security and stability

Measuring crime

Prevention

10.1 Introduction

What is the future of international criminal justice? What are the priorities in the fight against transnational crimes? What are the emerging themes, the key players in the next few years? Is there going to be a clarification of what an international criminal justice system should deliver? This is going to be discussed considering two variables: first, the role of nation-states and international institutions; and second, control of society and the criminology of the dangerous other.

10.2 Background

It is often heard that crime has 'gone global'. The reality is that there are well-established connections between local and global criminal activities. This is an integral part of globalization, as discussed in Chapter 2. We can find various attempts to track down the origin and evolution of transnational crimes. For instance, the Opium War between China and Britain to assert control over Hong Kong and the African slaves deported in America are good historical case studies that highlight the evolution of trafficking in drugs and human beings. Contemporary transnational crimes are certainly a product of historical developments. What has changed is this is a more integrated, globalized era, and therefore events can have wider effects than before. A good example is the 2008 Global Financial Crisis, which had massive repercussions in a number of countries. This has affected the distribution of wealth and the creation of a new layer of poverty mainly in some Western countries, such as the US, Canada and Britain, and brought an entire nation-state, Iceland, to bankruptcy (Friedrichs 2013; and see Case Study 3.1 for a discussion of the impact of the crisis on Iceland). This has inevitably triggered a new momentum in crime at a local and global level. It has also clearly illustrated the interconnections between criminal activities and socio-political and economic factors.

Hence, it is worth stressing that one main feature of the future of transnational criminal matters and international criminal justice is not only crime as such, but also economic and non-economic factors. Policy makers, academics and practitioners could not just concentrate on reactive transnational collaboration in crime prevention in order to organize human and financial resources, but also look systematically at those emerging themes such as poverty, education, a lack of resources and unemployment. The United Nations has already highlighted the link between transnational organized crime and humanitarian crises in a 2010 report on *Crime and instability* (UNODC 2010c). Reading this report, one is urged to reflect on the fact that priorities in the area of transnational crime are indicated by how such priorities are negotiated, rather than the 'crime' crisis reflecting the reality and the need worldwide. Definitions and understandings of transnational crime priorities are the products of diplomacy and networking of power brokers at an international level. To give an example, global civil society has changed its technique from outside protest to inside negotiation, through building up a network, and using momentum to persuade international organizations (the UN, IMF, ICC to name but a few) and states to introduce policies or act in a certain way. An example of this is the emphasis on human trafficking since the introduction of the 2000 Trafficking Protocol: there has been much political action and human and financial investment in the crime of human trafficking despite a clear lack of data on the crime and other pressing cases of crime and harm occurring at transnational and international levels (see for example, Wise & Schloenhardt 2014).

Yet, the human trafficking example is one that talks about how we can shape an effective response at global level to transnational crimes. The UN Congresses provide clear evidence that we share the belief that isolated nation-states' responses are no longer sustainable in response to crimes that cross borders. Every five years the United Nations holds a Crime Congress where policy makers and practitioners gather together to talk about crime prevention and criminal justice. In 2010 the United Nations had an opportunity to reflect on the first 55 years of 'Crime Congresses' (UNODC 2010b). By looking at the titles and keywords, it is evident that the discussion embraced clear international dimensions since the 1990s, when the Congress was titled *International Crime Prevention and Criminal Justice in the Twenty-first Century* and the recommendations focused on more international cooperation against organized crime and terrorism. In 2015, the Congress discussed ways to promote the rule of law and how to support sustainable development. Both topics are very important and interconnected.

10.3 In Search of 'Global' Justice

There is great difficulty in measuring transnational crime. Despite this, based on available evidence, and factoring in a large hidden component, we have to admit that the problem is immense. There is no single body or source that can offer data on all aspects of transnational crime. The United Nations has positioned itself quite prominently in some aspects, such as drugs and human trafficking, but it does not offer a comprehensive view on all types of transnational crime. Some academics such as Van Dijk (2008) have attempted to offer comparative data of crime across a number of nation-states. He admits that even if there has been international growth in transnational crime statistics, collected by various national and international organizations, the area of crime and criminal justice has not enjoyed the same trend. Further, he points out that we cannot rely on traditional methods to measure transnational crimes. This is because often domestic crime statistics are based on data from police and the courts as they respond to crimes and process criminal cases. Obviously, such a developed infrastructure does not exist at an international level, making the collection and analysis of data difficult and extremely piecemeal. Accordingly, Barbaret (2014) highlights the need for more methodological literature for the purpose of studying transnational crime.

In line with methodological constraints, it is worth reminding ourselves of the Salvador Declaration of the Twelfth UN Congress in April 2010 (UNODC 2010d). This declaration addresses the need to adapt national criminal justice systems to international standards. This point helps us reflect on the existence of many systems of justice and several networks of agents (a point discussed in Chapters 1 and 4). Looking at the international environment through a dualistic UN-based framework of national/international levels is clearly too simplistic to capture the confluence of multiple, overlapping systems and networks, and the various levels and layers of actors and agencies that make up the international environment. There are many players, alongside, below and above the state, that are contributing to a better and more comprehensive understanding of 'justice' understood beyond national territories. Nevertheless, there are other legal enterprises that are benefiting from such a chaotic system, such as corporations that are able to navigate legal loopholes at an international level and profit from the chaotic international environment to pursue their goals. This remains a core issue that is underplayed at the international level, for example in the UN Congresses.

Criminal justice should not be solely understood and pursued as justice against the other evils, for instance the traffickers or the terrorists. Global criminal justice is often translated in producing and introducing more security at national and international levels. In this way, we move the attention to the punishment after the crime approach in a reactive manner. Preventative measures should also be considered. These preventative measures should go beyond a criminal justice approach: a truly systematic and comprehensive programme of prevention in order to pursue global criminal justice should consider what global criminal justice means. In this discourse, the emphasis rests on the work of national and international governmental bodies as well as the plethora of external organizations.

This is why emerging themes of global justice refer to wealth and income. It has little to do with criminal justice, crime and punishment, and more with an egalitarian conception of justice: it is just and fair that every human being lives a dignified life, well above the level of life-threatening poverty (see **Southern Criminology**). But this sort of distributive justice is not directly linked to criminal justice which is often based on retribution. We have to appeal to moral values when we intervene in conflicts (such as in Iraq or the former Yugoslavia). We invest billions in wars and conflicts where international or transnational criminal activities are detected (ethnic cleansing in former Yugoslavia, hiding terrorists in Iraq). And yet, we have seen less serious international and sustainable programmes to eradicate famine and poverty, which has killed millions and millions of human beings. Starvation, the lack of basic local infrastructure to guarantee safe water, sanitation and basic services, should be made priorities by developed nation-states and international agencies. Attending to these priorities would ensure a truly preventative approach to transnational and international crimes. But the real challenge is having a broader vision in intergenerational and future issues, such as the shaping of law and governance with different priorities, stability and peace, access to a clean environment, and socio-economic opportunities rather than criminalizing the next group of deviant others.

Tackling poverty, helping socio-politically and economically fragile states, and establishing eco-targets, are key objectives. In this area, supranational bodies could achieve more, and their initiatives could have better impact-assessments – assessments which take into account both the results achieved and the impact on local economies. Introducing debt relief on IMF and World Bank loans is not sufficient; introducing and restructuring the aid programmes to include a better assessment of the impact on natural and human resources of receiver countries would help reduce short- and long-term negative or criminogenic effects.

Marginalizing developing countries is adding to an ongoing crisis of security and mobility. Often in international criminal justice, the ideal of common 'justice' and the central role of the network of national and supranational states are emphasized. The same trend can be traced in the area of transnational crime: the state operates to defend their people against terrorists, traffickers and virtual or real pirates. The idea of common understanding of justice is defended on the basis of shared values. In this area we can apply the same Gramscian hegemonic approach discussed in Chapter 9. National and supranational governmental agencies operate in the interests of all, to protect universal values undermined by global forms of crime. It is common sense to pursue the application of human rights and defence of shared interests. Solutions dictated by the governmental agencies are therefore aimed to protect all of us, the global society. In both areas, international crimes and transnational crimes, the national and supranational layering of states is essential in defining strategies to do this. But this is a hegemonic rather than consensual approach to global governance and crime and public policy. In this fight against global crimes (international crimes and transnational crimes), marginalized, militarized and poorer regional areas are left behind or defined as 'enemies', and 'others'. The ruling institutions appear to serve common, shared universal interests, but we end up serving sectional – Western – interests only.

The role and task of students interested in these aspects require a more comprehensive understanding of and engagement with not only conventional forms of crimes but also global forms of crimes. The separation between these two forms of crimes is, at times, an artificial paradigm.

Further Reading

Carrington, K, Hogg, R and Sozzo, M 2016, 'Southern Criminology', *British Journal of Criminology*, vol. 56, pp. 1–20.

Glossary

Adjunct protocol   refers to agreements that supplement or expand upon more formal treaties or conventions.

Aggression (crime of)   the use of force by one state against another without legal justification, such as self-defence.

Alien conspiracy view   a theoretical approach to **Organized crime** that focuses on ethnicity, suggesting that foreigners, the alien others, are causing disturbance and instability. It originated from the depiction of Sicilian migrants to the US as Mafia members responsible for the foundations of American organized crime.

Americanization   the spreading influence of American culture, including popular culture, financial systems, and political systems, on other cultures around the world. It is alternatively referred to as McDonaldization or Disneyization.

Amnesty   pardon granted by an authority (traditionally the government or head of state) to an individual or group of people, forgiving offences, granting immunity from prosecution and removing criminal punishment. It usually involves pardoning political crimes.

Anomie (anomic)   conditions in which there is a breakdown of social bonds, a sense of normlessness, and little moral guidance for individuals within society, meaning individuals do not feel part of a collective and society has minimal influence on citizens. The term is associated with the work of sociologists Emile Durkheim and Robert Merton. Merton used the term to describe a disaccord between societal goals and the legitimate means available for reaching them.

Anti-globalization movement   a disparate global social movement that is critical of globalization and, in particular, global corporate capitalism.

Border securitization   the process by which borders are linked with security discourses as groups and individuals are identified as hostile and dangerous and are therefore criminalized resulting in punitive measures that seek to secure national territory.

Civil society (or global civil society) the vast array of non-government organizations and societal institutions (including community groups, religious organizations, unions, professional associations etc.) that have a presence in public life and reflect the will of their members and, more broadly, citizens.

Commodification the transformation of something (goods, services, ideas, entities etc.) into a commodity, that is, a marketable or saleable item. The idea of commodity played a key role in Marxist theory (see **Marxist criminology**).

Constitutive criminology a postmodernist-influenced theory introduced by Stuart Henry and Dragan Milovanovic that conceives of crime as a core part of the production of subjects (human agents) and the social structures within which they simultaneously exist and create.

Cosmopolitanism the notion that all human beings belong to one inclusive community based on shared morals, values and norms.

Crime control the collection of strategies and structures designed to manage crime and achieve social control in response to crime.

Crimes against humanity This is one of the four **International crimes** included in the Roma Statute (or Rome Statute). Crimes against humanity are defined acts (including, but not limited to murder, extermination, enslavement, deportation, and imprisonment) that are committed as part of a widespread or systematic, purposeful attack against a civilian population.

Crimes of globalization the harmful consequences that are caused by the policies and practices of international financial institutions. These harms, which can be defined as crimes through a **Critical criminology** framework, often disproportionately affect the global south.

Criminogenic actions, behaviour or situations that produce criminality or cause or promote crime.

Critical criminology linked to **Marxist criminology**, it explains criminality as a result of an uneven distribution of resources and power, rather than individual causation. It also expands the horizon of crime to include harm.

Cryptocurrencies such as Bitcoin, are digital forms of alternative currency that use cryptography to control transactions. These currencies are typically decentralized.

Cryptomarkets are digital platforms that facilitate the trade of goods and services between anonymous online individuals (using software such as Tor) using cryptocurrencies such as Bitcoin.

Cultural cleansing   the deliberate and systematic destruction of a group and their cultural heritage with the intent of eliminating not only people but also all traces of their culture and history (including artworks, historical sites, museums etc.).

Cybercrime   an umbrella term that refers to a wide array of offences that involve the internet, computers or computer technology.

Cyberspace   the notional environment or space created by computer-based communication networks and the internet. Events and interactions that occur via online communication networks are said to occur within this space rather than in a physical location.

Cyber-terrorism   the use of computers, networks and the internet to cause harm for political or ideological purposes. This includes acts of disruption of computer networks and attacks against information, data and computer systems.

Dark Net   also called the 'deep web', refers to the hidden recesses of the internet accessed via anonymizing software (such as TOR). The hidden websites on the Dark Net are not discoverable by the major search engines.

Debt bondage   described as a modern day form of slavery, debt bondage describes the practice by which a person's labour or services are used as security for the repayment of a debt or other obligation.

Destination country   trafficked goods (including drugs and people) move from origin countries (or source countries), through transit countries and on to destination countries. Destination country refers to the end point or the destination of the goods, services or people being transported or trafficked.

Ecocide (or geocide)   widespread destruction of the natural environment and extensive damage to the ecosystem of a territory that significantly diminishes the ability of the population to survive or thrive in that territory.

Extraordinary rendition   the transfer, without legal process, of a detainee to another country for the purposes of interrogation. This practice has also been referred to as government-sponsored abduction and is used to circumvent human rights laws by transferring detainees to jurisdictions where practices such as torture are permitted.

Feminist criminology   a stream of criminology developed in the 1960s and 1970s that highlights the patriarchal domination of the field of criminology and emphasizes the contribution of aggressive masculinity to violent forms of crime. Feminist criminology views crime as a product of the inequalities within society and is closely linked to **Critical criminology**.

Fragmentation of state power (also defragmentation) describes how state powers are being diffused, reconfigured and spread across different institutions and organizations at local, regional and international levels under conditions of globalization.

Gendercide is the systematic, mass killing of members of a specific gender group (most often women). It is evidenced by assault, murder and violence based on gender. Practices such as sex-related abortion or infanticide (murder of a child) can also be classified as gendercide.

Geneva conventions refers to the four treaties and three additional protocols that establish the standards of international law for humanitarian treatment during war. The Geneva conventions were negotiated and updated in 1949 following World War II and seek to limit the impact of war on civilian populations.

Genocide this is one of the four **International crimes** included in the Roma Statute. Genocide is the systematic elimination of a national, ethnic, racial or religious group. It includes crimes such as murder, causing physical or mental harm, preventing births and forcibly removing children, when these acts are committed as part of a widespread plan to destroy a group.

Geopolitics conceptualizes the relationship between political power, strategic interests, decision making and geographic space. It studies the effects of geography on politics and international relations.

Global civil society refers to the existence and operation of **Civil society** at a global level.

Global north; global south the differentiation between the global north and south divides countries based on socio-economic and political distinctions. The term 'global north' (also referred to as the West, the first world or the developed world) denotes the economically developed countries of Western Europe, North America, Australia, New Zealand and South Africa. The term 'global south' (also known as the third world) refers to the developing countries of Africa, South America, and developing parts of Asia and the Middle East. See Southern Criminology

Global Transformationalists a broad grouping of theorists that argue that globalization is creating new, dynamic political, economic and social contexts which are transforming state powers and the environment within which states operate.

Globalization a complex and contested term. In this book we use Held et al's (1999 p.2) definition of globalization as: 'the widening, deepening and speeding up of worldwide interconnectedness in all aspects of contemporary life'. See Chapter 2 for a more in-depth discussion of globalization.

Globalization sceptics disagree that the current era is defined by globalization, viewing international processes as fragmented and regionalized and high-lighting that global interactions have been a part of life for centuries.

Glocalization describes the adaptation of global ideas, products, and trends to suit local conditions and the specificities of local culture.

Green criminology a stream of criminology that studies crimes against the environment, broadly conceiving harms to the environment as crimes and ana-lysing environment law through a criminological lens.

Hegemony (also hegemonic) Political, economic and/or socio-cultural domi-nance of a social group over others. See **Sovereignty**.

Human smuggling the organization of human beings' entry to a country without documents in exchange of a fee usually paid in advance.

Human trafficking the trade in human beings who are kept in debt-bondage for the purpose of sexual, labour or other exploitation until the repayment of their 'cost' (travel, boarding documents, and others) is achieved.

Hybrid courts (also known as internationalized courts) a blend of national and international courts to try cases that infringe international crimes. They are also known as a 'third-generation' criminal courts, following the Nuremberg and Tokyo Tribunals (first generation), and the ICTY, ICTR and ICC (second genera-tion). Currently they comprise the courts in East Timor, Kosovo and Sierra Leone.

Inter-governmental organizations bodies created usually by treaties or other formal agreements, and composed by two or more nation-states or by other intergovernmental organizations for the pursue of a common object, for exam-ple to strengthen security, economic and social issues. Among these bodies we count the United Nations, the World Bank, the North Atlantic Treaty Organization (NATO), the European Union, the African Development Bank (ADB).

International crimes extreme forms of mass violence that affect the peace and stability of one or more states. Since the Roma Statute establishing the International Criminal Court came into force in 2002, international crimes comprise **Genocide**, **Crimes against humanity**, **War crimes** and the crime of aggression.

International criminal law a branch of international public law that deals with criminal responsibility in cases of international crimes. It is closely linked to international human rights since it aims to protect fundamental human rights such as life, freedom and security.

International law a body of rules established by formal agreement (i.e. by treaty) or by custom to regulate relationships between nation states and intergovernmental organizations. The branch of international law more applicable to transnational criminal matters is categorized as 'public' (as opposed to 'private' international law).

Late modernity a way to define the contemporary and globally connected society as a succession to and an intensification of modern times (see **Modernity**). Late modernists believe that objective knowledge is important to improve society and minimise or remove threats and risk (see **Risk society**), unlike the views on a postmodern society (see **Postmodernity**).

Liquid modernity A term coined by Bauman to signify the condition of constant change (hence 'liquidity') of global socio-economic and political conditions. This is in opposition to the certainty predicated by **Modernity** and, to a certain extent, **Late modernity**.

Lustration historically understood as a purification ceremony, in **International criminal law** it is referred to as a process whereby those participating into a regime which had caused instability or criminal violations are removed from power or barred from accessing powerful positions.

Marxist criminology a school of criminology that explains the ways in which criminality is a product of the society and why crime is used as a social control tool by the ruling state. It states that a capitalist society produces an unjust divide between those who rule, owning the means of production, and the proletariat, whose labour is diverted and exploited according to the needs of the ruling class. It is closely linked to **Critical criminology, Radical criminology** and **Feminist criminology.**

Modernity a term used to indicate a period (17th century to the age of Enlightenment) where a rational approach to society brought progress and contributed to challenge traditions. This in turn produced stability and structure, security and identity.

Money-laundering the process of disguising the origin of the proceeds from criminal activities through a cycle of layering, with the final result of obtaining legitimate money.

Neoconservative a political ideology that favours a technocratic rational approach to crime, which involves practical and cost-effective policy making; it focuses on the moral culture of contemporary society and aims at controlling crime rather than tackling the roots of crime. See **Neoliberalism** and **Penal populism.**

Neoliberalism/neoliberal a political ideology that values free trade, privatization and deregulation allowing space for tradition, order, and authority. Risk is seen as victim-focused and individualistic. See **Neoconservative** and **Late modernity.**

Network theory   an approach used to understand the links not just between humans but also between elements and concepts, generating a network of relations which shape outcomes. In **Globalization**, this theory refers to global interconnected nodes.

New world order   often used as an opposed concept to, or a new stage of, the **Westphalian order**, it refers to the entrance of new political counterparts such as **Inter-governmental organizations** and **Non-governmental organizations** alongside nation-states in the arena of world politics.

Non-governmental organizations   otherwise known as NGOs, these are not for profit bodies, and do not belong to government or for profit business enterprises. These are normally based on volunteering work and can be sub-national, national or international.

Organized crime   a criminal enterprise organized by a group of people across a period of time for a specific purpose, often being profit and/or power. When its strategic and operational functions reach beyond national borders this is referred to as **Transnational organized crime**.

Penal populism   a terminology to summarize the political stance in embracing what is believed to be a public's generally punitive approach to criminals for the purpose of electorate advantage. See **Punitiveness**.

Policy transfer   a process where knowledge and experience of a criminal justice approach or system are applied directly, or used to develop closely related policies, in another system.

Postmodernity   differently from **modernity** and **late modernity**, postmodernists believe that the rational approach to explain and improve society is a challenging task due to a constant overthrowing of traditions.

Punitiveness   The new wave of toughness in punishment that has characterized a move away from rehabilitation to focus on incapacitation, through, for example, mass incarceration, 'three strikes' laws and mandatory sentencing. See **Penal populism**.

R2P (Responsibility to Protect)   linked to the notion of **State sovereignty**, the duty of a state (and increasingly the international community) to protect people from gross violations of human rights such as **Genocide**.

Radical criminology   Closely linked to **Marxist criminology**, it focuses on the power to enact laws used by the owners of the means of production to control the working class rather than the individual criminal. Reductions in crime therefore would occur only if profound structural changes in our society take place.

Radical globalists (also hyper-globalists) take an optimistic position on globalization, viewing developments such as free trade, open markets, global financial systems and the spread of democracy as positive, and highlighting how these trends are increasingly defining global space and contemporary social life.

Realpolitik politics based on power, strategic self-interest and practical and material considerations, rather than ideological or moral considerations.

Reflexivity a key term in social theory and particularly in **Late modernity**. It refers to the way in which social practices are continuously examined and reformed in light of new knowledge and information. Individuals also monitor and change their beliefs, behaviours based on self-reflection and recognition of social forces. These practices lead to constant change and evolution and undermine the solid, set social structures and identities established in **Modernity**.

Responsibility to Protect see R2P.

Restorative justice an approach to justice that prioritizes rehabilitating the offender, reconciling them with the victim and the community, and restoring or repairing the harm cause by crime.

Risk society (See **World risk society**) **Late modernity** is also described as a risk society (see Beck and Giddens) to emphasize the manufactured risks we face.

Social harm a means of defining crime. The social harm definition of crime defines behaviour that causes some form of social harm (harm to society or the environment) as crime. This type of crime may or may not be codified in existing criminal law.

Southern Criminology a new line of enquiry that challenges production of criminological knowledge which affirms the global North's approaches to theories and methods and minimizes the Global South. It is not just geographical division of the word but a power relation between what is considered 'periphery' and 'centre'.

Sovereignty the absolute right of a governing body such as a state (see **State sovereignty**) to govern itself legitimately; this power is traditionally understood as existing without any interference from outside bodies (see **Hegemony**), but in a networked society this concept is becoming more fluid (see **New world order**).

Speciesism the belief that humans should have greater moral rights than non-humans (animals) based on the fact that they are human.

State crime when the national or international governmental body acts against its people and in breach of international human rights.

State sovereignty the power of a state to rule itself and its people with legitimacy and autonomy (see **Sovereignty**).

Terror-genic an environment prone to **Terrorism**.

Terrorism violent acts against the state to subvert stability and instil fear (hence, terror) in civilians for various reasons, from political and ideological to economic and religious (see **War on terror**).

Time-space distanciation the reduction of distance among people, government and events via a better networked and technological society. Knowledge therefore travels in a faster manner than in the past. See **Globalization**.

Transitional justice processes and mechanism of transition from mass atrocity to society based on the rule of law and can involve judicial and non-judicial measures.

Transnational crimes criminal or harmful activities that originate or have effects across national borders.

Transnational organized crime a term used to refer to **Organized crime** across national borders.

War crimes crimes committed during an international armed conflict and in other conflicts listed in the Rome Statute. This is one of the four **International crimes** included in the Roma Statute.

Victimology the study of victimization, the victims of crime and their interaction with and treatment by the criminal justice system.

War on terror international military campaign that followed the attack in the US on 11 September 2001 (9/11) to track down and punish terrorists affiliated to al-Qaeda's group. See **Terrorism**.

Westphalian order the peace of Westphalia in 1648 has been recognized by international law and relations' scholars as bringing, in central Europe first and then worldwide, a new system of political order based on sovereign states who would recognize each other's national borders; it has since been referred to as the Westphalian order in contrast to the **New world order**.

World risk society following from **Risk society**, there is a shared view that risks are not spacially or temporarily circumscribed. Therefore risks are shared, from which is expected to follow a rational approach on solutions, which ought to be shared as well.

World System Theory a theoretical perspective that focuses on the dynamics of the capitalist world economy, a world economic system in which some countries benefit while others are exploited.

References

Aas, KF 2007a, 'Analysing a world in motion: Global flows meet "criminology of the other" ', *Theoretical Criminology*, vol. 11, no. 2, pp. 283–303.

Aas, KF 2007b, *Globalization and crime*, Sage, London.

Aas, KF & Bosworth, M (eds) 2013, *The borders of punishment: Migration, citizenship, and social exclusion*, Oxford University Press, Oxford.

ABC 2014, 'Four corners: The Dancing Shiva', *Australian Broadcasting Corporation Transcripts*, 24 March, accessed 2 July 2015, www.abc.net.au/4corners/stories/2014/03/24/3968642.htm

ABC News 2015, 'National Gallery of Australia to receive $1.2 million refund for "stolen" Buddha statue', *Australian Broadcasting Corporation News*, 6 March, accessed 2 July 2015, www.abc.net.au/news/2015-03-06/national-gallery-of-australia-to-receive-1-2m-refund-for-statue/6285060

ACC (Australian Crime Commission) 2013a, *Cyber and technology enabled crime*, ACC Commonwealth of Australia, Canberra, accessed 2 July 2015, pp. 1–4, www.crime-commission.gov.au/sites/default/files/CYBER%20AND%20TECHNOLOGY%20ENABLED%20CRIME%20JULY%202013.pdf

ACC (Australian Crime Commission) 2013b, *Organised crime in Australia*, Commonwealth Australia, Canberra.

Accord 2015, Accord on Fire and Building Safety in Bangladesh website: Signatories, accessed 2 July 2015, bangladeshaccord.org/signatories/

Adam, B, Beck, U & Van Loon, J (eds) 2000, *The risk society and beyond: Critical issues for social theory*, Sage, London.

Adler, E & Haas, PM 1992, Conclusion: Epistemic communities, world order, and the creation of a reflective research program, *International Organisation*, vol. 46, no. 1, pp. 367–390.

Agnew, R 2013, 'The ordinary acts that contribute to ecocide: A criminological analysis', in N South & A Brisman (eds), *The Routledge International Handbook of Green Criminology*, Routledge, London, pp. 58–72.

AIC (Australian Institute of Criminology) 2015, 'Definitions and general information – Cybercrime', Australian Government, AIC website, accessed 2 July 2015, aic.gov.au/crime_types/cybercrime/definitions.html

Albanese, J 2007, *Organized crime in our times*, LexisNexis, Newark, NJ.

Albanese, J 2015, *Organized Crime from the Mob to Transnational Organized Crime*, Abingdon: Routledge.

Alexander, H 2014, 'Second group of Amazonian Indians makes contact with outside world', *The Telegraph*, 14 August, accessed 30 June 2015, www.telegraph.co.uk/news/worldnews/southamerica/brazil/11033712/Second-group-of-Amazonian-Indians-makes-contact-with-outside-world.html

Anderson, A 2003, 'Risk, terrorism, and the Internet', *Knowledge, Technology & Policy*, vol. 16, no. 2, pp. 24–33.

Arendt, H 1992, 'Letter to Karl Jaspers. 17 August 1946', in L Kohler & H Saner (eds), *Hannah Arendt/Karl Jaspers correspondence 1926–1969*, Harcourt Brace, New York, pp. 54–55.

Arnold, AM 1998, 'Rape in cyberspace: Not just a fantasy', *Off Our Backs,* vol. 28, no. 2, pp. 12–13.

Arquilla, J & Ronfeldt, D 2001, *Networks and netwars: The future of terror, crime and militancy*, Rand Corporation, Santa Monica, CA.

Atrans, S 2006, 'The moral logic and growth of suicide terrorism', *Washington Quarterly*, vol. 29, no. 2, pp. 127–147.

AUSTRAC (Australian Transaction Reports and Analysis Centre) 2012, *Typologies and case studies report 2012*, AUSTRAC, Canberra.

AUSTRAC 2014, *Submission to the Inquiry into Financial Related Crime, Parliamentary Joint Committee on Law Enforcement, May 2014*, AUSTRAC, Canberra.

Australian 2011, 'Tourists airlifted from Tunisia riot zone', *The Australian*, 17 January, accessed 1 July 2015, www.theaustralian.com.au/archive/travel-2015-pre-life/tourists-airlifted-from-tunisia-riot-zone/story-e6frg8ro-1225989245031

Balais-Serrano, E 2007, 'Rome Statute of the International Criminal Court ratification and implementation in Asia: Some prospects and concerns', *Symposium on the International Criminal Court*, Beijing, China, 3–4 February, accessed 2 February 2010, www.icc.inseconline.org/download/Rome%20Statite%20Ratification%20and%20Implementation%20in%20Asia.pdf

Bales, K 1999, *Disposable people: New slavery in the global economy*, University of California Press, Berkeley.

Banks, D, Davies, C, Gosling, J, Newman, J, Rice, M, Wadley, J & Walravens, F 2008, *Environmental crime: A threat to our future*, Environmental Investigation Agency, London.

Barack, G (ed) 1991, *Crimes by the capitalist state: An introduction to state criminality*, State University of New York Press, Albany, NY.

Barbaret, R 2014, 'Measuring and researching transnational crime', in P Reichel & J Albanese (eds), *Handbook of transnational crime and justice*, Sage, Thousand Oaks, CA, pp. 47–60.

Bassiouni, MC 1995, 'Establishing an International Criminal Court: Historical survey', *Military Law Review*, vol. 149, pp. 49–63.

Bauman, Z 1998, *Globalization: The human consequences*, Columbia University Press, New York.

Bauman, Z 2000, *Liquid modernity*, Polity Press, Cambridge.

Bauman, Z 2003, *Liquid love: On the frailty of human bonds*, Polity Press, Cambridge.

BBC News 2012, 'Who, What, Why: In which countries is Coca-Cola not sold?, *BBC News Magazine*, 11 September, accessed 11 December 2015, www.bbc.com/news/magazine-19550067

BBC News 2015, 'Democratic Republic of Congo country profile – overview', BBC, 23 January, accessed 1 July 2015, www.bbc.com/news/world-africa-13283212

bdnews24.com 2014, 'Rana Plaza owner finally prosecuted', *bdnews24.com*, 15 July, accessed 12 February 2015, bdnews24.com/bangladesh/2014/07/15/rana-plaza-owner-finally-prosecuted

Bearnot, E 2013, 'Bangladesh: A labour paradox', *World Policy Journal,* vol. 30, no. 3, pp. 88–97.

Beck, U 1992, *Risk society: Towards a new modernity*, Sage, London.

Beck, U 1999, *World risk society*, Polity Press, Cambridge.

Beck, U 2002, 'The terrorist threat: World risk society revisited', *Theory, Culture & Society*, vol. 19, no. 4, pp. 39–55.

Beck, U 2006, *Living in the world risk society*, Hobhouse Memorial Public Lecture, LSE, London, 15 February 2006, accessed 2 July 2015, via Taylor & Francis Online, www.tandfonline.com/doi/abs/10.1080/03085140600844902

Beck, U, Giddens, A & Lash, S (eds) 1994, *Reflexive modernization: Politics, tradition and aesthetics in the modern social order*, Stanford University Press, Stanford, CA.

Beirne, P & South, N 2007, 'Introduction: Approaching green criminology', in P Beirne & N South, *Issues in green criminology: Confronting harms against environments, humanity and other animals*, Willan, Cullompton, pp. 3–31.

Belasco, A 2008, *CRS report for Congress: The cost of Iraq, Afghanistan, and other global war on terror operations since 9/11*, Congressional Research Service, Washington, DC.

Bennett, CJ 1991, 'Review article: What is policy convergence and what causes it?', *British Journal of Political Science*, vol. 21, no. 2, pp. 215–233.

Bhui, HS 2013, 'Introduction: Humanizing migration control and detention', in KF Aas & M Bosworth (eds), *The borders of punishment: Migration, citizenship, and social exclusion*, Oxford University Press, Oxford, pp. 1–20.

Bisschop, L 2015, 'Facilitators of environmental crime: Corporations and governments in the Port of Antwerp', in J van Erp, W Huisman & G Vande Walle (eds), *Routledge Handbook of White-Collar Crime in Europe*, pp. 246–259.

Boland, M 2015, 'NGA gets refund as Buddha goes home', *The Australian*, 6 March.

Brack, D 2002, 'Combatting international environmental crime', *Global Environmental Change*, vol. 12, no. 2, pp. 143–147.

Bratton, W 1997, 'Crime is down in New York City: Blame the police', in N Dennis (ed.), *Zero tolerance policing in a free society*, Institute of Economic Affairs, London, pp. 29–42.

Brereton, D 1999, 'Zero tolerance and the NYPD: Has it worked there and will it work here?' Paper presented to the Australian Institute of Criminology Conference, *Mapping the Boundaries of Australia's Criminal Justice System*, Canberra, 22–23 March 1999.

Bronitt, S, Harfield, C & Hufnagel, S 2013, *Cross-border law enforcement: Regional law enforcement cooperation – European, Australian and Asia-Pacific perspectives*, Routledge, London.

Brown, G 2009, 'We are about to take the war against terror to a new level', *The Observer*, 22 March, accessed online via Guardian.co.uk: www.theguardian.com/commentisfree/2009/mar/22/gordon-brown-terrorism.

Brungs, M 2002, 'Abolishing child sex tourism: Australia's contribution', *Australian Journal of Human Rights*, vol. 8, no. 2, pp. 101–124.

Budiani-Saberi, D & Delmonico F 2008, 'Organ trafficking and transplant tourism: A commentary on the global realities', *American Journal of Transplantation*, vol. 8, no. 5, pp. 925–929.

Bumillier, K 2008, *In an abusive state: How neoliberalism appropriated the feminist movement against sexual violence*, Duke University Press, Durham, NC.

Burke, J 2013, 'Bangladesh factory collapse leaves trail of shattered lives', *The Guardian*, 6 June, accessed 12 February 2015, www.theguardian.com/world/2013/jun/06/bangladesh-factory-building-collapse-community

Buttel, FH 2003, 'Some observations on the anti-globalization movement', *Australian Journal of Social Sciences,* vol. 38, no. 1, pp. 95–116, search.informit.com.au. ezproxy.flinders.edu.au/fullText;dn=770571619320499;res=IELAPA

Byassee, WS 1995, 'Jurisdiction of cyberspace: Applying real world precedent to the virtual community', *Wake Forest Law Review,* vol. 30, no. 1, pp. 197–220.

Cadwalladr, C 2013, 'How I bought drugs from "dark net" – it's just like Amazon run by cartels', *The Guardian,* 6 October, accessed 1 July 2015, www.theguardian.com/society/2013/oct/06/dark-net-drugs

Campbell, D & Davison, N 2012, 'Illegal kidney trade booms as new organ is "sold every hour" ', *The Guardian,* 28 May, accessed 1 July 2015, www.theguardian.com/world/2012/may/27/kidney-trade-illegal-operations-who

Cantor, D 2014, 'The new wave: Forced displacement caused by organized crime in Central America and Mexico', *Refugee Survey Quarterly,* vol. 33, no. 3, pp. 34–68.

Cape Argus 2015, 'Sold into a life of misery', *Cape Argus,* 26 February, accessed 30 March 2015, via Factiva.

Casey, L 2002, 'The case against the International Criminal Court', *Fordham International Law Journal,* vol. 25, no. 3, pp. 840–872.

Cassese, A 2003, *International criminal law,* Oxford University Press, Oxford.

Castells, M 2000, *The information age, economy, society and culture, vol. 1, The rise of the network society,* Blackwell, Cambridge, MA.

Castells, M 2004, *The network society: A cross-cultural perspective,* Edward Elgar, Cheltenham.

Caufield, C 1996, *Masters of illusion: The World Bank and the poverty of nations,* Macmillan, London.

Centre for Management and Policy Studies (CMPS) 2002, Beyond Horizons: Using International Comparisons in Policy Making: Toolkit, Cabinet Office, accessed 10 December 2015, http://people.bath.ac.uk/hssgjr/documents/sumprin.pdf

Chambliss, WJ 1989, 'State-organized crime', *Criminology,* vol. 27, no. 2, pp. 183–204.

Charlesworth, H 2002, 'International law: A discipline of crisis', *The Modern Law Review,* vol. 65, no. 1, pp. 377–392.

Chazal, N & Pocrnic, A 2016, 'Kony 2012: Intervention narratives and the saviour subject', *International Journal for Crime, Justice and Social Democracy,* vol. 5, no. 1.

Chow-White, P 2006, 'Race, gender and sex on the net: Semantic networks of selling and storytelling sex tourism', *Media, Culture & Society,* vol. 28, no. 6, pp. 883–905.

Christie, N 2000, *Crime control as industry: Towards gulags, western style,* 3rd edn, Routledge, New York.

CICC 2015, Coalition for the International Criminal Court website, accessed 12 June 2015, www.iccnow.org

Clifford, J 1997, *Routes: Travel and translation in the late twentieth century,* Harvard University Press, Cambridge, MA.

Cohen, S 1990, 'Intellectual scepticism and political commitment: The case of radical criminology', Institute of Criminology, University of Amsterdam.

Cohen, S 1993, 'Human rights and crimes of the state: The culture of denial', *Australian and New Zealand Journal of Criminology,* vol. 26, no. 2, pp. 97–115.

Cohen, S 2001, *States of denial: Knowing about atrocities and suffering,* Polity Press, Cambridge.

Cooney, R & Lang, A 2007, 'Taking uncertainty seriously: Adaptive governance and international trade', *The European Journal of International Law,* vol. 18, no. 3, pp. 523–551.

Crawshaw, M, Fronek, P, Blyth, E & Elvinet, A 2014, 'What are children's "best interests" in international surrogacy?', accessed 26 April 2015, cdn.basw.co.uk/upload/basw_123433-9.pdf

Cruvellier, T 2010, *Court of remorse: Inside the International Criminal Tribunal for Rwanda*, University of Wisconsin Press, Madison.

Culley, L & Hudson, N 2010, 'Fertility tourists or global consumers? A sociological agenda for exploring cross-border reproductive travel', *International Journal of Interdisciplinary Social Sciences*, vol. 4, no. 10, pp. 139–150.

Daems, T & Robert, L 2007, 'Crime and insecurity in liquid modern times: An interview with Zygmunt Bauman', *Contemporary Justice Review: Issues in Criminal, Social, and Restorative Justice*, vol. 10, no. 1, pp. 87–100.

Dalton, D 2014, *Dark tourism and crime*, Routledge, Abingdon.

D'Amato, A, Mazzanti, M & Nicolli, F 2015,'Waste and organized crime in regional environments: How waste tariffs and the mafia affect waste management and disposal', *Resource and Energy Economics*, vol. 41, pp. 185–201.

DEBKAfile 2015, 'DarkNet: A thriving marketplace for criminal transactions – from narcotics to terrorism', *DEBKAfile*, Exclusive Report, 23 February, accessed 18 March 2015, www.debka.com/article/24419/DarkNet-A-thriving-marketplace-for-criminal-transactions---from-narcotics-to-terrorism-

de Goede, M 2008, 'Beyond risk: Premeditation and post-9/11 security imagination', *Security Dialogue*, vol. 39, no. 2–3, pp. 155–176.

de Lint, W & Virta, S 2004, 'Security in ambiguity: Towards a radical security politics', *Theoretical Criminology*, vol. 8, no. 4, pp. 465–489.

Dembour, M & Kelly, T (eds) 2011, *Are human rights for migrants? Critical reflections on the status of irregular migrants in Europe and the United States*, Routledge, Abingdon.

Denton, F 2002, 'Climate change vulnerability, impacts and adaptation: Why does gender matter?', *Gender & Development,* vol. 10, no. 2, pp. 10–20.

Der Derian, J 2002, 'In terrorem: Before and after 9/11', in K Booth & T Dunne (eds), *Worlds in collision: Terror and the future of global order*, Palgrave Macmillan, Basingstoke, pp. 101–17.

Dibbell, J 1994, 'Rape in cyberspace or how an evil clown, a Haitian trickster spirit, two wizards, and a cast of dozens turned a database into a society', *Annual Survey of American Law*, vol. 3, pp. 471–490.

Dolowitz, DP & Marsh, D 2000, 'Learning from abroad: The role of policy transfer in contemporary policy-making', *Governance: An International Journal of Policy and Administration*, vol. 13, no. 1, pp. 5–23.

Downie, D & Chasek, P 2013, *Global environment politics*, Westview Press, Colorado.

Duffield, M 2007, *Development, security and war: Governing the world of peoples*, Polity Press, Cambridge.

Durlacher, J 2000, *Cocaine*, Carlton Books, London.

Dwyer, M 2013, 'Where did the anti-globalization movement go?', *New Republic,* 25 October, accessed 2 July 2015, www.newrepublic.com/article/115360/wto-protests-why-have-they-gotten-smaller

Economist 2013a, 'Disaster in Bangladesh: Rags in the ruins', *The Economist (Dhaka and Savar)*, 4 May, accessed 12 February 2015, www.economist.com/news/asia/21577124-tragedy-shows-need-radical-improvement-building-standards-rags-ruins

Economist 2013b, 'Prosecuting bankers: Blind justice: Why have so few bankers gone to jail for their part in the crisis?', *The Economist*, 4 May, accessed 24 May 2015, www.economist.com/node/21577064/print

Economist 2013c, 'The origins of the financial crisis: Crash course', *The Economist*, 7 September, accessed 24 May 2015, www.economist.com/news/schoolsbrief/21584534-effects-financial-crisis-are-still-being-felt-five-years-article

Economist Intelligence Unit, 2015, 'Thailand industry: Here be monsters', *ViewsWire*, 14 March, accessed 30 March 2015, via Factiva.

Edwards, A & Gill, P (eds) 2003, *Transnational organised crime: Perspectives on global security*, Routledge, London.

Eilstrup-Sangiovanni, M 2005, 'Transnational networks and new security threats', *Cambridge Review of International Affairs*, vol. 18, no. 1, pp. 7–13.

EJF (Environmental Justice Foundation) 2013a, *The hidden cost: Human rights abuses in Thailand's shrimp industry*, Environmental Justice Foundation, London, ejfoundation.org/sites/default/files/public/shrimp_report_v44_lower_resolution.pdf

EJF (Environmental Justice Foundation) 2013b, *Sold to the sea: Human trafficking in Thailand's fishing industry*, Environmental Justice Foundation, London, ejfoundation.org/sites/default/files/public/Sold_to_the_Sea_report_lo-res-v2.pdf

Elliot, A 2002, 'Beck's sociology of risk: A critical assessment', *Sociology*, vol. 36, no. 2, pp. 293–315.

Elliot, A (ed.) 2007, *The contemporary Bauman*, Routledge, Abingdon.

Elliot, A 2009, *Contemporary social theory: An introduction*, Routledge, Abingdon.

Elliot, A & Urry, J 2010, *Mobile lives*, Routledge, Abingdon.

Elliott, L 2004, *The global politics of the environment*, New York University Press, New York.

Elliot, L 2012, 'Fighting Transnational Environmental Crime', *Journal of International Affairs*, vol. 66, no. 1, pp. 87-xii

Ericson, R 2007, *Crime in an insecure world*, Polity Press, Cambridge.

Escobar, R 2009, *Escobar: The inside story of Pablo Escobar, the world's most powerful criminal*, Hodder, London.

Europol 2013, *EU serious and organised crime threat assessment 2013*, European Police Office, The Hague, accessed 2 July 2015, via Europol website, www.europol.europa.eu/content/eu-serious-and-organised-crime-threat-assessment-socta

Faust, KL & Kauzlarich, D 2008, 'Hurricane Katrina victimization as a state crime of omission', *Critical Criminology*, vol. 16, no. 2, pp. 85–103.

FBI 2015, 'Ross Ulbricht, the creator and owner of the Silk Road website, found guilty in Manhattan Federal Court on all counts', The Federal Bureau of Investigation, Press Release, 5 February, accessed 18 March 2015, www.fbi.gov/newyork/press-releases/2015/ross-ulbricht-the-creator-and-owner-of-the-silk-road-website-found-guilty-in-manhattan-federal-court-on-all-counts

Feeley, M & Simon, J 1994, 'Actuarial justice: The emerging new criminal law', in D Nelken (ed.), *Futures of criminology*, Sage, London, pp. 173–201.

Felbab-Brown, V 2009, *Shooting up: Counter-insurgency and the war on drugs*, Brookings Institution, Washington, DC.

Ferguson, CH et al. 2010, *Inside job*, motion picture, Sony Pictures Home Entertainment, Culver City, CA.

Finckenauer, J 2007, *Mafia and organized crime*, OneWorld Books, Oxford.

Findlay, M 2008, *Governing through globalised crime: Futures for international criminal justice*, Willan, Portland, OR.

Flynn, A & Fitz-Gibbon, K 2010, 'The honeymoon killer: Plea bargaining and intimate femicide: a response to Watson', *Alternative Law Journal*, vol. 35, no. 4, pp. 203–207, dro.deakin.edu.au/eserv/DU:30043976/fitzgibbon-honeymoonkiller-2010.pdf

Fotopoulos, T 2001, 'Globalisation, the reformist Left, and the anti-globalisation "movement" ', *Democracy & Nature*, vol. 7, no. 2, pp. 233–280.

Franzen, C 2013, 'Ill-gotten gains: How many museums have stolen objects in their collections?', *The Verge.com*, 13 May, accessed 2 July 2015, www.theverge.com/2013/5/13/4326306/museum-artifacts-looted-repatriation

Friedrichs, D 2007a, 'White-collar crime in a postmodern, globalized world' in H. N. Pontell & G. Geis (eds.), *International handbook of white-collar and corporate crime*, Springer, New York, pp. 163–184.

Friedrichs, D 2007b, 'Transnational crime and global criminology: Definition, typological and contextual conundrums', *Social Justice*, vol. 34, no. 2, pp. 4–18.

Friedrichs, D 2013, 'Wall Street: Crime never sleeps', in S Will, S Handelman & D Brotherton (eds), *How they got away with it: White collar criminals and the financial meltdown*, Columbia University Press, New York, pp. 3–25.

Friedrichs, D & Friedrichs, J 2002, 'The World Bank and crimes of globalization: A case study', *Social Justice*, vol. 29, no. 1–2, pp. 1–12.

Gallagher, A 2015, 'Two cheers for the trafficking protocol', *Anti-Trafficking Review*, vol. 4, pp. 14–32.

Gambetta, D 2006, *The Sicilian Mafia: The business of private protection*, Harvard University Press, Cambridge, MA.

Ganjanakhundee, S 2014, 'Thailand reverses earlier decision, backs ILO protocol on forced labour', *The Sunday Nation*, 15 June, accessed 30 March 2015, www.nationmultimedia.com/national/Thailand-reverses-earlier-decision-backs-ILO-proto-30236260.html

Garland, D 1996, 'The limits of the sovereign state: Strategies of crime control in contemporary society', *The British Journal of Criminology*, vol. 36, no. 4, pp. 445–471.

Garland, D 2001, *The culture of control*, Oxford University Press, Oxford.

Garland, D & Sparks, R 2000, 'Criminology, social theory, and the challenge of our times', in D Garland and R Sparks (eds), *Criminology and social theory*, Oxford University Press, New York, pp. 1–22.

Gauger, A, Rabatel-Fernel, M, Kulbicki, L, Short, D & Higgins, P 2012, The Ecocide project 'Ecocide is the missing 5th Crime Against Peace', Human Rights Consortium, London.

Gerhards, J & Rucht, D 1992, 'Mesomobilization: Organizing and framing in two protest campaigns in West Germany', *American Journal of Sociology*, vol. 98, no. 3, pp. 555–595.

Ghods, AJ & Savaj, S 2006, 'Iranian model of paid and regulated living-unrelated kidney donation', *Clinical Journal of the American Society of Nephrology*, vol. 1, no. 6, pp. 1136–1145.

Gibbons, DC 1994, *Talking about crime and criminals: Problems and issues in theory development in criminology*, Prentice-Hall, Englewood Cliffs, NJ.

Giddens, A 1981, *A contemporary critique of historical materialism, vol. 1, Power, property and the state*, University of California Press, Berkeley.

Giddens, A 1990, *The consequences of modernity*, Stanford University Press, Stanford, CA.

Giddens, A 1991, *Modernity and self-identity: Self and society in the late modern age*, Stanford University Press, Stanford, CA.

Giddens, A 2002, *Runaway world: How globalisation is reshaping our lives*, Profile Books, London.

Giddens, A & Pierson, C 1998, *Conversations with Anthony Giddens: Making sense of modernity*, Polity Press, Cambridge.

Glasius, M 2006, *The International Criminal Court: A global civil society achievement*, Routledge, New York.

Glenny, M 2008, *McMafia: Crime without frontiers*, Bodley Head, London.

Goldsmith, A 2007, 'Preparation for terrorism: Catastrophic risk and precautionary criminal law', in A Lynch, E McDonald & G Williams (eds), *Law and liberty in the war on terror*, Federation Press, Sydney, pp. 59–73.

Goldsmith, A 2008, 'The governance of terror: Precautionary logic and counter-terrorism reform after September 11', *Law & Policy*, vol. 30, no. 2, pp. 141–167.

Goldsmith, A. & Dinnen, S 2007, 'Transnational police building: Critical lessons from Timor-Leste and Solomon Islands', *Third World Quarterly*, vol. 28, no. 6, pp. 1091–1109.

Goldsmith, A & Sheptycki, J (eds) 2007, *Crafting transnational policing: Police capacity-building and global policing reform*, Hart, Oxford.

Goldsmith, J 2003, 'The self-defeating International Criminal Court', *University of Chicago Law Review*, vol. 70, no. 1, pp. 89–104.

Goncalves, R, Lourenco, A & da Silva, S 2015, 'A social cost perspective in the wake of the Portuguese strategy for the fight against drugs', *International Journal of Drug Policy*, vol. 26, no. 2, pp. 199–209.

Goodman, K 2013, 'The Dark Net: The new face of black markets and organized crime', *The Huffington Post*, 16 October, accessed 1 July 2015, www.huffingtonpost.com/kevin-goodman/internet-black-markets_b_4111000.html

Gramsci, A 1971, *Selections from the prison notebooks*, Lawrence & Wishart, London.

Green, P & Ward, T 2004, *State crime: Governments, violence and corruption*, Pluto Press, London.

Greenhouse, S 2013, 'Major retailers join Bangladesh safety plan', *The New York Times*, 13 May, accessed 10 February 2015, www.nytimes.com/2013/05/14/business/global/hm-agrees-to-bangladesh-safety-plan.html?_r=1&

Gregory, P 2013, 'Dangerous ethics', *The Institute of Public Affairs Review: A Quarterly Review of Politics and Public Affairs*, vol. 65, no. 3, pp. 26–27.

GSDRC (Governance and Social Development Resource Centre) 2008, 'Helpdesk research report: Climate change and social exclusion', accessed 25 June 2015, www.gsdrc.org/docs/open/HD501.pdf

Guild, E 2005, 'The legal framework: Who is entitled to move?', in D Bigo & E Guild (eds), *Controlling frontiers: Free movement into and within Europe*, Ashgate, Farnham, pp. 14–48.

Gupta, D 2011, 'Inside India's surrogacy industry', *The Guardian*, 7 December, accessed 1 July 2015, www.theguardian.com/world/2011/dec/06/surrogate-mothers-india

Hall, M 2014, 'The roles and use of law in green criminology', *International Journal for Crime, Justice and Social Democracy*, vol. 3, no. 2, pp. 96–109.

Halsey, M 2006, 'Social explanations for crime', in A Goldsmith, M Israel & K Daly (eds), *Crime and justice: A guide to criminology*, 3rd edn, Lawbook Co., Pyrmont, NSW.

Harfield, C 2006, 'SOCA: A paradigm shift in British policing', *British Journal of Criminology*, vol. 46, no. 4, pp. 743–761.

Harris, G 2013, 'Bangladeshi factory owners charged in fatal fire', *The New York Times*, 23 December, accessed 17 February 2015, www.nytimes.com/2013/12/23/world/asia/bangladeshi-factory-owners-charged-in-fatal-fire.html?_r=0.

Hart-Landsberg, M 2013, 'Lessons from Iceland: Capitalism, crisis and resistance', *Monthly Review*, vol. 65, no. 5, 1 October, accessed 24 May 2015, monthlyreview.org/2013/10/01/lessons-iceland/

Harvey, D 1990, *The condition of postmodernity: An enquiry into the origins of cultural change*, Blackwell, Cambridge, MA.

Hawley, S 2015, 'Baby Gammy, one-year-old at centre of Thai surrogacy scandal, granted Australian citizenship', *The Australian*, 20 January, accessed 1 July 2015, www.abc.net.au/news/2015-01-20/baby-gammy-granted-australian-citizenship/6026600

Head, M 2002, ' "Counter-terrorism" laws: A threat to political freedom, civil liberties and constitutional rights', *Melbourne University Law Review*, vol. 26, no. 3, pp. 666–689.

Heaphy, B 2007, *Late modernity and social change: Reconstructing social and personal life*, Routledge, Abingdon.

Hehir, A 2007, 'The myth of the failed state and the war on terror: A challenge to the conventional wisdom', *Journal of Intervention and State-building*, vol. 1, no. 3, pp. 307–332.

Held, D 2004, *Global covenant: The social democratic alternative to the Washington Consensus*, Polity Press, Cambridge.

Held, D & McGrew, A 2007, *Globalization/anti-globalization: Beyond the great divide*, Polity Press, Cambridge.

Held, D, McGrew, A, Goldblatt, A & Perraton, J 1999, *Global transformations: Politics, economics and culture*, Stanford University Press, Stanford, CA.

Henry, S & Milovanovic, D 1996, *Constitutive criminology: Beyond postmodernism*, Sage, London.

Hodal, K 2015, 'Thailand failing to tackle fishing industry slavery, says rights group', *The Guardian*, 18 February, accessed 30 March 2015, via Factiva.

Hodal, K, Kelly, C & Lawrence, F 2014, 'Revealed: Asian slave labour producing prawns for supermarkets in US, UK', *The Guardian*, 10 June, accessed 30 March 2015, www.theguardian.com/global-development/2014/jun/10/supermarket-prawns-thailand-produced-slave-labour

Holzapfel, M & Konig, K 2002, 'A history of the anti-globalisation protests', *Eurozine. com*, 5 April, accessed 2 July 2015, www.eurozine.com/articles/2002-04-05-holzapfel-en.html

Horowitz, M, Rosensweig, J & Jones, C 2007, 'Medical tourism: Globalization of the healthcare marketplace', *Medscape General Medicine*, vol. 9, no. 4, pp. 33–42.

Hugo, G 2004, *A new paradigm of international migration: Implications for migration policy and planning in Australia*, Research Paper 10, Parliamentary Library, Commonwealth of Australia, Canberra.

Human Rights Watch 2011, 'Justice compromised: The legacy of Rwanda's community-based Gacaca courts', 31 May, accessed 1 July 2015, www.hrw.org/report/2011/05/31/justice-compromised/legacy-rwandas-community-based-gacaca-courts

Human Rights Watch 2014, 'Global treaty to protect forced labor victims adopted', 11 June, accessed 30 March 2015, www.hrw.org/news/2014/06/11/global-treaty-protect-forced-labor-victims-adopted

Huntington, S 1996, *The clash of civilizations and the remaking of world order*, Simon & Schuster, New York.

Husain, E 2007, *The Islamist*, Penguin, London.

IBA (International Bar Association) 2015, 'Launch of eyeWitness to Atrocities app announced by IBA President', International Bar Association website, accessed 2 July 2015, www.ibanet.org/Article/Detail.aspx?ArticleUid=fea850c7-6f8e-4c75-9ee2-0d9af1e053ac

Ikemoto, L 2009, 'Reproductive tourism: Equality concerns in the global market for fertility services', *Law and Inequality: A Journal of Theory and Practice*, vol. 27, no. 2, pp. 277–309.

ILO (International Labour Office) 2012a, 'Global estimate of forced labour: Executive summary', International Labour Office, Geneva.

ILO 2012b, 'Questions and answers on forced labour', ILO website: Analysis, 1 June, accessed 30 March 2015, www.ilo.org/global/about-the-ilo/newsroom/comment-analysis/WCMS_181922/lang--en/index.htm

ILO 2015, 'Forced labour, human trafficking and slavery', ILO website, accessed 1 July 2015, www.ilo.org/global/topics/forced-labour/lang—en/index.htm

Interpol 2006, *Assessing the links between organised crime and pollution crimes*, Pollution Crime Working Group, Environmental Crime Programme, Lyon.

Interpol 2013, *Strategic analysis report on illegal export of electronic waste to non-OECD countries*, Pollution Crime Working Group, Lyon.

Interpol 2015, 'About Interpol: Vision and mission', Interpol website, accessed 2 July 2015, www.interpol.int/About-INTERPOL/Vision-and-mission

Ireland-Piper, D 2012, 'Extraterritorial criminal jurisdiction: Does the long arm of the law undermine the rule of law?', *Melbourne Journal of International Law*, vol. 13, no. 1, pp. 122–157.

IRIN Asia English Service 2011, 'Cambodia-Thailand: Men trafficked into "slavery" at sea', *IRIN News*, 29 August, accessed 30 March 2015, www.irinnews.org/report/93606

IRIN Asia English Service 2012, 'Cambodia: No recourse for enslaved migrant workers', *IRIN Asia English Service*, 27 June, accessed 20 March 2015, via ProQuest.

Irwin, N 2013, 'This is a complete list of Wall Street CEOs prosecuted for their role in the financial crisis', *Washington Post,* 12 September, accessed 24 May 2015, www.washingtonpost.com/blogs/wonkblog/wp/2013/09/12/this-is-a-complete-list-of-wall-street-ceos-prosecuted-for-their-role-in-the-financial-crisis/

Jamieson, R & McEvoy, K 2005, 'State crime by proxy and juridical othering', *The British Journal of Criminology*, vol. 45, no. 4, pp. 504–527.

Jennings, R & Watts, A 1996, *Oppenheim's International Law, vol. 1, Peace*, 9th edn, Longman, London.

Justice UK 2014, 'Contracted-out prisons', Justice UK website, 7 January, accessed 1 July 2015, www.justice.gov.uk/about/hmps/contracted-out

Kamali Dehghan, S 2012, 'Kidneys for sale: Poor Iranians compete to sell their organs', *The Guardian*, 28 May, accessed 1 July 2015, www.theguardian.com/world/2012/may/27/iran-legal-trade-kidney

Kauzlarich, D 2008, 'Victimisation and supranational criminology', in A Smeulers & R Haveman (eds), *Supranational criminology: Towards a criminology of international crimes*, Intersentia, Antwerp, pp. 435–453.

Kauzlarich, D, Matthews, RA & Miller, WJ 2001, 'Toward a victimology of state crime', *Critical Criminology: An International Journal*, vol. 10, no. 3, pp. 173–194.

Kenny, M 2007, *From Pablo to Osama: Trafficking and terrorist networks, government bureaucracies, and competitive adaptation*, Penn State Press, University Park, PA.

Kirsch, P & Holmes, J 1999, 'The Rome Conference on an International Criminal Court: The negotiating process', *The American Journal of International Law*, vol. 93, no. 1, pp. 2–12.

Klein, N 2007, *The shock doctrine: The rise of disaster capitalism*, Penguin, London.

Kleinman, R & Dhillon, A 2014, 'The National Gallery of Australia dances into trouble with Shiva', *The Sydney Morning Herald*, 18 March, accessed 2 July 2015, www.smh.com.au/national/the-national-gallery-of-australia-dances-into-trouble-with-shiva-20140317-34xui.html

Kline, H 1999, *State-building and conflict resolution in Colombia*, University of Alabama Press, Tuscaloosa.

Kramer, R & Michalowski, R 2005, 'War, aggression and state crime', *The British Journal of Criminology*, vol. 45, no. 4, pp. 446–469.

Kramer, R, Michalowski, R & Rothe, D 2005, ' "The supreme international crime": How the U.S. war in Iraq threatens the rule of law', *Social Justice*, vol. 32, no. 2, pp. 52–81.

Kucera, D, Roncolato, L & von Uexkull, E 2011, 'The trade and financial crisis in India and South Africa', in International Labour Organization (ed.), *The global crisis: Causes, responses and challenges*, ILO, Geneva.

Kuttner, R 2013, 'Sweat & tears', *The American Prospect*, vol. 24, no. 4, pp. 60–65.

Lambert, R 2008, 'Empowering Salafis and Islamists against al-Qaeda: A London counter-terrorism case study', *Political Science & Politics*, vol. 41, no. 1, pp. 31–35.

Latin American Commission on Drugs and Democracy 2008, *Drugs and democracy: Toward a paradigm shift*, accessed 2 July 2015 via Open Foundations website, www.opensocietyfoundations.org/publications/drugs-and-democracy-toward-paradigm-shiftvia

Legal Information Institute n.d., '18 U.S. Code 2113 – Bank robbery and incidental crimes', Cornell University Law School, accessed 24 May 2015, www.law.cornell.edu/uscode/text/18/2113

Lenzner, NR 1994, 'The illicit international trade in cultural property: Does the Unidroit Convention provide an effective remedy for the shortcomings of the UNESCO Convention?', *University of Pennsylvania Journal of International Business Law*, vol. 15, no. 3, pp. 469–507.

Levi, M 2004, 'The making of the United Kingdom's organised crime control policies', in C Fijnaut and L Paoli (eds), *Organised crime in Europe: Concepts, patterns and control policies in the European Union and beyond*, Springer, Dordrecht, pp. 413–34.

Levi, M & Maguire, M 2004, 'Reducing and preventing organised crime: An evidence-based critique', *Crime, Law & Social Change*, vol. 41, no. 5, pp. 397–469.

Lin, T 2013, 'Born lost: Stateless children in international surrogacy arrangements', *Cardozo Journal of International and Comparative Law*, vol. 21, no. 2, pp. 545–588.

Louw, A 2010, 'S Africa: Police probe theft of body parts for sale to Far East', BBC Monitoring Africa, 2 July, accessed 1 July 2015, via Factiva.

Lunt, N, Horsfall, D & Hanefeld, J 2015, 'The shaping of contemporary medical tourism and patient mobility', in N Lunt, D Horsfall & J Hanefeld (eds), *Handbook on medical tourism and patient mobility*, Edward Elgar, Cheltenham, pp. 3–15.

Lynch, M 1990, 'The greening of criminology: A perspective on the 1990s', *Critical Criminologist*, vol. 2, pp. 3–11.

Mackenzie, S 2011, 'The market as criminal and criminals in the market: reducing opportunities for organised crime in the international antiquities market', in S Manacorda and D Chappell (eds), *Crime in the Art and Antiquities World: Illegal Trafficking in Cultural Property*, Springer, New York, pp. 69–86.

Mackenzie, S & Green, P 2008, 'Performative regulation: A case study in how powerful people avoid criminal labels', *British Journal of Criminology*, vol. 48, no. 2, pp. 138–153.

Macnaghten, P 2006, 'Environment and risk', in G Mythen & S Walklate (eds), *Beyond the risk society: Critical reflections on risk and human security*, Open University Press, Maidenhead, pp. 132–148.

Manager Magazin Online 2013, 'Silk Road: Deep inside the internet hides a booming market for any kind of drug', *Manager Magazin*, 11 January, accessed 18 March 2015, via Factiva: www.manager-magazin.de/unternehmen/international/a-877878.html.

Mann, M 2001, 'Globalisation and September 11th', *New Left Review*, vol. 12, November/December, pp. 51–72.

March, S 2014, 'Indian police call on National Gallery of Australia to return 900-year-old statue of deity', *Australian Broadcasting Corporation News*, 21 March, accessed 2 July 2015, www.abc.net.au/news/2014-03-21/an-indian-police-call-on-national-gallery-of-australia-to-retur/5335174

Martin, C 2003, 'Globalization and national environmental policy: The influence of WWF, an international non-governmental organization', in F. Wijen, K. Zoeteman, & J. Pieters (eds), *A handbook of globalisation and environmental policy: National government interventions in a global arena*, Edward Elgar, Cheltenham, 2005, pp. 392–420.

Martin, J 2014, *Drugs on the dark net: How cryptomarkets are transforming the global trade in illicit drugs*, Palgrave Macmillan, Basingstoke.

Massari, M & Monzini, P 2004, 'Dirty businesses in Italy: A case-study of illegal trafficking in hazardous waste', *Global Crime*, vol. 6, no. 3–4, pp. 285–304.

Matthews, R & Kauzlarich, D 2007, 'State crimes and state harms: A tale of two definitional frameworks', *Crime, Law & Social Change*, vol. 48, no. 1–2, pp. 43–55.

McCulloch, J 2003, ' "Counter-terrorism", human security and globalisation: From welfare to warfare state?', *Current Issues in Criminal Justice*, vol. 14, no. 3, pp. 283–298.

McCulloch, J & Pickering, S 2009, 'Pre-crime and counter-terrorism: Imagining future crime in the "war on terror" ', *British Journal of Criminology*, vol. 49, no. 5, pp. 628–645.

McDonald, J M 2008, 'Restorative justice process in case law', *Alternative Law Journal*, vol. 3, pp. 340–44.

McLuhan, M and Powers, B 1989, *The global village: Transformations in world life and media in the 21st century*, Oxford University Press, New York.

Melossi, D 2003, '"In a peaceful life": Migration and the crime of modernity in Europe/Italy', *Punishment & Society*, vol. 5, no. 4, pp. 371–397.

Melossi, D 2004, 'The cultural embeddedness of social control', in T Newburn & R Sparks (eds), *Criminal justice and political cultures: National and international dimensions of crime control*, Willan, Cullompton, pp. 80–103.

Michals, D 1997, 'Cyber-rape: How virtual is it?', *Ms Magazine*, vol. 7, no. 5, pp. 68–72, accessed 24 February 2015, via ProQuest, search.proquest.com.ezproxy.flinders.edu.au/docview/204301496/fulltextPDF?accountid=10910

Milward, HB & Raab, J 2006, 'Dark networks as organizational problems: Elements of a theory', *International Public Management Journal*, vol. 9, no. 4, pp. 333–360.

Morozov, E 2009, 'The brave new world of slacktivism', *Foreign Policy*, 19 May, accessed 21 March 2013, neteffect.foreignpolicy.com/posts/2009/05/19/the_brave_new_world_of_slacktivism

Morselli, C 2009, *Inside criminal networks*, Springer, Dordrecht.

Motlagh, J 2014, 'The ghosts of Rana Plaza', *The Virginia Quarterly Review*, vol. 90, no. 2, pp. 44–89.

Mount, I 2014, 'Spain toughens up on financial criminals', *Fortune*, 24 October, accessed 24 May 2015, fortune.com/2014/10/24/spain-toughens-up-on-financial-criminals/

Muncie, J & McLaughlin, E (eds) 2001, *The problem of crime*, 2nd edn, Sage, London.

Mutua, M 2001, 'Savages, victims, and saviors: The metaphor of human rights', *Harvard International Law Journal*, vol. 42, no. 1, pp. 201–246.

Nadelmann, E 1993, *Cops across borders: The internationalization of US criminal law enforcement*, Penn State University Press, University Park, PA.

NATO 2015, 'What is Nato?', North Atlantic Treaty Organization website, accessed 2 July 2015, www.nato.int/nato-welcome/

NCA (National Crime Agency) 2014, *National strategic assessment of serious and organised crime 2014*, NCA, London.

Neate, R 2012, 'Iceland ex-PM Geir Haarde cleared of bank negligence', *The Guardian*, 24 April, accessed 24 May 2015, www.theguardian.com/world/2012/apr/23/iceland-geir-haarde-found-guilty

Newburn, T & Jones, T 2007a, 'Symbolizing crime control: Reflection on zero tolerance', *Theoretical Criminology*, vol. 11, no. 2, pp. 221–243.

Newburn, T & Jones, T 2007b, *Policy transfer and criminal justice: Exploring US influence over British crime control policy*, Open University Press, Maidenhead.

News.com.au, 2015, 'Investigation reveals slave link to supermarket seafood supply', *News.com.au*, 26 March, accessed 30 March 2015, via Factiva.

New York Times 2014, 'One year after Rana Plaza', *The New York Times.com Feed*, 28 April, accessed 12 February 2015, www.nytimes.com/2014/04/28/opinion/one-year-after-rana-plaza.html.

Nordstrom, C. 2000, 'Shadows and Sovereigns', *Theory, Culture & Society*, vol. 17, no. 4, pp. 35–54.

Norris, P 2001, *Digital divide: Civic engagement, information poverty, and the Internet worldwide*, Cambridge University Press, Cambridge.

Nouwen, S 2006, ' "Hybrid courts": The hybrid category of a new type of international crimes court', *Utrecht Law Review*, vol. 2, no. 2, pp. 190–214.

Nurse, A 2013, *Animal harm: Perspectives on why people harm and kill animals*, Ashgate, Farnham UK.

O'Brien, M 2011, 'Society is entitled to but one satisfaction: Ne bis in idem and jurisdiction questions in the Gabe Watson case', Conference Proceedings, Crime, Justice and Social Democracy: An International conference, 26–28 September 2011, School of Justice, Faculty of Law, Queensland University, pp. 61–78.

O'Driscoll, C 2008, 'Fear and trust: The shooting of Jean Charles de Menezes and the war on terror', *Millennium: Journal of International Studies*, vol. 36, no. 2, pp. 339–360.

Ohmae, K 1994, *The borderless world: Power and strategy in the global marketplace*, Harper Collins, London.

Ohmae, K 1995, *The end of the nation state: The rise of regional economies*, Simon & Schuster Inc., New York.

O'Malley, P 1999, 'Volatile and contradictory punishment', *Theoretical Criminology*, vol. 3, no. 2, pp. 175–196.

Oppermann, M 1999, 'Sex tourism', *Annals of Tourism Research*, vol. 26, no. 2, pp. 251–266.

Oppermann, M & McKinley, S 1997, 'Sexual imagery in the marketing of Pacific tourism destinations', in M Oppermann (ed.), *Pacific Rim tourism*, CAB International, New York, pp. 117–27.

Panitch, V 2013, 'Global surrogacy: Exploitation to empowerment', *Journal of Global Ethics*, vol. 9, no. 3, pp. 329–343.

Paoli, L 2003, *Mafia brotherhoods: Organized crime Italian style*, Oxford University Press, New York.

Paoli, L & Fijnaut, C 2004, 'Introduction to Part I: The history of the concept', in C Fijnaut & L Paoli (eds), *Organised crime in Europe: Concepts, patterns and control policies in the European Union and beyond*, Springer, Dordrecht, pp. 21–46.

Paoli, L, Greenfield, V & Reuter, P 2009, *The world heroin market: Can supply be cut?*, Oxford University Press, New York.

Pape, R 2005, *Dying to win: The strategic logic of suicide terrorism*, Scribe, Melbourne.

Passas, N 2005, 'Lawful but awful: Legal corporate crimes', *Journal of Socio-Economics*, vol. 34, no. 6, pp. 771–786.

Patrick, P 2010, 'Death on the reef', *The Age*, 17 July, accessed 2 July 2015, via Factiva.

Paul, R 2014, 'Bangladesh accuses 17 over garment factory collapse', Reuters, 15 June, accessed 2 July 2015, www.reuters.com/article/2014/06/15/us-bangladesh-rana-plaza-case-idUSKBN0EQ0KY20140615

Paulin, R 2003, 'Globalization and the sex trade: Trafficking and the commodification of women and children', *Canadian Women Studies/Les Cahiers de la Femme*, vol. 22, no. 3–4, pp. 38–43.

Peskin, V 2005, 'Beyond victor's justice? The challenge of prosecuting the winners at the International Criminal Tribunals for the Former Yugoslavia and Rwanda', *Journal of Human Rights*, vol. 4, no. 2, pp. 213–231.

Pianta, M 2001, 'Parallel summits of global civil society', in H Anheier, G Marlies & M Kaldor (eds), *Yearbook of global civil society 2001*, Oxford University Press, Oxford, pp. 169–194, www.lse.ac.uk/internationalDevelopment/research/CSHS/civilSociety/yearBook/contentsPages/2001.aspx

Pickering, S 2005, *Refugees and state crime*, Federation Press, Annandale, NSW.

Polhman, J 2014, 'The antiquities dealer accused in global art theft ring', CNBC, 16 January, accessed 2 July 2015, www.cnbc.com/id/101342238#

Potenza, A 2014, '21st century slavery: Millions of people around the world are living as modern-day slaves – including in the US (cover story)', *New York Times Upfront*, 17 March, vol. 146, no. 10, pp. 8–11, accessed 30 March 2015, via ProQuest, search.proquest.com.ezproxy.flinders.edu.au/docview/1508782040?OpenUrlRefId=info:xri/sid:primo

Pratt, J 2007, *Penal populism*, Routledge, Abingdon.

Preston, B J 2011, 'The use of restorative justice for environmental crime', *Criminal Law Journal*, vol. 35, no. 3, pp. 136–161.

Pryor, S 2015, 'Gallery to get refund after statue's return; Buddha going home to India', *The Canberra Times*, 7 March.

Raab, J & Milward, HB 2003, 'Dark networks as problems', *Journal of Public Administration Research and Theory*, vol. 13, no. 4, pp. 413–439.

Raban, J 2005, 'The truth about terrorism', *New York Review of Books*, vol. 52, no. 1, pp. 22–26.

Rakoff, JS 2014, 'The financial crisis: Why have no high-level executives been prosecuted?', *New York Review of Books*, 9 January, accessed 24 May 2015, www.nybooks.com/articles/archives/2014/jan/09/financial-crisis-why-no-executive-prosecutions/

Reed, V 2012, 'Due diligence, provenance research, and the acquisition process at the Museum of Fine Arts, Boston', *DePaul Journal of Art, Technology and Intellectual Property Law*, vol. 23, no. 2, pp. 363–373.

Richardson, L 2006, *What terrorists want: Understanding the terrorist threat*, John Murray, London.

Ritzner, G 1993, *The McDonaldization of society*, Pine Forge Press, Thousand Oaks, CA.

Robertson, R 2012, 'Globalisation or glocalisation', *The Journal of International Communication*, vol. 18, no. 2, pp. 191–208.

Robinson, W 2011, 'Globalization and the sociology of Immanuel Wallerstein: A critical appraisal', *International Sociology*, vol. 26, no. 6, pp. 723–745.

Rome Statute 1998, *Rome Statute of the International Criminal Court*, accessed 23 January 2013, www.icc-cpi.int/nr/rdonlyres/ea9aeff7-5752-4f84-be94-0a655eb30e16/0/rome_statute_english.pdf

Ross, J I (Ed.) 1995, *Controlling State Crime: An Introduction*, Garland Publishing, New York.

Ross, J I (Ed.) 2000, *Varieties of State Crime and Its Control*, Criminal Justice Press, Monsey, NY.

Roth, M 2014, 'Historical overview of transnational crime', in P Reichel & J Albanese (eds), *Handbook of transnational crime and justice*, Sage, Thousand Oaks, CA, pp. 5–22.

Rothe, D & Friedrichs D 2006, 'The State of the Criminology of Crimes of the State', *Social Justice*, vol. 33, pp. 147–161.

Rothe, D & Friedrichs, D 2015, *Crimes of globalization: New directions in critical criminology*, Routledge, London.

Rothe, D & Ross, J 2008, 'The marginalization of state crime in introductory textbooks on criminology', *Critical Sociology*, vol. 34, no. 5, pp. 741–752.

Rothe, D, Muzzatti, S & Mullins, C 2006, 'Crime on the high seas: Crimes of globalization and the sinking of the Senegalese ferry Le Joola', *Critical Criminology*, vol. 14, no. 3, pp. 159–180.

Rothe, D, Ross, J et al. 2009, 'That was then, this is now, what about tomorrow? Future directions in state crime studies', *Critical Criminology*, vol. 17, no. 1, pp. 3–13.

Roy, O 2006, 'Terrorism and deculturation', in L Richardson (ed.), *The roots of terrorism*, Routledge, London, pp. 159–70.

Ruggiero, V 2000, 'Transnational crime: Official and alternative fears', *International Journal of the Sociology of Law*, vol. 28, no. 3, pp. 187–199.

Ryan, C & Hall, MC 2001, *Sex tourism, marginal people and liminalities*, Routledge, London.

Sageman, M 2004, *Understanding terrorist networks*, University of Pennsylvania Press, Philadelphia.

Sageman, M 2008, *Leaderless jihad: Terror networks in the twenty-first century*, University of Pennsylvania Press, Philadelphia.

Salecl, R 2004, *On anxiety*, Routledge, Abingdon.

Salecl, R 2010, *Choice*, Profile Books, London.

Salter, M 2004, 'Passports, mobility, and security: How smart can the border be?', *International Studies Perspectives*, vol. 5, no. 1, pp. 71–91.

Samset, I 2002, 'Conflict of interests or interests in conflict? Diamonds and war in the DRC', *Review of African Political Economy*, vol. 29, no. 93–94, pp. 463–480.

Samuel, H & Russell, A 2005, 'We're all Londoners now', *The Telegraph*, accessed 23 June 2015, www.telegraph.co.uk/news/worldnews/northamerica/usa/1493626/Were-all-Londoners-now.html

Sanchez Taylor, J 2001, 'Dollars are a girl's best friend? Female tourists' sexual behaviour in the Caribbean', *Sociology*, vol. 35, no. 3, pp. 749–764.

Sanchez Taylor, J 2006, 'Female sex tourism: A contradiction in terms?', *Feminist Review*, vol. 83, no. 1, pp. 42–59.

Sandy, L 2014, *Women and sex work in Cambodia*, Routledge, Abingdon.

Sassen, S 2001, *The global city: New York, London, Tokyo*, 2nd edn, Princeton University Press, Oxford.

Schabas, W 2006, 'International justice for international crimes: An idea whose time has come', *European Review*, vol. 14, no. 4, pp. 421–439.

Schmitt, C 1996, *The concept of the political*, trans. G Schwab, The University of Chicago Press, Chicago.

Schwendinger, H and Schwendinger, J 1970, 'Defenders of order or guardians of human rights', *Issues in Criminology*, vol. 5, no. 2, pp. 123–157.

Scrutton, A & Sigurdardottir, R 2015, 'Iceland convicts bad bankers and says other nations can act', *Reuters (UK)*, 13 February, accessed 24 May 2015, uk.reuters.com/article/2015/02/13/uk-iceland-bankers-idUKKBN0LH0OC20150213

Sennett, R 1998, *The corrosion of character: The personal consequences of work in the new capitalism*, Norton, New York.

Sennett, R 2006, *The culture of the new capitalism*, Yale University Press, New Haven, CT.

Shapiro, MJ 2015, *War crimes, atrocity, and justice*, Polity Press, Cambridge.

Shaw, M & Mangan, F 2015, *Illicit trafficking and Libya's transition: Profits and losses*, United States Institute of Peace, Washington, DC.

Sheller, M & Urry, J 2006, 'The new mobilities paradigm', *Environment and Planning*, vol. 38, no. 2, pp. 207–226.

Sheptycki, J 2003, *In search of transnational policing: Towards a sociology of global policing*, Avebury, Aldershot.

Siegle, L 2014, 'One year after Rana Plaza, the world is still addicted to fast fashion: Disaster took 1,133 workers' lives, but garment trade is rewarded with a boom', *The Observer*, 20 April, accessed 12 February 2015, www.theguardian.com/world/2014/apr/20/rana-plaza-bangladesh-disaster-anniversary.

Simon, D 2000, 'Corporate environmental crimes and social inequality', *American Behavioural Scientist*, vol. 43, no. 4, pp. 633–645.

Simon, J 2007, *Governing through crime: How the war on crime transformed American democracy and created a culture of fear*, Oxford University Press, Oxford.

Slaughter, AM 2004, *A new world order*, Princeton University Press, Princeton, NJ.

Smith, D 2012, 'South Africa still a chronically racially divided nation, finds survey', *The Guardian*, 7 December, accessed 1 July 2015, www.theguardian.com/world/2012/dec/06/south-africa-racially-divided-survey

SOCA 2007, Threat Assessment of Serious Organized Crime, Serious Organized Crime Agency, UK.

Solana, M C, Kilburn, C R J & Rolandi, G 2008, 'Communicating eruption and hazard forecasts on Vesuvius, Southern Italy', *Journal of Volcanology and Geothermal Research*, vol. 172, pp. 308–314.

South, N 2014, 'Green criminology: Reflections, corrections, horizons', *International Journal for Crime, Justice and Social Democracy*, vol. 3, no. 2, pp. 5–20.

Spitz, S 2014, 'Silence on surrogacy: Why the world's reproductive market needs regulation', *Juris Diction (Queen's Law Newspaper)*, 24 October, accessed 1 July 2015, juris-diction.ca/silence-on-surrogacy-why-the-worlds-reproductive-market-needs-regulation/

Spivak, GC 1994, 'Can the subaltern speak?', in P Williams & L Chrisman (eds), *Colonial discourse and post-colonial theory: A reader*, Harvester Wheatsheaf, Hemel Hempstead, pp. 90–105.

Stenson, K 2003, 'The new politics of crime control', in K Stenson & R Sullivan (eds), *Crime, risk and justice*, Willan, Cullompton, pp. 15–28.

Stothard, M 2012, 'Recovery and reconciliation; Iceland; The improving outlook for one of the earliest victims of the global crisis – also the first to try its former leader and bankers for their role – is being studied by policy makers worldwide', *Financial Times*, 30 March, accessed 20 May 2015, via Factiva.

Swart, AHJ, Zahar, A & Sluiter, G 2011, *The legacy of the International Criminal Tribunal for the Former Yugoslavia*, Oxford University Press, Oxford.

Tacconi, L 2007, 'The problem of illegal logging', in Tacconi L (ed.), *Illegal Logging: Law Enforcement, Livelihoods and the Timber Trade*, Earthscan: London, pp. 1–16.

Tallgren, I 1999, 'We did it? The vertigo of law and everyday life at the diplomatic conference on the establishment of an international criminal court', *Leiden Journal of International Law*, vol. 12, no. 3, pp. 683–707.

Tazreiter, C 2013, 'Temporary, precarious and invisible labour: The globalized migrant worker in Australia', in C Tazreiter and SY Tham (eds), *Globalization and social transformation in the Asia-Pacific: The Australian and Malaysian experience*, Palgrave Macmillan, London, pp. 163–177.

Tilly, C 1985, 'War making and state making as organized crime', in PB Evans, D Rueschemeyer & T Skocpol (eds), *Bringing the state back in*, Cambridge University Press, Cambridge, pp. 169–191.

TOC Convention 2000, United Nations Convention against Transnational Organized Crime, United Nations, Vienna.

Townsend, C 2002, *Terrorism: A very short introduction*, Oxford University Press, Oxford.

Transcrime 2014, 'Executive summary', Joint Research Centre on Transnational Crime, accessed 2 July 2015, www.transcrime.it/wp-content/uploads/2014/02/PON-Executive.pdf

Tuckman, J 2014, 'Surrogacy boom in Mexico brings tales of missing money and stolen eggs', *The Guardian*, 26 September, accessed 1 July 2015, www.theguardian.com/world/2014/sep/25/tales-of-missing-money-stolen-eggs-surrogacy-mexico

UN 1975, *Fifth United Nations Congress on the prevention of crime and the treatment of offenders: Working paper*, A/CONF.10/3, United Nations, New York.

UN 1995, *Ninth United Nations Congress on the prevention of crime and the treatment of offenders*, A/RES/50/145, United Nations, New York.

UN 2000, *Protocol to prevent, suppress and punish trafficking in persons, especially women and children, supplementing the United Nations Convention Against Transnational Organized Crime*, United Nations, Geneva.

UN 2007, International cooperation in preventing and combating illicit international trafficking in forest products, including timber, wildlife and other forest biological resources, Resolution 16/1, Commission on Crime Prevention and Criminal Justice, United Nations, New York.

UN 2015a, United Nations Security Council frequently asked questions webpage, accessed 2 July 2015, www.un.org/en/sc/about/faq.shtml#measures

UN 2015b, Member States of the United Nations, accessed 12 June 2015, http://www.un.org/en/members/index.shtml

UNESCO 2014, 'Fighting against illicit trafficking of cultural property: Statutory meetings of the 1970 convention', accessed 2 July 2015, www.unesco.org/new/en/culture/themes/illicit-trafficking-of-cultural-property/in-focus-july-2013/

UN.Gift (Global Initiative to Fight Human Trafficking) 2008, *Human trafficking: An overview*, UNODC, United Nations, New York.

UN.Gift 2015, *Trafficking for Organ Trade*. UNODC, United Nations, New York.

UNICRI 2015, United Nations Interregional Crime and Justice Research Institute website, accessed 23 June 2015, www.unicri.it/institute/

United Kingdom 2009, *Pursue prevent protect prepare: The United Kingdom's strategy for countering international terrorism*, CM7547 (March).

UNODC 2006, *Toolkit to combat trafficking in persons: Global programme against trafficking in human beings*, UN Office on Drugs and Crime, United Nations, New York.

UNODC 2010a, *The globalization of crime: A transnational organized crime threat assessment*, UN Office on Drugs and Crime, United Nations, Vienna, www.unodc.org/documents/data-and-analysis/tocta/TOCTA_Report_2010_low_res.pdf

UNODC 2010b, *United Nations congresses on crime prevention and criminal justice 1955–2010*, UN Office on Drugs and Crime, United Nations, Vienna, www.un.org/en/conf/crimecongress2010/pdf/55years_ebook.pdf

UNODC 2010c, *Crime and instability: Case studies of transnational threats*, UN Office on Drugs and Crime, United Nations, Vienna, www.unodc.org/documents/data-and-analysis/Studies/Crime_and_instability_2010_final_26march.pdf

UNODC 2010d, *Twelfth UN Congress on crime prevention and criminal justice*, UN Office on Drugs and Crime, United Nations, Vienna, www.unis.unvienna.org/pdf/2010-Crime_Congress/English_press_kit-factsheets.pdf

UNODC 2012a World Drug Report, United Nations, Vienna, accessed 1 July 2015, www.unodc.org/documents/data-and-analysis/WDR2012/WDR_2012_web_small.pdf

UNODC 2012b, *Global report on trafficking in persons*, UN Office on Drugs and Crime, United Nations, New York.

UNODC 2015a, Money-Laundering and Globalization, United Nations, Vienna, accessed 1 July 2015, https://www.unodc.org/unodc/en/money-laundering/globalization.html

UNODC 2015b, 'Human trafficking', accessed 1 July 2015, www.unodc.org/unodc/en/human-trafficking/what-is-human-trafficking.html?ref=menuside

UNSC 2001, Resolution 1373 (28 September 2001), United Nations Security Council, S/RES/1373, United Nations, New York.

UNSC 2011, Strategy for Combating Transnational Organized Crime, US National Security Council, accessed 10 December 2015, https://www.whitehouse.gov/sites/default/files/Strategy_to_Combat_Transnational_Organized_Crime_July_2011.pdf

Urry, J 2002, 'The global complexities of September 11th', *Theory, Culture & Society*, vol. 19, no. 4, pp. 57–69.

Urry, J 2003, *Global complexity*, Polity Press, Oxford.

Urry, J 2007, *Mobilities*, Polity Press, Cambridge.

US Department of State 2014, *Trafficking in persons report*, June 2014, accessed 1 July 2015, www.state.gov/j/tip/rls/tiprpt/2014/index.htm

US Department of State 2015, *Trafficking in persons report: Tier placements*, accessed 27 June 2015, www.state.gov/j/tip/rls/tiprpt/2014/226649.htm

Valier C 2002, *Theories of crime and punishment*, Longman, Harlow.

Van Dijk, JJM 2008, *The world of crime*, Sage, Thousand Oaks, CA.

Vidino, L 2009, 'Homegrown jihadist terrorism in the United States: A new and occasional phenomenon?', *Studies in Conflict & Terrorism*, vol. 32, no. 1, pp. 1–17.

Virilio, P 2005, *Negative horizon: An essay in dromoscopy*, Continuum, London.

Visible Measures, 2012, 'Update: Kony social video campaign tops 100 million views', *Visible Measures*, 12 March, accessed 5 April 2013, www.visiblemeasures.com/2012/03/12/update-kony-social-video-campaign-tops-100-million-views/

Walters, R 2004, 'Criminology and genetically modified food', *British Journal of Criminology*, vol. 44, no. 2, pp. 151–167.

Washington Post 2014, 'Garment factories in Bangladesh still have massive safety problems', *The Washington Post.com*, 24 October, accessed 10 February 2015, www.washingtonpost.com/opinions/bangladesh-still-needs-safer-conditions-in-garment-factories/2014/10/23/925d37f8-563a-11e4-892e-602188e70e9c_story.html.

Watts R, Bessant J and Hil R 2008, *International criminology: A critical introduction*, London, Routledge.

Weber, L 2006, 'The shifting frontiers of migration control', in S Pickering & L Weber (eds), *Borders, mobility and the technologies of control*, Springer: Dordrecht, pp. 21–44.

Weber, L & Bowling, B 2004, 'Policing migration: A framework for investigating the regulation of global mobility', *Policing and Society: An International Journal of Research and Policy*, vol. 14, no. 3, pp. 195–212.

Weimann, G 2005, 'Cyberterrorism: The sum of all fears?', *Studies in Conflict & Terrorism*, vol. 28, no. 2, pp. 129–149.

White, M 2010, 'Clicktivism is ruining leftist activism', *The Guardian*, 12 August, accessed 21 March 2013, www.theguardian.com/commentisfree/2010/aug/12/clicktivism-ruining-leftist-activism

White, R 2008, *Crimes against nature: Environmental criminology and ecological justice*, Willan, Cullompton.

White, R 2011, *Transnational environmental crime*, Routledge, Abingdon.

WHO 2007, *Second global consultation on critical issues in human transplantation: Towards a common attitude to transplantation*, World Health Organization, Geneva, apps.who.int/medicinedocs/documents/s15437e/s15437e.pdf

Williams, C 1996a, 'An environmental victimology', *Social Justice*, vol. 23, no. 4, pp. 16–40.

Williams, C 1996b, 'Environmental victims: An introduction', *Social Justice*, vol. 23, no. 4, pp. 1–6.

Williams, M 2000, 'Virtually criminal: Discourse, deviance and anxiety within virtual communities', *International Review of Law, Computers & Technology*, vol. 14, no. 1, pp. 95–104.

Wilson, JQ & Kelling, GL 1982, 'Broken windows', *Atlantic Monthly*, vol. 249, no. 3, pp. 29–38.

Wilson, M 2005, 'Precommitment in free-market procreation: Surrogacy, commissioned adoption, and limits on human decision making capacity', *Journal of Legislation*, vol. 31, no. 2, pp. 329–350.

Wise, M & Schloenhardt, A 2014, 'Counting shadows: Measuring trafficking in persons in Australia', *International Journal of Criminology and Sociology*, vol. 3, pp. 249–266.

Wonders, NA 2007, 'Globalization, border reconstruction projects, and transnational crime', *Social Justice*, vol. 34, no. 2, pp. 33–46.

Woodiwiss, M 2003, 'Transnational organised crime: The global reach of an American concept', in A Edwards & P Gill (eds), *Transnational organised crime: Perspectives on global security*, Routledge, London, pp. 13–27.

World Bank 2009, 'News & broadcast: Impact of the financial crisis on employment', Worldbank.org, accessed 24 May 2015, go.worldbank.org/Y0IXWC8T10

World Economic Forum 2011, *Global Risks 2011*, 6th Edition, accessed 3 March 2016, http://reports.weforum.org/wp-content/blogs.dir/1/mp/uploads/pages/files/global-risks-2011.pdf accessed 03/03/2016.

Wyatt, T 2013, *Wildlife trafficking: A deconstruction of the crime, the victims and the offenders*, Palgrave, Basingstoke.

Yardley, J 2013a, 'Report on deadly factory collapse in Bangladesh finds widespread blame', *The New York Times (late edition, East Coast)*, 23 May, accessed 10 February 2015, via ProQuest.

Yardley, J 2013b, 'Justice still elusive in factory disasters in Bangladesh', *The New York Times*, 29 June, accessed 12 February 2015, www.nytimes.com/2013/06/30/world/asia/justice-elusive-in-a-bangladesh-factory-disaster.html?_r=0

Zaitch, D 2002, *Trafficking cocaine: Colombian drug entrepreneurs in the Netherlands*, Kluwer, The Hague.

Zarsky, L 2002, 'Introduction: Conflicts, ethics and globalization', in L Zarsky (ed.), *Human rights and the environment*, Earthscan, London, pp. 1–8.

Zedner, L 2007, 'Pre-crime and post-criminology?', *Theoretical Criminology*, vol. 11, no. 2, pp. 261–281.

Zonnoor, B 2014, 'How to sell your kidney: A brief overview of the Iranian model for kidney transplantation', *in-Training*, 31 March, accessed 1 July 2015, in-training.org/sell-kidney-brief-overview-iranian-model-kidney-transplantation-5682

Index

Note: page numbers in *italic type* refer to figures, page numbers in **bold type** refer to glossary entries.

Christie, N., 74
citizenship, 110
civil society, **193**
  see also global civil society
civilization blocs, 39
climate change, 58, 166
clustered hierarchy, in organized crime, *118*
CMPS (Centre for Management and Policy
  Studies), 70
Coalition for the International Criminal
  Court, 20
Coca-Cola, *2*, 35, 125–6
coercive policy transfer, 71, 76
Cohen, S., 175–6, 178
Colombia, 125
colonialism, 104
commodification, 93, 103, 110, **194**
  see also human bodies
complementarity principle, 80
conferences, 20–1
consent, and surrogacy, 110
constitutive criminology, 174–5, **194**
consumerism, and globalization, 35, 36–7, 43
Cooney, R., 167
cooperation
  cosmopolitanism and cultural clashes,
    21–4, 120
  importance of, 77
  proliferation of actors, 18–21
  in responses to environmental crimes, 160
  in responses to organized crime, 120,
    129–30, 131–2
  in responses to terrorism, 144–5, 146–7
corporate responsibility, 37
corporations
  environmental responsibility, 162–5, 167
  harm caused by, 181–2
  and justice system, 191
  and social stratification, 34
corruption
  in garment industry, 36, 39, 43
  and organized crime, 123, 130
cosmopolitanism, 21–2, 120, **194**
Costa, A.M., 10, 12–13
counter-terrorism responses, 137,
  144–50, 151
crime
  in context of liquid modernity, 46
  defined by state, 172
  domestic, 5–6, 13, 39
  governing through, 60–2
  international, 6, 7–9, 13, 183
  parallels between state and conventional,
    175–6

crime *cont.*
  use of internet, 64–6
  see also organized crime; state crime;
    transnational crime
crime control, **194**
  and concept of risk, 54, 60–2
  policy convergence, 74
  policy transfer, 71–3
  responses to transnational crimes, 75–8
  see also criminal justice; law enforcement
crimes against humanity, 8, 176–7, 183, **194**
  see also atrocities
crimes of globalization, 14–15, 180–2, **194**
criminal justice
  global, 86–9, 190–3
  impact of globalization on, 139
  mechanisms and structures, 23–4, 78–86
  policy convergence, 71, 73–4
  policy responses to transnational crimes,
    75–8
  policy transfer, 70–5
  responses to environmental crime, 160
  responses to terrorism, 148–9
  see also law enforcement
criminal networks, 63–4, 119, 123
  see also terrorist networks
criminal responsibility, 88, 171, 183–4
criminalization
  of drug use, 125–6
  of migrants, 95–6
  of money laundering, 128
criminogenic, 140–1, 162, **194**
criminology
  approaches to environmental harm, 155–7
  approaches to state crime, 172–5
critical criminology, 172, 174, **194**
cryptocurrencies, 64, **194**
cryptomarkets, 64–5, **194**
cultural artefacts, 158–9, 161
cultural clashes, 21–4
cultural cleansing, 161, **194–5**
  see also ethnic cleansing
culture, and perceptions of risk, 59
cyber-terrorism, 143–4, **195**
cybercrime, 66–7, **195**
cyberspace, 65–7, **195**

Dancing Shiva case study, 158–9
dark net, 64–5, **195**
dark networks, 140
death penalty, 22–3
debt-bondage, 100
deception, and human trafficking, 100
deforestation, 163

defragmentation of power, 177, **195–6**
  see also fragmentation
Democratic Republic of Congo (DRC),
    13, 80, 177
Der Derian, J., 143
destination countries
  for migrants, 47, 48
  for sex tourism, 105
  for trafficking, 76, **195**
developed countries *see* Western countries
developing countries
  environmental protection in, 156–7
  as exploited, 185
  help for, 191–2
  impact of climate change in, 58
  impact of globalization on, 2, 34–5, 36–7
  marginalized, 192
  and sex tourism, 105
  and surrogacy, 109–10
  see also global south
development assistance *see* capacity
    building
digital currencies, 64, 129
digital divide, 63
digital networks, 62–3
Disneyization, 35
distributive justice, 191
Dolowitz, D.P., 70
domestic crimes, 5–6, 13, 39
domestic justice, alongside international
    justice, 78–9, 80–2, 84–5
domestic law enforcement
  impact of globalization on, 35, 39, 43–4
  and organized crime, 131–3
  and terrorism, 148–50
double jeopardy, 6
Downie, D., 165
DRC (Democratic Republic of Congo),
    13, 80, 177
Dread Pirate Roberts (DPR), 65
drug laws, 125–6
drug trade, 4, 22–3, 124–6
  cryptomarkets, 65
  responses to, 75, 120, 129–31
drugs, tackling demand for, 130–1
Duffield, M., 148

East Timor, capacity building in, 77
East Timor Tribunal, 81
ecocide, 164, **195**
ecological risks, 55, 157
ecological sovereignty, 157
elite networking, 70
Elliot, A., 48
Elliott, L., 161, 162

employment, 45–6
  see also working conditions
emulation, policy transfer by, 70
enforced cosmopolitanism, 120
environmental crimes
  defining, 154–7
  individual responsibility, 158, 160–1
environmental harm, 4, 153–4
  corporate and state responsibility, 157,
    162–5, 167
  criminological approach, 155–7
  global approach, 166
  legal-procedural approach, 154–5
  micro-macro approach, 158–65
environmental risks, 55, 157, 166
Escobar, P., 127
ethnic cleansing, 170, 176
  see also cultural cleansing; genocide
ethnic identity, 115–17, 122–3, 126
Eurojust, 19–20
Europe, radicalization in, 141–2
European Union (EU), 19, 71, 160
Europol, 19
evidence, 74–5, 121–2, 190
Extraordinary Chambers in the Courts of
    Cambodia (ECCC), 81
extraordinary rendition, 179–80, **195**

fashion industry *see* garment industry
Faust, K.L., 183
feminist criminology, 173, **195**
fertility industry, 108–10
Financial Action Task Force (FATF), 127
financial crises, 4, 55–6, 189
financial institutions
  and 2008 crisis, 55–6
  harm caused by, 182
  and money laundering, 128–9
  see also International Monetary Fund;
    World Bank
first world *see* Western countries
fishing industry, 101–2, 164
food supplies, 60
forced labour, 101–2
forced migration, 96, 184
fragmentation of power, 42–4, **195–6**
  see also defragmentation
Friedrichs, D.O., 12, 181

G7 Summit (1984), 38
Gacaca Courts (Rwanda), 84–5
Garland, D., 60, 74
garment industry, 31, 32–3, 34–5, 36, 39, 43
gendercide, 169, **196**
Geneva conventions, 8, **196**

genocide, 8, 84–5, 86, 170, **196**
  see also ethnic cleansing
geocide, 164, **195**
geopolitics, 17, 185, **196**
  and environment, 157, 162, 163, 166
  of international courts, 82–3
  and state crime, 180, 183
  see also developing countries; Western
    countries
Ghodse, H., 131
Giddens, A., 29, 41–2, 45, 57–8, 166
'girlfriend trade', 105
Global Alliance Against Traffic in
  Women, 20
global cities, as nodes, 62
global civil society, 20, 177, 189, **196**
global criminal justice, 86–9, 190–3
global financial crises, 55
  2008 crisis, 4, 55–6, 189
global north, 33, 47, **196**
  see also Western countries
global sceptic view, 30, 38–40, **196**
global south, 33, 47, 88, **196**
  see also developing countries
global transformationalist view, 30, 40–5
globalization, **196**
  anti-globalization, 36–8
  complex effects of, 40–1
  concepts of, 31–2
  crimes of, 14–15, 180–2
  fragmentation and integration in, 42–4
  impact on state accountability, 176
  link with transnational crime, 2–4, 10,
    12–13, 103, 189
  and mobilities, 45–50
  negative effects of, 2–4, 12–13, 14, 35,
    36–7, 181
  and paradox of jihadist terrorists, 138
  positive effects of, 1–2, 34–5
  risks linked to, 55, 57
  terrorism, counter-terrorism and, 150–1
globalization theories
  global sceptics, 38–40
  global transformationalists, 40–5
  radical globalists, 33–5
  types of, 30, 40
glocalization, 44–5, **197**
governance
  crime, risk and, 59–62
  of cyberspace, 66, 67
  see also crime control; law enforcement;
    regulation
governing through crime, 60–2
Gramsci, A., 173
green criminology, 155–7, **197**

Hague Convention, 110
harm
  caused by globalization *see* globalization
  caused by organized crime, 120–2
  caused by state *see* state crime
  constitutive criminology concept of,
    174–5
  need to consider, 14–15
  see also environmental harm
harmonization of policy, 70, 71, 76–7
Harvey, D., 42
hegemony, 173, 192, **197**
Hehir, A., 141
Held, D., 41
Henry, S., 174–5
heroin, 131
hierarchies
  in criminal organizations, 118–19
  in dark networks, 140
high-consequence risks, 57
Holocaust, 86
home-grown terrorism, 141–2, 145–6
homogenization, 74
human bodies (markets in), 94
  human smuggling, 96–9
  human trafficking, 96–102
  labour exploitation, 99, 101–2
  organ trafficking, 106–8
  responses to, 76, 77, 93–4, 111, 189
  surrogacy and adoption, 108–10
  tourism industry, 103–6
human rights
  discourse of, 79, 83, 88, 168–9, 175–6
  in global justice context, 88
  and international crimes, 7–9
  interventions justified by, 16, 88
  need to consider, 14
  and prevention of terrorism, 61
  protection of, 177
  see also crimes against humanity
human rights video, 63
human smuggling, 93–4, 96–9, **197**
human trafficking, 96–9, **197**
  experiences of, 99–100
  labour exploitation, 99, 101–2
  responses to, 76, 77, 93–4, 189
  statistics, 99
humanitarian interventions, 16, 88
Huntington, S., 39
Husain, E., 142
hybrid courts, 81–2, **197**
hyper-globalist *see* radical globalist view

IBA (International Bar Association), 176–7
ICC *see* International Criminal Court

Iceland, 56
ICTR (International Criminal Tribunal for Rwanda), 7, 17, 79, 84
ICTY (International Criminal Tribunal for the Former Yugoslavia), 7, 17, 79, 176
ideology, and terrorism, 139
illicit enterprise view, 116
ILO Convention 29 on Forced Labour, 102
IMF (International Monetary Fund), 19, 37, 103, 177
IMT (International Military Tribunal), 78
IMTFE (International Military Tribunal for the Far East), 79
India, surrogacy in, 109
Indian antiquities, 158–9
Indonesian National Police (INP), 22
industrial accidents, 32–3, 35, 36–7, 39, 43–4
inequality
    in access to mobility, 46–7, 95–6
    in access to technology, 63
    effects of, 14
    and environment, 157, 162, 163, 166
    and impact of globalization, 36, 37
    and impact of risk, 58
    and markets in bodies see human bodies
    in power and law, 172–3, 174, 180
    see also social stratification
INGOs (international non-governmental organizations), 20, 42–3
institutional development, 78–83
integration
    and fragmentation in globalization, 42–4
    in money laundering process, 127
inter-governmental agreements, 162
inter-governmental organizations, 18–20, 42, **197**
International Bar Association (IBA), 176–7
International Court of Justice, 7
international courts, 7, 34, 78–83
    see also International Criminal Court
international crimes, 6, 7–9, 13, 183, **197**
International Criminal Court (ICC), 7–8, 17, 34, 75, 79–81, 177, 183
international criminal justice
    economic and social context, 189
    mechanisms and structures, 23–4, 78–86
    move towards, 189–90
    and national systems, 190–1
    and state crime, 171
international criminal law, 7, **197**
International Criminal Tribunal for the Former Yugoslavia (ICTY), 7, 17, 79, 176
International Criminal Tribunal for Rwanda (ICTR), 7, 17, 79, 84

International Labour Association (ILO), 102
international law, 7, **198**
    interventions legitimized by, 17
    and state crime, 175
International Military Tribunal for the Far East (IMTFE), 79
International Military Tribunal (IMT), 78
International Monetary Fund (IMF), 19, 37, 103, 177
International Narcotics Control Board, 131
international non-governmental organizations (INGOs), 20, 42–3
international organizations
    as criminal actors, 180–2
    involved in Rana Plaza collapse, 43–4
    proliferation of, 18–19, 20–1, 42
international tribunals, 7, 17, 78, 79, 81–2, 176
internationalization, 31–2
internationalized courts see hybrid courts
internet
    criminal use of, 64–6
    online networks, 62–3
    regulating, 66, 67
    role in sex tourism, 104
    role in terrorism, 143–4
Interpol, 19, 161
interventions
    humanitarian, 16, 88
    and sovereignty, 16–17
Invisible Children, 63
Iran, 108
Iraq, 16, 83, 147, 178
irregular migration, 4, 95–6, 184
Islamic State, 161
Italian Mafia, 115, 118, 119

Jamieson, R., 178, 179–80
jihadist terrorism
    paradox of, 138
    responses to, 144–50, 151
    understanding, 138–44
Jones, T., 72
jurisdiction
    cosmopolitanism and clashes, 21–4
    and domestic crimes, 5, 6
    international and regional actors, 18–21
    and sovereignty, 15–18
    and state crime, 179–80
justice
    relationship with peace, 85
    see also criminal justice

Kapoor, S., 158–9
Kauzlarich, D., 183

Kelling, G.L., 71
kidney donation, 108
Klein, N., 164
Kony 2012 campaign, 63
Kramer, R., 170–1

labour exploitation, 36–7, 43, 99, 101–2
labour trafficking, 99, 101
LambdaMOO, 67
Lang, A., 167
late modernity, 41, 42, 45, **198**
Latin American Commission on Drugs and
    Democracy, 134
law enforcement
  impact of globalization on, 35, 39, 43–4
  responses to environmental crime, 160–1
  responses to human trafficking, 77,
      93–4, 111
  responses to organized crime, 119, 128–33
  responses to terrorism, 146, 148–50
laws, drug laws, 125–6
layering, in money laundering process, 127
Le Joola case study, 182
lebanon, 81
legal-procedural approach to environment,
    154–5
legalization of drugs, 126
Levi, M., 133
Libya, 114–15
liquid modernity, 45–6, **198**
local *see* domestic crimes; domestic justice;
    glocalization
London terrorist attacks (2005), 141
lustration, 85, **198**
Lynch, M., 166

McDonaldization, 35
McEvoy, K., 178, 179–80
Mafia, 115, 118, 119
Maguire, M., 133
maps, *49, 50*
markets
  in bodies *see* human bodies
  and organized crime, 116
Marsh, D., 70
Martin, C., 162
Marxist criminology, 173, **198**
measurement and analysis, of crime, 74–5,
    121–2, 190
media, role in terrorism, 143
medical tourism, 106
  see also reproductive tourism
Melossi, D., 73
memorialization, 86
Menezes, J.C. de, 150

Mexico, 109, 110, 125
Michalowski, R., 170–1
micro-macro approach to environmental
    responsibility, 158–65
migrants
  criminalization of, 95–6
  differential mobilities, 47–8
  and labour exploitation, 101–2
  and organized crime, 115–17, 122–3, 126
  regular and irregular, 95–6
  see also human smuggling
migration
  factors leading to, 94–5
  irregular, 4, 95–6, 184
military interventions, 16–17, 88
  as response to terrorism, 145, 147, 151
Milovanovic, D., 174–5
Milward, H.B., 140, 141
mobility
  and globalization, 45–50
  and networks, 62
  unequal access to, 46–7, 95–6
modernity, 41–2, 45, **198**
money laundering, 123, 126–9, **198**
Multi-User Dungeon/Dimension
    (MUD), 67
multinational corporations, 34, 37
  see also transnational corporations

'naming and shaming', 76, 129, 161
National Crime Agency, 132
NATO (North Atlantic Treaty Organization), 19
natural disasters, 164
neo-conservativism, 87, **198**
neoliberalism, 33, 74, 87, 88, **199**
network analysis, 63, 139–40
network theory, 54, 62, **199**
network warfare, 143
networking, impact on policy, 70, 71, 189
networks, 62–5
  dark networks, 140
  of new world order, 170
  and organized crime, 119, 123
  terrorist, 137, 139–40, 142–3
new world order, 170, 175–80, **199**
Newburn, T., 72
nodes, 62, 140
non-governmental organizations (NGOs),
    20, **199**
non-intervention principle, 16, 17
Nordstrom, C., 64
north *see* global north
North Atlantic Treaty Organization
    (NATO), 19
Nuremberg Trials, 78

Ohmae, K., 33
O'Malley, P., 87
online behaviour, 67
online networks, 62–3
organ donation, 108
organ trafficking, 106–8
organizational capacity building, 77
organizations *see* international
    organizations
organized crime
  actors, activities and networks, 122–4
  areas of, 124–9
  assessing extent of, 121–2
  defining, 117–19, **199**
  drug trade, 120, 124–6, 129–31
  and environmental crime, 160–1
  and globalization, 3
  historical and political context, 114–17, 185
  and human trafficking and smuggling,
    96–7
  money laundering, 126–9
  responses to, 119, 120, 128–33
  threat of, 119–22
  transnational, 12, 117, 119–20
othering, 178–9, 184, 191
  see also alien conspiracy view

Palermo Convention *see* United Nations
  Convention against Transnational
  Organized Crime
Palermo Protocols, 75–6, 77, 96
Paulin, R., 104
peace, relationship with justice, 85
penal populism, 74, **199**
penetration, policy transfer by, 71
personal relationships, 46
Pickering, S., 184
placement, in money laundering process, 127
police
  capacity building in East Timor, 77
  cooperation between, 22–3
  international and regional, 19
policing
  counter-terrorist, 150
  of organized crime, 131–2
  zero tolerance, 71–2
policy convergence, 71, 73–4
policy process, 73
policy transfer, 70–5, 76, **199**
political instability, 12–13, 77, 114–15, 141
pollution, 161, 162
population resettlement, 157
Portugal, 131
post-modernist theories, 174–5
post-modernity, 86–7, 139, **199**

power
  and criminality at supranational level,
    180–2
  defragmentation of state, 177
  in international order, 17–18
  relationship with law, 172–3, 174–5,
    180, 183
Preston, B.J., 165
preventative detention, 61, 74, 148
preventive approach, 191
  to cybercrime, 66
  to drug trade, 131
  to organized crime, 131, 132–3
  to terrorism, 61, 148
prisons
  Abu Ghraib, 178, *179*
  private, 72, 73
profit motivation of crime, 138–9
Prohibition era, 115
prostitution, 100
  sex tourism, 103–6
protection by state, 16, 59, 60
protection rackets, 114
public fear of terrorism, 143, 149, 150
pull factors in migration, 95
punitiveness, 46, 71–2, 74, **199**
push factors in migration, 94

al-Qaeda, 16, 138, 143, 147

R2P (responsibility to protect), 16, **200**
Raab, J., 140, 141
Raban, J., 147
racketeering, 115
radical criminology, 172–3, 174, **200**
radical globalist view, 30, 33–5, 40, **200**
radicalization, 141–2, 143, 150
Rana Plaza collapse, 32–3, 35, 36–7, 39,
  43–4
Rana, Sohel, 32–3, 36, 39
rape, in online MUD, 67
realpolitik, 17, 76, **200**
reflexivity, 42, 54, **200**
refugees/asylum seekers, 47, 96, 184
regional hierarchy, in organized crime, *118*
regional organizations, 19–20
regionalization, 71
Regulation 64 Panels in the Courts of
  Kosovo, 81
regulation
  impact of globalization on, 35, 39
  related to commercial surrogacy, 109
  related to environment, 157, 160–1
  see also crime control; governance; law
    enforcement

religion, and terrorism, 139
reproductive tourism, 108–10
resettlement of populations, 157
resilience, of networks, 140
responsibility
  individual, 88
  state, 171, 183–4
responsibility (environmental), 157
  of corporations and states, 157,
    162–5, 167
  of individuals, 158, 160–1
  micro-macro approach to, 158–65
responsibility to protect (R2P), 16, **200**
restorative justice, 83–5, 87, 165, **200**
retributive justice, 85, 87, 88
reverse market, 95
Richardson, L., 138
risk(s), 53–4
  environmental, 55, 157, 166
  governance, crime and, 59–62
  interconnection of, *57*, 58, 62
  as non-calculable, 57
  and penal populism, 74
  threat of organized crime, 119–20
  types of, 55
risk society, 53, **200**
  see also world risk society
Robertson, R., 44–5
Rome Conference (1998), 8, 79
Rome Statute (1998), 7–9, 79–80
Rothe, D., 12, 181, 182
Roy, O., 139
Ruggiero, V., 12
Rwanda
  Gacaca Courts, 84–5
  International Criminal Tribunal, 7, 17,
    79, 176
  memorialization in, 86

Sageman, M., 139, 142, 143
Sandy, L., 100
Sassen, S., 62
satellite companies, 162
'seafood slaves' case study, 101–2
Senegal, 182
September 11th attacks, 145, 146
Serious Organized Crime Agency (SOCA), 132
sex tourism, 103–6
sex tourists, 105–6
shadow networks, 64
Sicilian Mafia, 115
Sierra Leone, 81
Silk Road, 65
slaughter, A.M., 170
Slavery Footprint, 101

smuggling
  of art, 159
  of humans, 93–4, 96–9
  of wildlife, 160
SOCA (Serious Organized Crime
    Agency), 132
social harm, 154
social movements (online), 63
social stratification
  at global level, 30, 33, 34, 37, 48
  and mobility, 46–8
  see also inequality
south see global south
South, N., 164, 165
South African Truth and Reconciliation
    Commission, 83–4
sovereignty, 15–18, 157, **200**
Sparks, R., 60
Special Court for Sierra Leone, 81
special investigative measures, 132
special measures (counter-terrorist), 148–9
Special Panels of the Dili District Court, 81
Special Tribunal for Lebanon (STL), 81
speciesism, 163–4, **200**
speed, 42
Spivak, G.C., 88
standard hierarchy, in organized crime, *118*
state crime
  concept and definition, 169, 170–2, **200**
  in context of new world order, 170
  examples of, 170
  parallels with conventional crime,
    175–6
  theories of, 172–5
  and transnational crime, 183–5
  visibility and accountability, 175–80
  see also atrocities; crimes of globalization
state power, defragmentation of, 177, **195–6**
state regulation, 35, 39
state sovereignty, 15–16, **201**
state-building, 147–8
states
  denial of harm by, 178–9, 185
  environmental responsibility, 157,
    162–5, 167
  international/regional organizations
    founded on, 20
  naming and shaming of, 76, 129, 161
  national justice in international contexts,
    190–1
  organized crime and development of, 114
  protection of citizens by, 16, 59, 60
  relationship with terrorists, 138
  responses to transnational crime, 75
  terror-genic environment of, 140–1

states *cont.*
    theories of globalization and, 33, 39, 40,
        41, 42–4
    see also domestic justice; domestic law
        enforcement
stratification *see* social stratification
suicide terrorism, 141–2
supply chains
    in garment industry, 31, 32, 34–5, 36, 43
    and organized crime, 119
supranational bodies
    as criminal actors, 180–2
    role of, 191–2
    and state crime, 172
    see also international organizations
surrogacy, 108–10

technology
    global sceptic view of, 38–9
    and jihadist terrorism, 138, 143–4
    and money laundering, 129
    unequal access to, 63
    and visibility of state crime, 176–7
    see also cyberspace; internet
television, role in terrorism, 143
territory, and terrorism, 140–1
terror-genic environments, 140–1, 143, **201**
terrorism
    controlling risk of, 59, 61
    defining, 137, **201**
    environment, 140–1, 143
    home-grown terrorism, 141–2, 145–6
    jihadist terrorist groups, 138–44
    motivations, 138–9, 142
    responses to, 137, 144–50, 151
    role of technology, 138, 143–4
    suicide terrorism, 141–2
    transnational and global, 3, 137, 138
terrorist alert systems, 59
terrorist networks, 137, 139–40, 142–3
textile industry, 31, 32–3, 34–5, 36, 39, 43
Thailand, 101–2, 109–10
third generation criminal courts *see* hybrid
    courts
third world *see* developing countries; global
    south
timber trade, 163
time-space compression, 42
time-space distanciation, 42, **201**
TOC Convention *see* United Nations
    Convention against Transnational
    Organized Crime
Tokyo Trials, 79
Tor (The Onion Router), 64, 65
torture, 180

tourism
    and markets in bodies, 103–6
    medical tourism, 106
    reproductive tourism, 108–10
tourists
    Bauman's concept of, 46–8
    sex tourists, 105–6
trafficking *see* drug trade; human trafficking;
        organ trafficking
transitional justice, 83–5, **201**
Transnational Adoption Convention, 110
transnational corporations, 181–2
    see also multinational corporations
transnational crime(s)
    consideration of wider harms, 14–15
    defining, 6–7, 9–13, **201**
    and domestic crimes, 5–6
    economic and social context, 12–13, 189
    evolution, 10, 189
    and international crimes, 6, 7–9
    link with globalization, 2–4, 10, 12–13,
        103, 189
    measuring, 190
    overlap and connections, 13
    politics of, 13–14
    responses to, 12, 75–8
    and state crime, 183–5
transnational environmental crime
    defining, 154–7
    and responsibility, 160, 162–3
transnational organized crime
    context of, 119–20, 185
    defining, 12, 117, **201**
    drug production and trafficking, 126
    responses to, 129–31
transnational terrorism, 137, 138
    jihadist terrorism, 138–44
    responses to, 137, 144–50, 151
tribunals *see* international tribunals
Truth and Reconciliation Commission
    (South Africa), 83–4
Tunisia, 59

uncertainty
    and liquid modernity, 45–6, 48
    and risk, 54, 59, 60, 61, 157
unemployment, 55
United Kingdom (UK)
    counter-terrorism strategy, 149
    policy transfer to, 72, 73
    state accountability, 177
United Nations (UN)
    harm caused by, 181
    international tribunals, 7, 79, 81–2
    nature and purpose of, 18–19

CPSIA information can be obtained
at www.ICGtesting.com
Printed in the USA
JSHW011611261219
3190JS00003B/118

9 781412 919258